Dear Hannah & Tre[...] [...] the you

May God richley [...]

marriage [...]

could have been [...]

your special day; I pra[...]

Father and Lord Jesus Christ [...]

and will bless you with peace! Eph 1:2 CEV

love, Aunt Karla :)

The Blessing Book

God's Story: Blessing-by-Blessing

Karla Kay Minick

To broaden our understanding of the concept of bless in God's Story, I have used the following Bible translations.

The personal stories interspersed throughout The Blessing Book are true, however some names have been changed.

There have been times over the past five years that I have wished someone else had already written The Blessing Book because I really want to read a book that tells the blessings of God chronologically. But, I believe God entrusted me to write it and for that I have been blessed.

I have been blessed by countless hours spent in God's Story as I sought and collected each blessing, and in prayer as I wrote and rewrote each entry. I could never have done this alone. Thank You God for guiding me through. You are the blessing.

I'm thankful for my husband, Russell. His support, encouragement and technical ability made the project available online a whole year before it went to print. Next to Jesus, Russell is my favorite teacher and I'm so thankful that we get to serve God as one. Thanks Russ for reminding me of the blessings we share and I'm thankful to God for the blessings with you that are yet to come.

My children Hannah, Sophie, and Isaiah: each of you is a continual source of joy and blessing, and this book has allowed me to relive God's past faithfulness in our lives. Thank you kiddos, for traveling with us around the world and for your willingness to let our stories be shared. Many thanks to my son-in-law Andrew, who encouraged me to add more personal entries, which connect God's big Story with our little one, making this a better book.

For those of you whose lives have overlapped with mine, I am blessed. Thanks for allowing me to include you in the story.

Kristina, your keen insight as you prayerfully read each entry and offered wonderful suggestions for clarity and flow is a gift to me and to each person who reads The Blessing Book. Thank you my friend, where would I be without you?

To Cecil, our team's added pair of eyes, thank you for meticulously reading and editing. I'm grateful to you for giving your time and expertise.

Dear family, friends and friends who I have not yet met, thank you for communicating how certain entries have blessed you. This has certainly blessed me.

Chris, I love your work and I knew you would do a wonderful job with the cover design. Thanks for partnering with me on another book.

Thank you Jesse for taking all our efforts and putting together a great layout and for moving the project on through to completion. I'm so glad you are on our team.

Introducing: The Blessing Book. May God bless you as you see His blessings unfold from the first blessings in the Garden of Eden through to the Garden City where the blessed ones have access to the Tree of Life and forever live in blessedness.

January

Blessed to Sing God's Praises, like the Birds

Genesis 1:21b-22 NIV

JANUARY 1

Long before the sun is up, the birds awake to sing God's praises for the new day. Creation rises to bless God their Creator and the Author of all blessings. The Bible overflows with blessings yet the first of all blessings that appear is reserved not for humankind but for birds and fish. After He formed the water creatures and every kind of bird, *God saw that it was good. God blessed them and said, "Be fruitful and increase in number and fill the water in the seas, and let the birds increase on the earth."* This is the first blessing that occurs in God's Story. God knows goodness when He sees it and from the very beginning He blessed creation to multiply so that the goodness that He created would fill the earth. From the depths of the sea to the heights of Heaven the first blessing continues to point our hearts to God.

But we will see that God is much more than a Creator who is content to sit back and enjoy His handiwork. We will experience the King through history and through His promises for the future. As we encounter blessings in places both familiar and surprising, it is my prayer that we'll look back by faith and forward with hope and choose to serve in love, seeking His Presence daily.

Made in God's Image and Blessed!

Genesis 1:28 AMP

JANUARY 2

During the sixth day of creative creations, the Master of Everything did something extraordinary: He created mankind in His own image! *And God blessed them and said to them, "Be fruitful, multiply, and fill the earth, and subdue it [using all its vast resources in the service of God and man];*

and have dominion over the fish of the sea, the birds of the air, and over every living creature that moves upon the earth." We are created in the very image of God, and blessed! It is important for us to remember that God blessed humanity before there was any opportunity to earn that blessing. Yet being blessed entails a call to action. We were not called to be passive but to take dominion over the earth that God made. Let us then live wisely because we know that we are blessed by the Creator, who created us in His image. As He blessed us, so we should bless the world around us. God is love; it only makes sense that being created in His image means that we were made for love and designed to be loving.

Blessed to Rest

Genesis 2:3 NIV

JANUARY 3

What a spectacular universe the Lord has made! Day after day He adds more splendor to the mix. By the seventh day of creation, God had completed His masterpiece. Seeing that it was good, He stopped and He rested. *Then God blessed the seventh day and made it holy, because on it he rested from all the work of creating that he had done.* God rested. Be blessed to rest. Trust that our heavenly Father knows best what we need, and we need time to set work aside and to rest. Reflecting on His goodness refreshes us.

It was while in Spain during my enlistment in the Marine Corps, that I was first introduced to the concept of "siestas", a time in early afternoon when business stopped and the Spaniards enjoyed naps. Years later, when our family moved to China, we embraced an activity in the culture called "xiu xi". For an hour or so, in the afternoon, doors would not be knocked upon and all of China could rejuvenate for the evening interactions yet to take place. These resting principles are similar to rest in God's Story. Sadly, many societies value work but do not value rest. Often people try to get ahead by pushing through, seeking to fit more into a day already packed full, leaving little room for margin. From the beginning, however, God demonstrated that He valued rest a great deal. It is good to work, and it is good to rest. God did both. May we have wisdom to do the same.

Blessing upon Blessing

John 1:15b-18 NLT

JANUARY 4

God the Father created the world out of nothing, but He was not alone. Jesus was there too, one with God from before time began. In the opening of John's Gospel he makes it clear just who Jesus is: the Word that was with God from the very beginning, the Maker of all things, the Source of life and light, through whom a relationship with God the Father is established. Jesus became flesh and lived among humanity on earth. Referring to Jesus, John the apostle recorded the excitement of John the baptizer: *"This is the one I was talking about when I said, 'Someone is coming after me who is far greater than I am, for he existed long before me.'" From his abundance we have all received one gracious blessing after another. For the law was given through Moses, but God's unfailing love and faithfulness came through Jesus Christ. No one has ever seen God. But the unique One, who is himself God, is near to the Father's heart. He has revealed God to us.* May we be aware of one blessing after another today because of the grace that Jesus gives. We will read more of His life on earth later, but it is good to remember that Jesus was with the Father right from the start. He, like His Father, treasures giving good gifts. Our God is not stingy; He is not a miser. All goodness comes from Him. He is the source of blessing upon blessing.

Bless the Lord All My Days

Psalms 104:1, 35b NKJV

Psalm 104 echoes God's creation story. Written many years after the establishment of the world we can join the psalmist in singing praise to God for the wonders of His handiwork and for His provision. The song starts out with, *"Bless the Lord, O my soul! O Lord my God, You are very great: You are clothed with honor and majesty..."* And verse after verse tells of God's wonderful work in creation and how the earth is filled with goodness because God is a good God worthy of all praise. In many places throughout the Psalms the use of the words "bless" and "praise" are intertwined. Isn't it great how we, the creation, can bless the Lord, the Creator? The author of this astonishing praise song exclaims how he will sing praise to the Lord all his life. "I will sing to the Lord as long as I live; I will sing praise to my God while I have my being."

These verses blessed me in January of 1998 as I read them while waiting for the results of an extensive procedure including tests for cancer. I resolved that no matter how many days were yet before me, my lips would sing praise to God. Russell and I sat across a worn wooden desk from a Chinese doctor in a Thai hospital to hear, "I so happy, you no cancer." My reply: "I so happy too!" From that appointment, we resumed our family vacation on a beach in Thailand. My senses were newly alive. God's love was deeper than the salty ocean that we splashed in with the kiddos. Heavy elephants ambled while horses galloped across the sand under a brilliant blue expanse and all was framed by vibrant green mountains. When I heard my children's laughter I smiled with thankfulness. Time transformed day to night and warm air blew through a bejeweled sky. My gratitude was made complete as I held Russell's hand, so glad for the husband God gave to me to enjoy His goodness with. The conclusion to Psalm 104 rings out loud and clear what we as those blessed by God are to do: *"Bless the Lord, O my soul! Praise the Lord!"*

Blessed to Start Again

Genesis 5:1-2 MSG

JANUARY 6

From the beginning of time we find God's bountiful goodness in everything. But the goodness He provided in the Garden of Eden was not enough for Adam and Eve. Falling for the temptation offered by the serpent, humanity's rebellion against God began. Adam and Eve were forced to leave Eden because they chose to trust the creation rather than the Creator. In between the tragic story of Adam's first two sons and the birth of his third son, Seth (when Adam was 130 years old), we can read again of the original creation of mankind. *This is the family tree of the human race: When God created the human race, he made it godlike, with a nature akin to God. He created both male and female and blessed them, the whole human race.*

Could it be that Seth was a kind of re-start? At the birth of Seth's son Enoch, God's Story states that people began to call on the name of the Lord. Do we not need to hear afresh, and often, that God blessed and continues to bless those who call on His name? Jesus will later describe this phenomenon to a teacher named Nicodemus as a "born again encounter" that comes from trusting in the One whom the Father has sent to rescue. Thank You, Lord, that You do not leave us like we are but You continue to provide for us a way to have new life, full life, blessed life in You. Amen.

Blessed to Be Fruitful

Genesis 9:1 NLT

JANUARY 7

One generation followed another and things turned bad. Mankind's wickedness grew to the point that there were only evil thoughts and utter corruption at the heart of man. God grieved that He had made the human race and with an aching heart He planned to wipe out everyone and everything that was alive. Now enter the story of Noah, his family, the ark, animals coming in pairs and how they were spared as a great flood washed away everything else. A rainbow was placed in the sky as a sign of the promise God made that a flood will never again destroy the earth. *Then God blessed Noah and his sons and told them, "Be fruitful and multiply. Fill the earth."* This new beginning began with a blessing.

In 2010 I taught Noah's story with joy to a dozen young ladies in a Thai juvenile detention center. Several in our group had been there long enough to contemplate the actions that led to their incarceration, which would interrupt life as they knew it for many years. The world cast them off, but God was able to use their confinement for His goodness to be experienced. On Tuesday and Thursday mornings they would meet with a team of ladies dedicated to sharing and showing God's unconditional love. Sitting in a circle on a cement floor, adding colors to a paper rainbow, I could see the beginning of hope in some faces as they took in the truth that God cares about justice and yet He offers the possibility of redemption- a new start even for those who feel as though their lives are over. Please pray with me for one teenager in particular named Rain; may she trust in the God who made the rainbow and live in His blessings.

Blessed Be the Lord

Genesis 9:25-27 ESV

JANUARY 8

After the great flood the ground dried and Noah and his family began to work the land. Noah drank some wine from a vineyard he had planted and he became drunk. In his drunkenness, his son Ham disrespected him. Noah then cursed Ham's son, Canaan. *"Cursed be Canaan; a servant of servants shall he be to his brothers." He also said, "Blessed be the Lord, the God of Shem; and let Canaan be his servant. May God enlarge Japheth, and let him dwell in the tents of Shem, and let Canaan be his servant."* One grandson was cursed and two sons benefitted but the account does not give much more detail than that. Sometimes stories like these help us, centuries later, to get a feel for the grittiness of life and offer some hope in our messed up situations too. Although Shem and Japheth profited, Noah says it is the Lord who is to be blessed.

We Are Blessed to Bless

Genesis 12:2-3 NIV

JANUARY 9

We now fast forward several generations to the time of a man named Abram. God calls Abram to leave the familiar to go to where He will show him. God then makes an extraordinary promise to Abram: *"I will make you into a great nation, and I will bless you; I will make your name great, and you will be a blessing. I will bless those who bless you, and whoever curses you I will curse; and all peoples on earth will be blessed through you."* God's Story goes on to say that Abram left, as the Lord had told him. Oh, the blessings that obedience brings!

An old timey gospel chorus comes to my mind, *"Wherever He leads, I'll go."* I wonder what came to Abram's mind as he stepped out in faith. He could have ignored God, and gone on living as before. Aren't you glad he obeyed? We are blessed because he listened and followed God. God blessed Abram to be a blessing and we too are blessed to bless. How are we extending God's blessing today? Think about the many ways we are loved and cared for by God. His Presence is with us always. Blessing continues to be God's plan for all people so let's not miss out on His strategy, but look for ways to join Him in blessing.

Rescued into Blessing

Genesis 14:19b-20a NLT

Abram's nephew, Lot, traveled with Abram and his wife, Sarai, and over time both men prospered with their herds. After a while, it became necessary for the men to separate. It was best that they went different ways so that the land could support their large flocks and herds. Lot pitched his tents near Sodom because the valley was well watered. Unfortunately, this was a volatile area and during a war involving several kings, Lot and his family were captured in the mix of battle. Uncle Abram and 318 trained men bravely rescued Lot and his family. Then Melchizedek, king of Salem and priest of God Most High, blessed Abram, saying, *"Blessed be Abram by God Most High, Creator of heaven and earth. And blessed be God Most High, who has defeated your enemies for you."* I can imagine Lot and his family being really thankful for the God of Abram and for the mighty rescue. How wonderful when blessings from God return to God in praise. We can sing about receiving a blessing from the Lord and giving back to Him praise for it, and that is a wonderful principle to live by. Sometimes singing how we ought to live is a great start to form up our mindset. We can then move it from principle to practice and live from a grateful heart.

Blessed to Believe

Genesis 15:2 NLT

God called out to Abram in a vision to reassure him that the Lord is his shield and his great reward. But Abram replied, *"O Sovereign Lord, what good are all your blessings when I don't even have a son? Since you've given me no children, Eliezer of Damascus, a servant in my household, will inherit all my wealth."* God said again that Abram's descendants will be more than the sand of the earth and the stars in the sky. Abram believed

Him, and God affirmed this righteousness. We will read several accounts of how belief and blessings can go hand in hand. Abram is just the beginning. Is there a truth about God that we are struggling to believe? Let God's Word reassure us and grow our trust. Believe, obey, be blessed. This is one pattern that appears throughout God's Story, and still applies. "O Sovereign Lord" is more than stating a title, it is a declaration that God has absolute authority and nothing happens without His direction or permission. God is trustworthy. He was the source of Abram's blessings and He blesses His children today.

Blessed to Change

Genesis 17:15-16 NIV

JANUARY 12

Can you imagine what it would be like if you received a name change in your nineties? That is what God gave Abram and Sarai. Abram was ninety-nine when he got his new name, Abraham, to remind him that he would be the father of many nations. The covenant was to be an everlasting one between God, Abraham and the descendants who were yet to come. God also said to Abraham, *"As for Sarai your wife, you are no longer to call her Sarai; her name will be Sarah. I will bless her and will surely give you a son by her. I will bless her so that she will be the mother of nations; kings of peoples will come from her."* Never give up on a promise God gives. He is faithful and can change more than just our names.

I've been called by a variety of names through the years. Back in the summer of 1965 my parents named me Karla Kay. After graduating high school I lived with a host family in Germany as a summer exchange student and my "dad" changed my name to Speedy because I liked to run. Marine Corps friends shorted my name to K.K., which I liked so much better than being called by my last name, as was the Marine custom. Many women take their husband's last name when they marry, and my name changed from Spindler to Minick in 1989. In our early married years, when Russ and I served among Spanish-speakers in Dallas, I was called Karlacita, a term of endearment. As each of our babies were born, their names were lovingly changed too by those wonderful people in our first church for Hispanics. We moved to China in 1996 and one of my Chinese friends took it upon herself to rename me Ming Yang Yan. In China, people are called by their last name first, so Ming was chosen because it is close to Minick. Ming means bright and Yang Yan translates to sunshine. It is hard not to be cheerful when you are called Bright Sunshine! Our ministry to the minorities in China moved us to Thailand and my name changed yet again. To the ears of most Thai people the letters "r" and "l" sound the same, so I answer to Kaalaa or Kaaraa when I'm in Thailand, that wonderful land of smiles.

I have lived in many interesting places but I always thank God that my citizenship is in Heaven. We read in the second chapter in the book of Revelation that those who overcome will be given a white stone with a new name on it. I can't wait to receive the name that God will bless me with on that day when I see Him face-to-Face!

Not All Blessings Are the Same
Genesis 17:18-20a NLT

JANUARY 13

Backtrack a few chapters and thirteen years earlier in the life of Abraham. He had seen the power of God and knew His promises. Yet he remained childless and so Sarah came up with a plan to offer her maidservant to Abraham to start a family through her. Abraham was eight-six years old when Hagar gave birth to Ishmael. Now Ishmael is a teenager and Sarah is soon to be expecting her first child. Abraham had just been retold that the blessing (all nations would be blessed through him) would come through the son born of Sarah. Listen to the concern and dilemma in this father's voice regarding his first son as Abraham said to God: *"May Ishmael live under your special blessing!" But God replied, "No—Sarah, your wife, will give birth to a son for you. You will name him Isaac, and I will confirm my covenant with him and his descendants as an everlasting covenant. As for Ishmael, I will bless him also, just as you have asked."* May we learn this lesson from Abraham that God's ways and His timing are best. We cannot always make sense of the natural order of situations in our life. I believe this is to grow our trust and it aids us in seeking God's Presence for guidance. If we saw everything clearly, we would be walking by sight, but God calls us to walk by faith, trusting Him with each step.

We missed out on a blessing once. Russell sensed that God was leading our young family to Costa Rica, but we could not figure out why. Isaiah was a baby, and his sisters were just one and two years old. All was going well with the Hispanic church we started, and Russ had just completed Bible College and had been ordained. Costa Rica? Pushing the thought from his mind, we packed up and took the next logical step; seminary. We may never know of the blessings God had in store for us had we moved to Costa Rica at that time, but the experience grew us to trust Him more, even when we don't have the full picture before us. Later, when the opportunity to serve in communist China came up, we pursued God's leading. Lots of prayer and preparation went into this life-changing decision, yet confirmation that we were truly following God's plan for that time came on the airplane, somewhere over the Pacific Ocean. We would get to participate in the blessing of Abraham, that all nations would be blessed by God, including those that had never even heard of His name.

Repeated Blessings

Genesis 18:18-19 NIV

JANUARY 14

The grievous sins of Sodom and Gomorrah reached an all-time high and destruction by the Lord was at its doorstep. Abraham's nephew Lot and his family still lived in that area and Abraham bartered with the Lord not to destroy the righteous along with the wicked. During this conversation with Abraham, God restated His promise. *"Abraham will surely become a great and powerful nation, and all nations on earth will be blessed through him. For I have chosen him, so that he will direct his children and his house-hold after him to keep the way of the LORD by doing what is right and just so that the LORD will bring about for Abraham what he has promised him."*

Does keeping the way of the Lord make a difference to God when we ask Him for His help? It did for Abraham, and because of it, Lot was spared again. How we live our life matters. Abraham knew that righteousness and justice were important to God. He could choose to obey the commands that God gave to him or reject His instruction. Obedience was the only wisdom he had. Let's be wise and learn to listen to God's voice. Obeying God leads us to wisdom. Lord, may we seek to make progress on changing according to Your plan rather than repeating the sins of Sodom and Gomorrah. Amen.

Blessed to Pass the Test

Genesis 22:15-18 NLT

JANUARY 15

In the ancient near-East, child sacrifice was an unfortunately common practice. People believed that the gods demanded the blood of children as signs of worship. As horrific as that seems to us, this was the world that Abraham and Sarah inhabited. It is crucial to remember this point when reading about Abraham's most difficult test. One day, God called out to Abraham and asked him to sacrifice his son Isaac. In addition to being a heartbreaking request, this must also have been confusing to Abraham. Wasn't Isaac the child God had promised? Hadn't Abraham waited for years to have a son? These thoughts undoubtedly raced through his mind, but Abraham again obeyed God.

As a parent of three beautiful children, I cannot even imagine Abraham's heavy heart as he and Isaac climbed the mountain together. My heart grows heavier still when I think of how he had to then tie Isaac down to the altar, and how, with a trembling hand, he drew the knife to slay his son. This is horrible to imagine. But God had something besides death in store, for He is different from the pagan gods. At the last minute, just as Abraham was about to sacrifice Isaac, the angel of the Lord stopped Abraham and said that now it was known that Abraham feared God above all else. *Then the angel of the LORD called again to Abraham from heaven. "This is what the LORD says: Because you have obeyed me and have not withheld even your son, your only son, I swear by my own name that I will certainly bless you. I will multiply your descendants beyond number, like the stars in the sky and the sand on the seashore. Your descendants will conquer the cities of their enemies. And through your descendants all the nations of the earth will be blessed—all because you have obeyed me."* What an incredible test. Again, Abraham obeyed God, and God's blessing followed his obedience.

To prepare to serve God in China, our family received a series of injections, some of which could actually infect us with enough virus to make us extremely sick and even die. Although we sensed God's leading to move our young family to the other side of the world, our trust in Him was truly tested when our four-year-old child, Sophie, began to show an adverse response to the injections. In some ways, like Abraham, we needed to obey God fully before we saw His provision. We intentionally reflected on the truth that our children were given to us from God, but that they belonged to Him. God, I pray that we continually trust You with the lives of those we love most dearly. Loving You and living obediently will never disappoint us even when the situation at hand may not be what we would naturally choose. In the end, Sophie was okay and with grateful hearts we boarded the plane, blessed to grow closer to God than ever before.

Blessed with Marriage

Genesis 24:1 NLT

JANUARY 16

Thirty-seven years have passed since the birth of Isaac. Sarah, Abraham's faithful wife, has just died. Abraham mourned the loss of his wife, who was his partner, companion and friend through life. By this time, *Abraham was now a very old man, and the LORD had blessed him in every way.* When his grieving subsided, the next thing on Abraham's mind was to find a wife for Isaac. He did not want Isaac to marry a local girl from the pagan land where they now lived, but instead Abraham looked to his hometown to find a mate suitable for his son. I picture Abraham reminiscing about the years of life lived with his dedicated wife and he must have desired his son to be blessed with a godly wife as well. As we will find out in the story of Isaac's wife, it is a good and godly thing to pray for the future marriage partner of the children God has blessed us with. Lord, I pray we would honor You by living faithfully with the spouse You have given to us and in doing so be a godly example for the next generation. Please provide for our children marriage partners who love You above all else. May we live with the joy and blessing that comes when marriage is built on Your foundation. Amen.

Blessed Be the Lord for Answered Prayer

Genesis 24:26-27 ESV

Abraham asked one of his servants to be the matchmaker for his son and so he traveled to Abraham's hometown in search of a wife for Isaac. As the servant journeyed he prayed to God for guidance and success. When a beautiful maiden gave him water to drink from the spring and watered his camels too he knew God had answered this specific request. *The man bowed his head and worshiped the Lord and said, "Blessed be the Lord, the God of my master Abraham, who has not forsaken his steadfast love and his faithfulness toward my master. As for me, the Lord has led me in the way to the house of my master's kinsmen."*

In order to get an answer from a specific prayer we need to go to God and voice our specific needs. Sometimes the answer comes quickly as it did for Abraham's servant and sometimes our faith is grown as we wait upon God's timing. Our young family had a great lesson in faith growing during our second time of living in a Chinese village. Duke, an adorable puppy brought lots of joy to our household, and Sophie was especially attached to the little guy. One afternoon right out of the blue, a man walked into our courtyard, picked up Duke and ran away before we could catch him. Duke's "dognapping" led to several trips to the local market in hopes of finding him and nightly prayers were lifted to God, pleading to bring Duke back. Thirty days later, Sophie still leading the prayer campaign, a local friend called saying they spotted Duke with a thug. Russell rushed to the rescue, decisively dealt with the drug dealer and Duke returned to our home with much rejoicing to God! God cares about our cares, whether they be dog-sized or concerning a new bride. Blessed be the Lord!

Blessed by the Lord

Genesis 24:31, 34-35a NLT

JANUARY 18

The servant shared the interesting wedding proposal situation with Rebekah, the beautiful girl at the spring, and gave her jewelry. She excitedly passed on this unexpected news to her mother and brother Laban. Laban rushed back to the well and invited the servant to their home. *"Come and stay with us, you who are blessed by the Lord! Why are you standing here outside the town when I have a room all ready for you and a place prepared for the camels?"* Inside, with the family gathered, the servant told them the reason for his visit. *"I am Abraham's servant,"* he explained. *"And the LORD has greatly blessed my master; he has become a wealthy man."* He added that Isaac was his master's son and he was sent to bring back a wife for him. If you were Rebekah's parents how would you take such news? Life was going along with normal activities, then one day, one visit, and all that would be customary for the future of your daughter, could potentially be radically different. Did Rebekah's parents have the boy-next-door picked out for her to marry? Would giving her hand in marriage to a man miles away mean never seeing their grandchildren grow up? What about Rebekah; would she be given a say in the matter?

Bless God Who Leads in the Way of Truth

Genesis 24:48 NKJV

Oh, to be a prayerful, faithful servant. When we start our day, do we ask for God's direction and then take time to pray specifically for His intervention as we go about on our mission? Abraham's servant is a wonderful role model to us. He not only prays but he wastes no time to praise God for providing an answer. God's Story records this account twice, first as the servant does it and then as he retells his story of God's faithfulness to Rebekah's family. *And I bowed my head and worshiped the Lord, and blessed the Lord God of my master Abraham, who had led me in the way of truth to take the daughter of my master's brother for his son.* The servant felt Rebekah was the answer to his prayer for Isaac but she still needed to respond. That was a huge decision to make all in one day. Her whole life could possibly change if she said yes. But that is how life works. One decision leads to a whole new set of possibilities.

What if a girl from Michigan never went to boot camp in South Carolina, and then on to training in Florida for an intelligence unit where she met a young Marine from Texas who was in Florida learning Morse code? What if he never pursued her to Spain? What if God did not intervene and reconcile each of them into His family? What if on a rainy night he never asked the marriage question? What if she did not reply, "Yes, I'll marry you!" As I have experienced in my own life, the journey offers several opportunities to respond and a different choice along the way brings about a very different conclusion. A whole lot was resting on how Rebekah and her family took in the news from Abraham's servant concerning a bride for Isaac.

Blessed Future

Genesis 24:60 NLT

Rebekah's father, brother and mother all gave permission for Rebekah to marry Isaac for they understood this opportunity was from the Lord. But the choice was left to Rebekah. When she said "yes", *they gave her this blessing as she parted: "Our sister, may you become the mother of many millions! May your descendants be strong and conquer the cities of their enemies."* Many were blessed with this arrangement and wedding plans were quickly formulated. Along with her childhood nurse, Rebekah left all that was familiar to her and traveled a long distance to be married to a man she had never met. Her future was unknown yet she trusted enough to get on a camel and begin the journey. It must have given her comfort and assurance to know that this wedding was arranged and blessed by God. May He be the foundation in each marriage.

Marriage is not an easy partnership as it will, maybe more than any other relationship, bring out what is really inside of us. Character traits, like the good, the bad and the changing are often shown most intensely to those we are the closest to. Some would say that marriage is not just meant to make us happy but that God uses marriage to make us holy. And even the most mature are still on a journey in becoming complete. I'm happiest when I am holy (pure, un-mixed) and enjoy the blessings that come with married life. As Rebekah entered into marriage she was given a blessing to be the mother of millions. Content with the three children God has blessed Russell and me with, I look forward to embrace those who may one day extend our family through additional marriages and grandchildren. This blessing promise that began with Abraham continues on through the ages.

Double Blessing: Twins!

Genesis 25:11 NIV

Isaac was meditating as he walked along his property when he first saw Rebekah approaching on the back of a camel. Whether or not it was love at first sight, we do not know, but God's Story does say that Rebekah was beautiful. Isaac was forty years old when he married Rebekah and she comforted him greatly in the loss of his mother. Isaac deeply loved his wife and the couple had quite a while to get to know each other for Rebekah was barren for twenty years. By this time Father Abraham lived until he reached the ripe old age of 175. When he died his two sons, Ishmael and Isaac, buried him in the same cave with his dear wife Sarah. *After Abraham's death, God blessed his son Isaac, who then lived near Beer Lahai Roi.*

One of the ways that God blessed Isaac was to answer his prayers on behalf of his wife who could not have children. After two decades of married life, twins were born to Isaac and Rebekah. What joy must have filled their tent! The brothers grew up and Esau, the older of the two, became a skillful hunter. Isaac loved the taste of wild meat, so of the two boys, Isaac favored Esau. Rebekah, however, favored their son Jacob as he quietly enjoyed time with her among the tents. Due to a famine in the land, the family moved to Gerar, yet God remained faithful in His promise to bless Isaac. In the days to come, we will see more clearly how God continued to bless Isaac.

God's Blessing Passed Down

Genesis 26:2-5 NIV

It was during this time of famine when *the LORD appeared to Isaac and said, "Do not go down to Egypt; live in the land where I tell you to live. Stay in this land for a while, and I will be with you and will bless you. For to you and your descendants I will give all these lands and will confirm the oath I swore to your father Abraham. I will make your descendants as numerous as the stars in the sky and will give them all these lands, and through your offspring all nations on earth will be blessed, because Abraham obeyed me and did everything I required of him, keeping my commands, my decrees and my instructions."* Isaac grew up hearing that his father Abraham was blessed by the Lord. There was God's promise that all nations would be blessed through Abraham. Now the Lord spoke this same blessing to Isaac, giving him confirmation and assurance. What peace Isaac must have felt knowing God would be with him. I pray we sense that kind of peace from our Father today. Lord, may we draw near to You and take time to reflect on Your many blessings in our own lives. We thank You for Your decrees that show us the way to truth and full life. Thank You for peace that over-comes the world. Amen.

Blessed Provisions

Genesis 26:12 NLT

JANUARY 23

God also blessed Isaac's finances. Substantially. *When Isaac planted his crops that year, he harvested a hundred times more grain than he planted, for the LORD blessed him.* The increase in Isaac's wealth and power caused the king of that land to be fearful of Isaac so he sent him away. Then there were conflicts over water rights and wells. These disagreements brought about many quarrels and more moving. It must have been a stressful time for the whole family. But in stressed-filled times we can draw near to God who desires our closeness at all times as He provides what we need.

What I needed for my family back in the winter of 1992 was diapers. God had blessed us with three babies in the span of twenty-eight months, which meant we went through a lot of diapers. At the end of one of those months there were no diapers, and no money to buy them. How we rejoiced when there was a check in our mailbox for just enough to get us through another round of diapers! Years later we had three kiddos in college; diapers are expensive but college even more so! Our mission board generously provided "X" amount toward scholarships but when we took a leave of absence from the mission field those scholarships were no longer available to us. We would have a tuition fund shortage. God knew this and the very next day a Marine Corps scholarship was presented to us for the exact amount that the mission board previously provided. God used the time we served in the Marine Corps as singles, to bless us as a family almost thirty years later. Isaac was blessed with grain. We were blessed with diapers and scholarships, and so much more. God likes to bless His children.

Surprise Blessing

Genesis 26:24, 29 HCSB

JANUARY 24

Isaac and his family were now in Beersheba, and the Lord appeared to him one night and said, *"I am the God of your father Abraham. Do not be afraid, for I am with you. I will bless you and multiply your offspring because of My servant Abraham."* Again, God blesses Isaac, and reminds him that He is faithful. He tells him that just as He was with Abraham, He will be with Isaac, too. Isaac had moved quite a bit and it must have felt good to be settling his family in Beersheba. He had just built an altar to worship the Lord and maybe Rebekah got the last picture hung on the tent wall before they received a surprise visitor. Remember the king who sent Isaac away because he felt threatened by Isaac's power? Well now he traveled to find Isaac. Was he coming for war or for peace? Did Isaac's recent dream flash through his mind, hearing afresh that he did not need to be afraid? The king came for peace and he wanted a treaty with Isaac because he could see that the Lord was with him. Along with other things the king said, *"You are now blessed by the Lord."* In life we will have surprises. There will be good times, hard times and times when we are astonished at how the times can change around. May we seek and stay near to God during our transitions as well as in times of settledness. Like Isaac, may we not be afraid, for He is with us.

Battle over the Blessing

Genesis 27:4, 8-10, 12b NIV

JANUARY 25

Generally speaking, having favorites is an unhealthy habit for parents. We can see this statement lived out in the lives of Jacob and Esau as their parents each had their favorite son. Even though Isaac's firstborn son Esau sold his birthright to his brother Jacob for a bowl of bean soup, Isaac still planned to give Esau his blessing. Just before he died, Isaac told Esau, *"Prepare me the kind of tasty food I like and bring it to me to eat, so that I may give you my blessing before I die."* Rebekah overheard Isaac and since she loved Jacob and wanted the best for him, she schemed with her favorite son, Jacob. *"Now, my son, listen carefully and do what I tell you: Go out to the flock and bring me two choice young goats, so I can prepare some tasty food for your father, just the way he likes it. Then take it to your father to eat, so that he may give you his blessing before he dies."* Jacob wasn't so sure the plan would work, for although Isaac had lost his eyesight, he hadn't lost his sense of touch. If Isaac touched Jacob he would know Jacob was not his hairy son Esau. Jacob's replied, *"I would appear to be tricking him and would bring down a curse on myself rather than a blessing."* The backdrop is set for the battle over the blessing.

Blessing of Heaven's Dew and Earth's Richness

Genesis 27:19b, 23b, 25, 27-29 NIV

So now we find Jacob posing as his brother Esau to gain the blessing of their father Isaac. After telling his father that he was his firstborn, Jacob urged, *"Please sit up and eat some of my game so that you may give me your blessing."* At first, Isaac is not convinced because the voice sounded like Jacob's but the fur that Rebekah had placed on Jacob's hands convinced him, and *he proceeded to bless him.* Isaac asked again if Jacob was really his firstborn son Esau and Jacob replied that he was. So Isaac continued, *"My son, bring me some of your game to eat, so that I may give you my blessing."* Jacob moved closer to his father and kissed him. *When Isaac caught the smell of his clothes, he blessed him and said, "Ah, the smell of my son is like the smell of a field that the LORD has blessed. May God give you of heaven's dew and of earth's richness—an abundance of grain and new wine. May nations serve you and peoples bow down to you. Be lord over your brothers, and may the sons of your mother bow down to you. May those who curse you be cursed and those who bless you be blessed."* This blessing should sound familiar to us as it is similar to the blessing that God gave to Abraham back in Genesis chapter twelve. We will see that this blessing story is far from over!

Grabby for Blessings?

Genesis 27:30-41 NIV

After Isaac finished blessing him, and Jacob had scarcely left his father's presence, his brother Esau came in from hunting. Esau approached his father with the meal he had freshly prepared and said, "My father, please sit up and eat some of my game, so that you may give me your blessing." This interaction really confused Isaac and he had to tell Esau that he had already given away the blessing to his brother Jacob: *"I blessed him—and indeed he will be blessed!"* Esau took this news really hard and with a loud and bitter cry he said: *"Bless me—me too, my father!"* Isaac answered, *"Your brother came deceitfully and took your blessing."* With growing hurt and anger Esau spoke what was on his mind, *"Isn't he rightly named Jacob? This is the second time he has taken advantage of me: He took my birthright, and now he's taken my blessing!"*

Esau asked his father, *"Haven't you reserved any blessing for me?"* Isaac told Esau plainly that he had given it all to Jacob. Can you hear the desperation in Esau's voice? *"Do you have only one blessing, my father? Bless me too, my father!" Then Esau wept aloud.* Esau received a sad "blessing" and held a grudge against Jacob *because of the blessing his father had given him.* When we think about the present and we reflect on this part of God's Story written years ago, the names may be different, but the challenge to living morally upright lives in complicated settings is the same. May we learn from the examples of others, and seek God for His guidance to lead us through the confusion.

Blessed to Be Spared

Genesis 28:1 HCSB

JANUARY 28

Tension continued to build in Isaac's family. Once again Rebekah tried to protect Jacob; this time, using marriage. When she heard that Esau wanted to kill his brother Jacob, she made a plan for Jacob's escape. Rebekah told Isaac that she didn't want Jacob to marry a Hittite woman but instead he needed to travel to her hometown to marry a woman from her family line. *Isaac summoned Jacob, blessed him, and commanded him: "Don't take a wife from the Canaanite women."* As a father, Isaac sends his son on the same journey that Abraham sent his trusted servant on years before. Isaac instructed Jacob to marry one of his mother's brother's daughters. And it will be intriguing how Rebekah's brother Laban again becomes a part of God's Story. I think that Laban might have had a challenge with greed and manipulation. It is interesting that Jacob, on the run from out-maneuvering his brother, finds himself on a journey to live with Uncle Laban. Uncle Laban was the needed shelter from this storm, however, God desires for there to be peace within our families. Because we are often stiff-necked and stubborn, sometimes a little time and space is required for that desired peace to come about. Jacob will find out later that pursuing peace is not for the cowardly. May we be brave in the Lord to offer and accept both forgiveness and apologies for the sake of peace.

Generational Blessing

Genesis 28:3-4 AMP

JANUARY 29

In 1990, on the first Christmas with our firstborn, Hannah, I gave my mom a daily scripture calendar by Dr. James Dobson called *The Heart of the Family*. The next Christmas, she gave a copy to each of her grown children so we could read the same passages day-by-day. Over the years I continue to use it to record special events. On a very meaningful Thanksgiving with our house church family in Thailand, I jotted down a blessing I did not want to forget. It was 2006 and our thankful hearts were quite aware that soon the oldest children in our group would be leaving for college. With the smells of special food filling the room it was great to hear different voices reflecting on holidays from the past. Looking over at the "kids' table" it was obvious that our kiddos had grown up and life was about to change as they each would head out on their own.

My calendar for that day held a blessing from Genesis 28. *"May God Almighty bless you and make you fruitful and multiply you until you become a group of peoples."* This original blessing was given by Isaac to his son Jacob, but I couldn't help but feel blessed by the Lord who had formed our group of families into a blessed church called Sojos. As Jacob was about to head out on his own, his father, talking about God, said, *"May He give the blessing [He gave to] Abraham to you and your descendants with you, that you may inherit the land He gave to Abraham, in which you are a sojourner."* In time we will see that the blessing from Isaac was passed down again from father to son. Present times will become memories but the future holds hope because of God's faithful promises. Even as sojourners, God provides the blessing of communion with Him and with others.

Pray for Blessed Marriages
Genesis 28:6 NLT

JANUARY 30

By being obedient to his parents and leaving when he did, Jacob's life was spared because his brother Esau was plotting to take it. *Esau knew that his father, Isaac, had blessed Jacob and sent him to Paddan-aram to find a wife, and that he had warned Jacob, "You must not marry a Canaanite woman."* By this time Esau had already married two Canaanite women and the pagan daughters-in-law made life bitter for Isaac and Rebekah. Esau added another wife to the mix, this one was from his dad's brother's family. For the hope of the generations to come, for those who would inherit the blessing of Abraham, a lot was resting on the need for a healthy wife for Jacob. I'm sure Isaac and Rebekah were hoping for some peaceful family reunions too. Just think of how the conflicts grew even more intense for the elderly couple due to the proximity of the tents in which their extended family lived. Family relational struggles can be a hindrance to the joy of living in peace and harmony, no matter what time period. Let's pray deliberately for those who will one day marry into our families and continue to pray for those who we are committed to through marriage. May we practice loving God now with all that we are, and may God bless our families with people who love and honor Him and one another.

Pillow to Pillar Blessing

Genesis 28:14 HCSB

Ready to find his wife, Jacob set out for his mother's land. Along the way, he grew tired and using a stone for a pillow he fell asleep and dreamed. During his unusual dream of a stairway to Heaven, God spoke to Jacob saying he would have many descendants. *"Your offspring will be like the dust of the earth, and you will spread out toward the west, the east, the north, and the south. All the peoples on earth will be blessed through you and your offspring."* God told Jacob that He would watch over him and give to him the land on which he slept. The blessing given to Abraham and Isaac has now been passed on to Jacob. Are we keen to listen when God speaks to us through dreams, His Word or through messengers He sends? What blessings are we passing on to the generations that follow us?

Jacob turned his "pillow" into a pillar, poured oil over it and after making a vow to God, continued his journey. It was a pivotal time in Jacob's life and he took ownership of his own faith in the Lord. The world offers many roads for young adults to choose as they venture out into life on their own. Wise discernment is needed now just as it was needed back in the days of Jacob. Father, we pray for ourselves and for the next generation. Please provide us with direction and increase our desire to choose to walk in step with Jesus. Open our ears to hear You speak, and then like Jacob, may we follow in obedience. Amen.

Reflections

We have traveled through a whole lot of blessings in January alone! God blessed humanity over and over and we were introduced to people like Adam and Eve, Noah, Abraham and Sarah, as well as Isaac and Rebekah. God's great covenant blessing in Genesis 12, that we are blessed to be a blessing, is now being passed on to Jacob. February holds some great stories of how God's Story continues to unfold, blessing after blessing. Read on, be blessed and bless! Feel free to pass along The Blessing Book to those you would like to bless. Love, Karla

February

Asher: Blessed to Be Happy

Genesis 30:12-13 AMP

FEBRUARY 1

Jacob fell head over heels in love with Rachel, his Uncle Laban's youngest daughter. Jacob worked hard for seven years to earn her hand in marriage only to discover on the morning after his wedding night that he had married her older sister, Leah instead! How did he handle this deception? How did Leah feel about the whole situation? I'm sure this state of affairs caused a little tension in Rachel's life too. Tricky Uncle Laban offered another work incentive program to Jacob and he worked an additional seven years for Rachel. As Jacob spent time shepherding did he reflect on his life and remember how he had deceived his own brother Esau out of his blessing?

Sometimes what goes around comes around. At any rate, the years had added up and by that point, Jacob had acquired many herds and flocks of animals, which meant his livelihood had grown. Jacob's family also grew. His wives who were sisters were in steady competition to give him sons. Rachel and Leah even provided Jacob with their maidservants to expand the family. *Zilpah, Leah's maid, bore Jacob [her] second son. And Leah said, I am happy, for women will call me blessed (happy, fortunate, to be envied); and she named him Asher [happy].* Jacob now had eight sons. His number was indeed increasing and this was just the beginning of the blessing passed down from God to Abraham to Isaac and now to Jacob coming to fruition.

Open Handed Blessings

Genesis 30:27, 30 NLT

FEBRUARY 2

Jacob wanted to leave Laban's control and start a life away from his uncle. Because Laban recognized the blessing of God upon the life of Jacob, he does not want Jacob to leave. Laban thinks that maybe God's blessing will go when Jacob goes. Laban tells Jacob, *"I have become wealthy, for the LORD has blessed me because of you. Tell me how much I owe you. Whatever it is, I'll pay it."* Jacob explained that he worked very hard (seven years for each wife then six more years for the flocks) and that during those two decades, Laban's wealth also increased enormously. Jacob then gives the credit to God. *"The LORD has blessed you through everything I've done. But now, what about me? When can I start providing for my own family?"* When Laban did not give his blessing for Jacob and his family to leave, Jacob left secretly. He packed up his wives, their maids, a dozen children (eleven sons and a daughter) and all he owned. The whole family headed back to the land of Jacob's father Isaac, like God had said to do.

As a young adult, Rebecca arrived in Thailand ready to serve only to find that her team leaders had resigned. We brought Rebecca on board with our team and began to invest in her life. We were blessed by Rebecca's friendship and by her contributions as she faithfully served her two year commitment. When the time came for her to decide her future service Rebecca chose to join a different team. We liked Rebecca; it would have been easy to want to hold on to her, or we could have let her go, but done so grudgingly. I'm glad we chose to bless her as she left and be thankful for how God matured her to go forth as a blessing to the new team that He had provided.

Laban was Jacob's provision when Jacob needed a fresh start in life. Jacob worked hard for Laban and the time had come for him to step out on his own. This type of a relationship dynamic continues in many ways still today. May we not turn it into an unhealthy form of co-dependency, but allow for good growth, even when it means change will be involved. It is best if we do not hoard blessings (especially those that come to us in the form of people) but to allow blessings to flow. I'm so thankful that in doing so with Rebecca we maintain a joyful friendship and she continues to bless so many through the experiences God keeps

giving to her.

A Parent's Blessing

Genesis 31:55 NIV

After a seven-day pursuit, Laban caught up with Jacob, and there was a heated confrontation and then a resolution, which ended with an oath that neither man would harm the other. A meal was eaten together and they all spent the night peacefully on the mountain. *Early the next morning Laban kissed his grandchildren and his daughters and blessed them. Then he left and returned home.* Although God's Story does not record it, I have a feeling the blessing of their father made for a better trip for his two grown daughters, Leah and Rachel. Let us never hold back on blessing those we love, especially when it involves our children as they start out for lives on their own.

I felt a lot of emotion the summer of 2011 when Isaiah, our last to fly from the nest, walked through security checks at the Chiang Mai airport to board the plane that would take him from our home in Thailand to a new life in America. I remembered Sophie making the same solo flight the year before and how a short time before that we helped Hannah unpack into her freshman dorm then we said good-bye and flew to a new nest in London. So many changes in such a short time, yet God remained faithful through it all. A part of me wanted to hang on with a long hug at each departure, but instead I kissed each of our kiddos good-bye, as parents have been doing for generations before me, and I thanked God through tears for the life and time we shared as a family. One thing I love about God is that He is everywhere. No matter what time zones we are scattered through, He is near those we love and our prayers are heard by Him who cares even more than we ever can.

Wrestling Blessing

Genesis 32:26, 29 HCSB

During our seminary days we wrestled with our calling. Were we to settle into our lives in rural North Carolina, go deeper into Hispanic ministry or take up a challenge to travel to the other side of the world to pioneer work with an unreached people group? Long talks and pro/con worksheets played their parts, but wrestling with God in prayer for direction is what led us to gather up our young kiddos and journey to China.

Jacob continued his journey with all that belonged to him and he too knew what it meant to wrestle. As he approached his brother's land it was inevitable that he would need to face Esau. Jacob had not seen Esau in over twenty years, ever since the time their father had blessed Jacob with Esau's blessing and Esau had threatened to take Jacob's life. This meet-up could be life threatening for Jacob and the family he loved. With this in mind, Jacob separated gifts of animals and people to go on ahead of him, then he placed his wives and children in the safest place he could find and he remained alone for the night.

He prayed to God reminding Him of the promises God had given and was thankful for God's great provision. But instead of his prayers leading to sleep, he had an all-night wrestling match with God. When the sun began to rise Jacob heard, *"Let Me go, for it is daybreak." But Jacob said, "I will not let You go unless You bless me."* Jacob was given a new name "Israel" and then the One he was wrestling with *blessed him there.* Do we value wrestling with God long enough for a breakthrough to come with a blessing? I pray we do even if it means sleepless nights.

The Blessing of Forgiveness

Genesis 33:11 NKJV

FEBRUARY 5

It was a very scary time for Israel (Jacob) and his large traveling family. Instead of being refreshed by a night of sleep he had just wrestled until dawn. It must have been encouraging to know God was near him, even blessing him, yet he did not know how Esau would respond to seeing him again. How relieved Israel must have been when Esau met him with forgiveness. With a big bear hug and weeping the two powerful men were filled with joy from their reconciliation and were genuinely happy to see each other again. Israel urged, *"Please, take my blessing that is brought to you, because God has dealt graciously with me, and because I have enough."* Esau accepted the gift then Israel and his family moved on to settle in Succoth. How completely wonderful is reconciliation! God is a God of forgiveness and He must beam with joy when His children forgive one another. Jesus came so that we could be reconciled to God Himself. What an amazing gift that is.

Remember Former Blessings in Hard Times

Genesis 35:9b-10 NIV

FEBRUARY 6

Just because we are blessed does not mean we will live life free of hard times. We see in the life of Jacob that some of his young adult children made some bad choices that led to bad consequences and challenging times, yet God did not leave Jacob. God faithfully led Jacob. He was told by God to move once more to Bethel and to build an altar where he had lived back in the day of the blessing from his father Isaac. When they arrived, *God appeared to him again and blessed him.* Restating what was told to Jacob during the all-night wrestling match, he was told by

God, "Your name is Jacob, but you will no longer be called Jacob; your name will be Israel." Another pillar was set up, like the time after Jacob's dream of the stairway, and with wine poured over it, Israel worshipped God. The recording of God's Story goes back and forth sometimes calling Jacob, "Jacob" and at other times "Israel". I wonder what name his wives used to call him by?

After God described the promise of a great nation with great land, Israel and his family moved on toward Bethlehem. On the way there, Benjamin was born but he lost Rachel, the wife he loved most, as she gave birth to his twelfth and last son. Israel held a brand new baby instead of the love of his life. This unexpected death must have been devastating. Even though we are blessed we will not be exempt from times of suffering. The world is a fallen, broken one, but remember, God is over this world and He gives us hope.

Blessed for the Sake of Another

Genesis 39:5 NLT

FEBRUARY 7

For some reason, Jacob (Israel) loved his eleventh son Joseph more than his other children. Maybe it was because Joseph was Rachel's firstborn. Things took a turn for the worse for Joseph when he was about seventeen years old. The favoritism of his father coupled with the seemingly arrogant dreams that Joseph had about his own brothers pushed his brothers over the edge. In a series of challenging events Joseph ends up in the bottom of a well and then sold to a man named Potiphar in Egypt, far from the father who loved him.

But Joseph found favor with the Lord. *From the day Joseph was put in charge of his master's household and property, the LORD began to bless Potiphar's household for Joseph's sake. All his household affairs ran smoothly, and his crops and livestock flourished.* Even in this far away land God did not forget Joseph and He blessed the work of his hands. At times we might ask ourselves, "What in the world am I doing here?" I bet

Joseph wondered that while down in the pits a few times in his life. Hold on, the story is not over yet. God is a God who redeems and blesses! The stark contrast between our darkness and His light is often the backdrop we read about in His Story as well as experience in our own lives.

God, may we be quick to turn to You when life does not make sense. Thank You for the precedent that has been set and lived over and over, that You are able to release us from the darkness of our own prisons and give beauty in place of ashes. Amen.

Blessing Others as a Result of Being Blessed

Genesis 47:7b-10 NIV

FEBRUARY 8

The handsome and well-built Joseph became quite the Egyptian ruler over the years but before that happened he finds himself thrown into prison because he did not give in to the advances of his master's wife. Although not as serious as the episode with Potiphar's wife, I'm grateful that Russell knew how to resist an unwanted approach. In broad daylight on a public street in our little Chinese town, a "professional" woman asked him to come into her shop for a haircut. He responded, "Uh, I don't have any hair." "That's ok," she purred, "I don't have any scissors."

Back in Egypt, Joseph was put in charge of the prison that he himself was thrown into. Through a series of dreams and interpretation of dreams Pharaoh is made aware that the spirit of God was in Joseph, so he promoted Joseph over all of Egypt. During this time there is an extreme famine and who comes asking for food, but Joseph's brothers. Long story short, there was great rejoicing when Joseph finds out that his father, Jacob, is still living.

When Jacob arrived in Egypt with the rest of his clan, Joseph presented his father before Pharaoh. *After Jacob blessed Pharaoh, Pharaoh asked him, "How old are you?" And Jacob said to Pharaoh, "The years of my pilgrimage are a hundred and thirty. My years have been few and difficult, and they do not equal the years of the pilgrimage of my fathers." Then Jacob blessed Pharaoh and went out from his presence.* I have a feeling that in his wildest dreams Jacob never thought that he would one day be blessing Egypt's number one man. Russell did not start out in a prison or end up in a royal palace, but he eventually led church planting work in five countries. When we stay near God, who knows how we may be led by Him to bless others.

End of Life Blessings

Genesis 48:3b-4 ESV

FEBRUARY 9

The Israelites (Israel's family) moved to Egypt and Israel (Jacob) lived the last seventeen years of his life there. Jacob made Joseph promise to bury his body where his father Isaac and grandfather Abraham were buried. I'm curious if Jacob thought back to the time of his own father's funeral and how he and his brother Esau had buried Isaac. When we know we are at the end of our lives, what will we look back on with joy?

A whole lot of blessing takes place at the end of Jacob's life and it begins with Jacob recalling the way in which God had blessed him. Jacob reminisced and told his son Joseph, *"God Almighty appeared to me at Luz in the land of Canaan and blessed me, and said to me, 'Behold, I will make you fruitful and multiply you, and I will make of you a company of peoples and will give this land to your offspring after you for an everlasting possession.'"* Who can forget a blessing like that?

The twelve tribes of Israel came from Jacob, and indeed the Promised Land would be theirs. God's good Story is worth passing down from generation to generation. What has He done in our lives that we are sharing with the generations that follow us? Are we purposefully leaving a legacy of thanksgiving? If not, it may not be too late to rethink and align afresh to God the giver of all blessings. We have been given the gift of life; I pray we would choose to live wisely.

Blessing Grandchildren

Genesis 48:9b, 15-16 NIV

Jacob asked about Joseph's two sons who were born to him in Egypt. The grandfather then said, *"Bring them to me so I may bless them."* Even though age had robbed Jacob of clear sight he hugged and kissed his two grandsons. With his hand on the heads of Joseph's sons, Ephraim (the younger) and Manasseh (the older), Israel began. *Then he blessed Joseph and said, "May the God before whom my fathers Abraham and Isaac walked faithfully, the God who has been my shepherd all my life to this day, the Angel who has delivered me from all harm—may he bless these boys. May they be called by my name and the names of my fathers Abraham and Isaac, and may they increase greatly on the earth."* It was a very moving time for the three generations of men, the descendants of Abraham and Sarah. This unexpected reunion was indeed a blessing from God. And blessings continued to flow from Israel's heart and lips.

One Day Our Ability to Bless Will End

Genesis 48:19b-20 NLT

When Jacob was blessing Joseph's sons, Joseph tried to correct his father about which son was older, for the older son was due the special blessing. Jacob however, refused Joseph's guidance and said, *"I know, my son; I know. Manasseh will also become a great people, but his younger brother will become even greater. And his descendants will become a multitude of nations." So Jacob blessed the boys that day with this blessing: "The people of Israel will use your names when they give a blessing. They will say, 'May God make you as prosperous as Ephraim and Manasseh.'" In this way, Jacob put Ephraim ahead of Manasseh.*

There in Egypt, in the land of Pharaoh, Jacob blessed his two grandsons from Joseph. Jacob then went on to bless the other men in his family. What a special occasion that must have been, but it was also bittersweet. These blessings were given at the end of Jacob's time on earth. Not all of us will be granted a time for giving bedside blessings. One of our saddest sacrifices was being overseas when Russell's mother, Ann, died. Though we spent the previous Christmas with her, it was difficult not to have one more chance to give and receive blessings before she passed from this world. We continue to learn to live each day extending blessings while we can.

Blessings like a Crown

Genesis 49:24b-26 HCSB

FEBRUARY 12

Before he died, Jacob gathered his sons around him to tell each one, in the form of a blessing, what would happen in the days to come. So he "blessed" all twelve of his sons in the order in which they were born. When he got to son number eleven (Joseph), again we can read the way Jacob loved him more because he blessed him more. Joseph will be fruitful and strong due to *the hands of the Mighty One of Jacob, by the name of the Shepherd, the Rock of Israel, by the God of your father who helps you, and by the Almighty who blesses you with blessings of the heavens above, blessings of the deep that lies below, and blessings of the breasts and the womb. The blessings of your father excel the blessings of my ancestors and the bounty of the eternal hills. May they rest on the head of Joseph, on the crown of the prince of his brothers.*

Now that is a whole lot of blessing! God did bless Joseph extra; He blessed him with humility to trust Him in the hard times and to forgive his brothers. Joseph had the wisdom to know that what his brothers had initially meant for evil, God turned to good. Out of God's goodness Israel's family did not die of famine but lived! God placed Joseph just where he needed to be. I want to be faithful to humbly live out my life where God places me.

Bless until You Die

Genesis 49:28 MSG

FEBRUARY 13

Israel said his final good-byes to his twelve sons, and as he did so he bless-ed each of them. *All these are the tribes of Israel, the twelve tribes. And this is what their father said to them as he blessed them, blessing each one with his own special farewell blessing.* Jacob (Israel) went on to repeat his burial desires while he had everyone assembled, and then he died. The whole community (both the Israelites and the Egyptians) mourned his death and a very impressive procession travelled from Egypt to Canaan. Jacob was buried next to his wife Leah since Rachel had been buried where she had died while giving birth to Benjamin on the journey to Bethlehem. Jacob's parents and grandparents were all buried together in the same cave back where it all began when God gave Abraham the promise and blessing that he would be a great nation and all nations would be blessed through him.

Three generations of God's blessed people have now died. But the blessing lives on. God blesses people to be a blessing. It is humbling to realize that we are a part of God's blessing cycle. Thank You, our Father for Your loving kindness toward us. Way beyond what we will ever know, You give to us good gifts. May we live lives that honor You as we share with others from the abundant favor You have supplied so that all can know You. Amen.

A Hard Heart toward God's Blessing

Exodus 10:10a MSG

FEBRUARY 14

About half a century later Joseph died. Joseph's death concludes the Gen-esis record and the first of many chapters in God's Story. Years passed and a new leader emerged in the Story; Moses. Family heritage is import-ant to God as we will often see in listed genealogies. It is interesting to know that Moses was a grandson of Levi, one of the twelve sons of Jacob. The youngest of three children, Moses was born in Egypt, rescued from the Nile River as a baby, grew up in the Egyptian palace, spent years in the outback as a shepherd for his father-in-law, and would be used by God to deliver His people from the hand of the Egyptians to be brought into the land of blessing and promise.

This would not be an easy rescue mission but a very fascinating one as God's provision, protection and blessing continually guided His people. By this time in history the Egyptians do not remember Joseph and all the good he had done for them. Even as slaves in the land, the Israelite community grew and because they were seen as a threat, they were mistreated. Moses, as God's spokesperson, asked that all the Israelites be given permission to leave to worship Yahweh and this new Pharaoh did not want to lose his workforce. Pharaoh said, *"I'd sooner send you off with God's blessings than let you go with your children."* Once again, Moses and Aaron (his brother and ministry partner) were thrown out of Pharaoh's sight. Pharaoh, with his hard heart, did not get a blessing from God and another plague of locusts filled his land. God, may our hearts be soft to Your ways in our days. Amen.

Bless Me as You Leave

Exodus 12:31b-32 NLT

FEBRUARY 15

Moses was eighty years old and the task before him must have seemed insurmountable. Pharaoh was not budging but God told Moses it would be that way for a reason: all would know that He is the Lord when the Story of God's miraculous power would be told. It took several devastating plagues for Pharaoh's eyes to be opened to see that God was in charge.

One night, Pharaoh finally summoned Moses and Aaron and said, *"Get out! Leave my people—and take the rest of the Israelites with you! Go and worship the Lord as you have requested. Take your flocks and herds, as you said, and be gone. Go, but bless me as you leave."* Pharaoh ultimately saw God as powerful. The leader of all of Egypt bowed to ask for God's blessing.

No matter if we see ourselves as weak or strong, the reality is that God is the most powerful and He is able. May He bless us today as we choose to connect with Him. May we then follow Him as we continue to make choices that come before us; the easy ones and the hard ones. Let's seek to see from God's perspective and bless people, even those who have hearts that to us may seem like stone.

Blessed by God Who Delivers

Exodus 18:10b-11 MSG

FEBRUARY 16

With the multitudes departing, the Exodus began. The Egyptians even gave the Israelites gold to take with them as they made their exit! As God guided him by a cloud and by fire, Moses led the people. The Israelites passed through the parted Red Sea, the Egyptians who pursued them were destroyed, and the liberated sang songs of praise to God. God provided water, manna, and quail and the Israelites journeyed on.

Moses had a wonderful family reunion when his wife, their two sons and Jethro, his father-in-law, met up with him in the desert. I love these little personal glimpses into the big Story, for they are like a small puzzle piece put into place and the whole picture is made more complete. Jethro was thrilled to hear that the Israelites were delivered from the oppression in Egypt and how it was all due to God's strength and goodness to bless His people. Jethro told Moses, *"Blessed be God who has delivered you from the power of Egypt and Pharaoh, who has delivered his people from the oppression of Egypt. Now I know that God is greater than all gods because he's done this to all those who treated Israel arrogantly."*

While we lived outside of the US, our family experienced a lighter version of this kind of a reunion during our annual group meetings. Christian workers would gather together representing extended families and tribes, and celebrate the Father's blessings from the past year. Fellow missionaries became uncles and aunts to our children, their own children were like cousins to ours, and to this day our family is blessed with those deep relationships forged from rejoicing in God's redemption. Reflecting upon and sharing God's blessings with others leads us to thank and bless God. A thankful life is a blessed life, and the goodness course continues.

Remember, We Are Blessed to Rest!

Exodus 20:8-11 NIV

FEBRUARY 17

It is hard to know exactly, but about 500-650 years have passed since God promised Abraham that he would be blessed and all peoples would be blessed through him. God's Story is a long one! Three months after God led the Israelites from Egypt, He was ready to make a very personal covenant with His people. Were His people ready to live out their part of the agreement?

At Mount Sinai, with dense smoke coming from the mountain, God spoke what we would later refer to as the Ten Commandments. Right before the commandment "Honor your mother and father", God gave this one: *"Remember the Sabbath day by keeping it holy. Six days you shall labor and do all your work, but the seventh day is a Sabbath to the LORD your God. On it you shall not do any work... For in six days the LORD made the heavens and the earth, the sea, and all that is in them, but he rested on the seventh day. Therefore the LORD blessed the Sabbath day and made it holy."*

The Israelites' leader was God Himself and they learned that loyalty and allegiance is shown through obedience, even when obeying is hard. Resting is a difficult thing for me. I think my issue with this command ultimately has to do with trust. Do I trust that God is really in control and that things will not fall apart if I put my lists aside to rest?

43

My head knows the right answer, but living out what I know is right is an on-going process.

During the years of raising our family while working in Asia, two of my most cherished rests were vacations only an hour's drive from home. Leaving behind the computer and language books and packing lots of snacks and board games we "camped out" at a mountain hotel near a British soccer camp that our kiddos attended. In the crisp morning air Russ took the kids to training and I took long runs in the countryside and allowed my mind to be refreshed in the beauty of God's creation. Afternoons and evenings were intentionally restful as we enjoyed being together as a family. God has blessed us to rest. In fact, as part of the Ten Commandments, He has commanded us to do so each week as we set aside time to purposely meet with Him. Just like the Israelites of the Old Testament, when we obey, we live out our loyalty.

Blessed Covenant

Exodus 20:24 HCSB

FEBRUARY 18

God proclaimed the Ten Commandments to the people. There was thunder, lightning, the sound of a trumpet and smoke surrounded the mountain. It was natural for the people to be afraid; I would have been too! Wise fear of God, as the One we certainly cannot control, can keep us from sinning. God told the Israelites not to craft any "gods" but instead, *"You must make an earthen altar for Me and sacrifice on it your burnt offerings and fellowship offerings, your sheep and goats, as well as your cattle. I will come to you and bless you in every place where I cause My name to be remembered."* Through Moses, God continued to talk to the Israelites about the covenant He established with His people clarifying many areas of life.

In hindsight we see how everything was leading up to a new covenant. Jesus is that new covenant. When we place our faith and trust in God's Son, the sacrificial substitute who takes away the sins of the world, we can come before Him clean and blessed by God Almighty. The fear of realizing we cannot control God is replaced by the assurance that we do not need to try to control Him. He is good. The Almighty blesses.

Blessing God Matters

Exodus 23:13 AMP

FEBRUARY 19

There were a wide variety of laws passed down from God to Moses and many of these same laws are recorded in the four books that follow Genesis: Exodus, Leviticus, Numbers, and Deuteronomy. God was crystal clear that other gods were not to be called upon (do not invoke the names of other gods) for He alone made the covenant with the people Israel. *"In all I have said to you take heed; do not mention the name of other gods [either in blessing or cursing]; do not let such speech be heard from your mouth."* Other "gods" are not God. That may seem straightforward to us, but many people struggle with this truth. A Chinese taxi driver and Russell had a conversation about God as the taxi crawled through afternoon traffic. When Russell had shared the new covenant hope through Jesus, the cab driver commented, "Gods are gods. Jesus? Buddha? Same-same". Russell responded, "People are people. When I get out someone else can pay. O.K.?" "What? I drove you; you pay me." "I guess you are right; it's not the same. There is only one God who has paid my debt and who provides for me. That is the only God I will honor." Who we say God is matters to God.

Blessings That Are Well with My Soul

Exodus 23:25-26 NIV

FEBRUARY 20

We can read pages of God's promises to the Israelites as His Story continues to unfold for His people during the time of Moses. Some of these blessings were very conditional. Do this and this will happen; if not, it won't. The next blessing is contingent on the people's choice to worship. *"Worship the LORD your God, and his blessing will be on your food and water. I will take away sickness from among you, and none will miscarry or be barren in your land. I will give you a full life span."*

God desired the Israelites to take over the land He had promised to them. This would require trust in God since the land was presently occupied by the enemies of God. Worship draws us near God; it gives us a proper perspective of the goodness and greatness of our Lord. Although the blessing mentioned above was specifically for those about to enter into the Promised Land, we as those living years later can still draw on the importance that God places on worship.

Choosing to worship God blesses us in many ways. Worshiping God is easy to do when our world is humming along smoothly. I remember thinking about this with heightened depth one Sunday morning. Several members of our house church family were enjoying a vacation together so we gathered to worship God on the beach. The waves were rolling in and before Russell preached, one of the young guys strummed his guitar as we sang a song called, *It is Well with my Soul.* My eyes welled up with tears, thinking of how the day before Sophie had nearly drowned as a rip tide took her further and further from the shore. Did I have the deep conviction that even in tragedy, God is worthy of worship? I sang on, sensing His nearness. Come what may, because of Him, it is well with my soul.

Painful Blessing of Loyalty

Exodus 32:29 NLT

All of Israel had just agreed whole-heartedly to the covenant with the Lord. This was not a small deal so God called Moses into an exclusive executive meeting and gave him massive amounts of information including specific plans so Moses could construct a tent of meeting where God's people would worship Him. The plans included instructions for the priests and described the items required inside the tabernacle too.

Moses was gone for over a month for this administrative meeting with God. He then came down the mountain with the first hard copy of the Ten Commandments, written on stone tablets. But while Moses was away, the people begged Aaron to give them "gods" they could see, so Aaron gave them what they wanted: a golden calf. The people chose to break the promises they had made to God and this made the Lord, and Moses, furious. God told Moses that He was going to destroy them all; however, Moses interceded on behalf of the Israelites. He demolished the god of gold and also broke the tablets of stone.

Moses then called those who were for the Lord to come to him and the tribe of Levi responded. With swords the Levites went through the camp killing 3,000 of the disobedient Israelites. Purity is not a small thing in the eyes of a holy God. I cannot begin to imagine the grief experienced in the camp that day. With great reverence to God, Moses spoke to the Levites, *"Today you have ordained yourselves for the service of the LORD, for you obeyed him even though it meant killing your own sons and brothers. Today you have earned a blessing."* What a sobering experience. The blessing earned would not be quickly forgotten.

The Blessing of a Job Done Well

Exodus 39:43 HCSB

FEBRUARY 22

The breach of contract that God's people found themselves in led to a very serious wake-up call. They needed to re-establish their relationship with the Lord so when Moses relayed the instructions that God had given to him about building the tabernacle, everyone listened carefully and followed God's instructions with great attention to detail. The tabernacle was to be an exceptionally special place where God met with His people and it was designed to be portable too. I love how the phrase, "all who were willing" is used several times to describe how people gave specific supplies and services. People gave from a willing heart to the extent that Moses had to say, "enough!"

Everything that was required to build the tabernacle had been received. *Moses inspected all the work they had accomplished. They had done just as the Lord commanded. Then Moses blessed them.* Oh, the joy of knowing that you have done a job well. The glory of the Lord then filled the tabernacle and that concludes the blessings from the book of Exodus, the Story of God's people rescued from the Pharaoh of Egypt to live life in a relationship with the God of the universe.

God has already blessed mankind immensely but there are a whole lot of blessings yet to come, and some of those blessings will depend on the faithfulness to the work God gave the Israelites to do. One of my jobs after my enlistment in the Marine Corps and before getting married, was to help people better understand their electric bills. My workdays were spent tethered to a phone line looking up records on microfiche, seeking to find resolutions to electric questions that were most commonly asked in the form of a complaint. Over the year I spent at Consumer's Power Company, I received several "people pleaser" awards as satisfied customers expressed gratitude for my service. Things like those are fun to get as they can represent doing your job to the best of your ability. God too has rewards in store for His faithful ones. Will we one day hear God say to us, "Well done, my good and faithful servant"? That hinges on whether or not we have lived a life of faithfully serving Him.

Cleansed from Sin and Blessed

Leviticus 9:22-23 HCSB

FEBRUARY 23

Moses, as God's leader for Israel, helped the people in many ways as they grew to understand and live out what it meant to be in a covenant love relationship with God. They needed to know how to deal with sins that separated them from God. *Aaron lifted up his hands toward the people and blessed them. He came down after sacrificing the sin offering, the burnt offering, and the fellowship offering. Moses and Aaron then entered the tent of meeting. When they came out, they blessed the people, and the glory of the Lord appeared to all the people.*

God's people in the time of Moses needed to be trained to be holy. We have that same need today. Through the sacrifice that Jesus made, once for all, on the cross, we are able to enter into in a deep relationship that depends fully on a holy God. But dealing correctly with our sin-nature does not come naturally to us. Like the Israelites, we too need training. Physical trainers are popular for fitness but we are more than physical beings.

God, please give us the coaches we need for our spiritual growth. May we be disciplined to value discipleship, may our spiritual muscles be strengthened by spending time in Your Word, and may we better understand Your Story. Help us to live out Jesus' teachings so our lives are not wasted but instead used so Your glory shines through us. Amen.

Blessed Not to Be Anxious

Leviticus 25:21 NIV

Over the next forty years or so, God, through Moses, sets in place many laws and standards which affected the religious duties, diet, hygiene, the political and social responsibilities, as well as the morality of this young nation. These laws guided the Israelites so they could function on a daily basis. One law that gave interesting direction was about farming. Every seventh year the land was to remain fallow; dormant and uncultivated.

I am blessed to have had grandparents who were farmers, for I feel a sense of special connection to the earth. While riding through the countryside in various seasons I like to see how crops are growing. When I fly and look upon farmland from the perspective I picture God having, I'm fascinated how fields cover the earth like a well-stitched quilt. Although I am not an expert, even I know that fallow land normally does not produce food. But so the people in the time of Moses didn't worry about starvation, God assured them: *"I will send you such a blessing in the sixth year that the land will yield enough for three years."*

When the Israelites followed the decrees and laws of God, they lived safely and were blessed with God's good provisions. God is still the provider of what we need today. Even though Russell and I have never owned a home, we have never been homeless in all our years of placing God's Kingdom first. Through many wonderful and varied situations we continue to be blessed by God's provisions. The faithfulness of our Father is good to remember, for He wants us to be anxious for nothing but to talk to Him in prayer for what it is we need. And in doing so, to be thankful.

Blessed to Know
That Pride Is Not the Answer

Leviticus 26:19 AMP

Over and over again God told His people that blessings would come from Him, and in specific ways, if only they would obey the good laws He had put in place which were for their benefit. Yet, God knows human hearts and so He also tells them how they will be punished if they choose to follow their own stubborn, prideful ways. *"And I will break and humble your pride in your power, and I will make your heavens as iron [yielding no answer, no blessing, no rain] and your earth [as sterile] as brass."* Even with the lessons of the past to learn from, today we are often no different than the generations before us. We are frequently bent in a sinful, selfishness direction. Oh, for the blessings that would flow if only we would choose to live in obedience to God.

Russell and I arrived in Texas during the drought of 2011. With the average rainfall for the year at about 11 inches, it made it the driest year of Texas history (and the history of droughts in the area goes back to the days of Spanish exploration in the 1500's). Traveling the dry and depressing land to preach and to support our son's soccer team, we read sign after sign, along the highways, in small towns and in bigger ones, with the words, "Pray for rain". The sky was like iron and rain was desperately needed. In times like these it seemed like everyone was calling out to God for His intervention. But when the rains come, do we thank Him, or return to our prideful thinking that says we can live without Him?

The Blessing of God's Smile

Numbers 6:22-27 NLT

FEBRUARY 26

One of my all-time favorite blessings in the Bible is the blessing that the Lord gave to Aaron to pass on to His people. I want this blessing of God's protection, His smile and His peace and I want it for everyone whom I love. Revel in the goodness of a good God who has good things to offer those He loves. If we try, we can almost feel the warmth of these ancient words, known as the priestly blessing, relayed from God to Moses to Aaron to us.

"Tell Aaron and his sons to bless the people of Israel with this special blessing: 'May the LORD bless you and protect you. May the LORD smile on you and be gracious to you. May the LORD show you his favor and give you his peace.' Whenever Aaron and his sons bless the people of Israel in my name, I myself will bless them." It is so good I want to bless again: May the Lord bless you and protect you. May the Lord smile on you and be gracious to you. May the Lord show you His favor and give you His peace. What a blessing! What a God!

Blessed to Be Guided by God

Numbers 10:29, 31-32 NLT

FEBRUARY 27

Everyone is packed up for the Promised Land and the marching orders have been given when Moses asked one of his relatives to come along as their guide. *One day Moses said to his brother-in-law, Hobab son of Reuel the Midianite, "We are on our way to the place the Lord promised us, for he said, 'I will give it to you.' Come with us and we will treat you well, for the Lord has promised wonderful blessings for Israel!" "You know the places in the wilderness where we should camp. Come, be our guide. If you do, we'll share with you all the blessings the Lord gives us."*

Hobab may have known where to camp, but it was the Lord who provided the guidance as the Israelites followed the cloud and fire over the tabernacle. In our life journey we are very tempted to seek out human guides and that may be helpful, but I pray we do not miss out on the ways God personally desires to mark the path before us. Destination is important, but so is the adventure of the journey as we learn and grow close to God along the way.

God Blesses Those He Chooses

Numbers 24:10 NIV

The next several chapters of God's Story show interesting interactions in the pursuits of blessings. Some of God's enemies wanted to bribe Balaam, a diviner, to get God to bless them and curse God's people. Fear causes people to do weird things; so does bribery. But as the account unfolds we read how God is God and He will bless those He chooses to bless and He will curse those He chooses to curse. He can even cause a donkey to speak to get His point across.

Balak, king of the Moabites, is afraid of God's people so he bribes Balaam to curse them. But just the opposite happened. *Then Balak's anger burned against Balaam. He struck his hands together and said to him, "I summoned you to curse my enemies, but you have blessed them these three times."* From the very beginning, the Bible records that God blesses His people. We need to stay close to Him especially when it may feel like our enemy has the upper hand and wants us to be cursed.

Leap Forward with Blessings!

Deuteronomy 1:11 NIV

Even if this year does not have a leap year day, you will not want to miss reading this blessing. The time had come! Years of wandering in the wilderness were over and God told Moses to tell all the Israelites to go and take possession of the land that He promised to them. The promise that God made to Abraham, Isaac and Jacob was about to become reality! The land was right before them. Moses continued, *"May the LORD, the God of your ancestors, increase you a thousand times and bless you as he has promised!"* Moses appointed leaders and encouraged the group not to be afraid but to trust God and take the land.

This is exciting! This is what everyone had been waiting for! Yet, even with years of faithfulness shown to them by a holy God, most of the assembly rebelled against the Lord, rather than obeyed Him. This was a shocker to me. Why didn't they take those final steps to victory? But are we any different? How do we respond to God's blessings? When things look a bit scary do we leap forward in obedience or go the way of rebellion?

—— Reflections ——

In February we wrap up the life and ministry of Joseph, Jacob's eleventh son. By reading of the many ways that Joseph was blessed, and how he used his position in Pharaoh's palace to bless the Israelites, we too are encouraged to bless. Moses is the next major character in God's Story. Excitement builds through the great escape from Egypt and God's chosen people, now in large numbers, learn how to follow Him. On our journey we are just steps away from entering the long awaited Promised Land.

March

Blessings Increase Trust in the Journey

Deuteronomy 2:7 NLT

MARCH 1

From time to time we all need to be reminded of God's past faithfulness. This helps us as we continue to journey with Him, stepping out in faith bravely marching into uncharted territory. The Israelites were venturing into uncharted territory so Moses gave a much-needed pep talk: *"the Lord your God has blessed you in everything you have done. He has watched your every step through this great wilderness. During these forty years, the Lord your God has been with you, and you have lacked nothing."* God was with them; He will be with us. Sometimes we get comfortable in the place that our last faith steps have taken us and we think we have arrived. But God yearns to move us out of the familiar and into a deeper trust of His guidance.

After our first year of living in a provincial city in China I was not excited about moving to the rural back woods near Burma. It was the summer of 1997 and I had grown to know the flower lady on the corner and the egg man in the market. I knew several ways to ride my bike across town to language school, our family had made local friends, and odd as it may seem, the bustling Chinese city, filled with foreign smells and sights and sounds, felt like home. Oh, the blessings we would have missed if we had not stepped forward with God's leading, leaving the newly familiar to pursue Him into the more unknown. When we focus on His Presence, the steps of faith are not taken alone for Jesus is right next to us along the way.

As we resettled, and made yet another new place home, relationships developed. We trusted in God in fresh ways, relying on Him to be our "Steadfast Constant" when so much around us was again uncharted. Over time, we had the joy to share truth with a minority tribal man. When he understood God's love and forgiveness, he asked, "God can understand my dialect? I can talk directly with Him?" If we had stayed in the familiar, how would this man have heard God's good news? I believe

God would have made a way, but we would have missed out on being a part of the blessing.

Blessed with Direction

Deuteronomy 4:37 NLT

MARCH 2

God blesses those He chooses to bless. Some blessings are not based on condition or obedience or situation but on the choice of the God who is Lord of all; the One who has the power to bless. Moses again reminded the Israelites of this truth about God. *"Because he loved your ancestors, he chose to bless their descendants, and he personally brought you out of Egypt with a great display of power."* Thank You Father God for the way You bless us with direction. You show us love and give us gifts just because You are good. You are the Mighty One, God, the Lord, and You are all powerful and all good and personal. You are a good and faithful Leader. What an awesome combination! Thank You for Your love. Amen.

Blessed to Obey

Deuteronomy 6:24 NLT

MARCH 3

Love the Lord your God with all you have; with all your heart, with all your soul and with all your strength. As you do this it will not be a chore but a joy to pass down God's teachings to your children, grandchildren, and to people God has blessed your life with. As we love completely and know that we are completely loved, we will be filled with the desire for others to have an opportunity to love in these good ways too. God gave us life and blessings and purpose. Moses emphasized the importance of not forgetting such a valuable truth.

The Shema, the confession of Jewish faith in God alone, found in portions of Deuteronomy chapters 6 and 11 and in Numbers chapter 15, adds further details that describe how one is to live as a follower of God. Moses ended this chapter by saying, *"And the Lord our God commanded us to obey all these decrees and to fear him so he can continue to bless us and preserve our lives, as he has done to this day."* Righteousness (a good and right way of life) is a blessing to those who carefully follow God's commands. We fear what we cannot control. Wisdom comes when we realize that it is God whom we cannot control, but we do not need to control Him because He is trustworthy. These are good lessons to pass on to the generation that will follow. May others not only hear our words but see our actions as we follow God wholeheartedly.

Sometimes the Blessings Follow an "If"

Deuteronomy 7:12-14a HCSB

MARCH 4

Moses told the Israelites that holiness has its privileges. And we will see how the little two-letter word "if" can have big implications. *"If you listen to and are careful to keep these ordinances... He will love you, bless you, and multiply you. He will bless your descendants, and the produce of your land—your grain, new wine, and oil—the young of your herds, and the newborn of your flocks, in the land He swore to your fathers that He would give you. You will be blessed above all peoples."*

All of these blessings (and there are a lot of them!) depend on the condition of carefully following the good laws that God has established for His people. God does bless, and the blessings are huge, but at times these blessings hinge upon the obedience of His people. Have we grown accustomed to the blessings but have we forgotten the obedience part? I remind myself: "You better check yourself before you wreck yourself!"

Don't Forget God When You Are Filled with His Blessings

Deuteronomy 8:10 ESV

Deuteronomy means "second law" and this part of God's Story contains a flowing history lesson for the Israelites. Moses didn't deliver a different or additional law, but the same law given a second time to a new generation of Israelites who were only children at the time the original Ten Commandments were presented. They needed to hear God's law fresh for they were about to go into the Promised Land. He described the many and specific ways that God had provided for His people and ended with a wonderful description of the land that would soon be theirs. How about a little foretaste of what was in store for the obedient? *"And you shall eat and be full, and you shall bless the Lord your God for the good land he has given you."*

Moses told those following him to remember God, and not to forget that it was He who brought them into this great situation. Several translations quote Deuteronomy 8:10 as "you shall praise the Lord..." which is a great thing to do, however, I like how the English Standard Version puts it: *"you shall bless the Lord."* God is the One who blesses us with all that we have, and we are to bless the Lord and be careful not to forget Him when we are filled with blessings.

Pronounce Blessings in God's Name

Deuteronomy 10:8 NIV

Do you remember that Moses smashed the original Ten Commandments when he saw those he was leading engaging in indisputable sin? Sin ruins so much but now the time had come for a renewed covenant between

God and His people. God told Moses to chisel out two stone tablets, like the first set. Then Moses carried these up the mountain where the Lord wrote the Ten Commandments upon the stone. How easy it is to read through portions of God's Story and not pause long enough to let it sink in. I wonder what it was like to have a blank writing tablet made of stone and then see the completed Commandments knowing the finger of God wrote them?

This time a wooden box, called the Ark of the Covenant, was also made and the stone tablets were stored in the box. Life went forward and blessings were pronounced. *At that time the LORD set apart the tribe of Levi to carry the ark of the covenant of the LORD, to stand before the LORD to minister and to pronounce blessings in his name, as they still do today.* What a job that must have been for the Levites! Imagine being set apart and responsible for pronouncing the blessings in the name of the Lord.

Who in our communities today have roles like these? Our children were blessed with godly soccer coaches. Life lessons were taught both on and off the playing fields and as a high school senior in Thailand, our son Isaiah helped lead devotional times for the younger players on his soccer team. There is something special about having a responsibility to lead and teach, not just agreeing with words about God's goodness, but being the one to speak those blessings to others. As we minister to one another I pray our words would be words of blessing. Let us give encouragement that instills courage, not discouragement that takes it away.

Time to Choose: Blessing or Cursing
Deuteronomy 11:26-28 NLT

MARCH 7

"Look, today I am giving you the choice between a blessing and a curse! You will be blessed if you obey the commands of the Lord your God that I am giving you today. But you will be cursed if you reject the commands of the Lord your God and turn away from him and worship gods you have not

known before." What commands did God give? These instructions include loving the Lord, walking in all His ways, and staying near to Him, wholeheartedly. God is very clear about what He thinks about other gods. Idols, foreign gods, pagan worship poles and practices may seem exotic and enticing, but they will not set us free. These will ensnare those who choose to live outside of God.

The Israelites have been on a long journey; they felt the oppression of the false gods of Egypt and received the rescue from God Almighty. They experienced victories against idolatrous nations when All-powerful God fought for them. They knew about child sacrifices and other evil behaviors required to appease pagan gods. God does not want His people to be ignorant of the importance of choosing wisely. When we live intentionally for God, we will enjoy a lifetime of the blessing of being close to Him, our Creator and the One who loves us most. Yet God gave His people a choice back in the days of Moses and we too have a choice to make: to be blessed or to be cursed. Our actions indicate to Him as we day-by-day, choice-by-choice decide.

Blessed to Be Joyful, Thankful and Prayerful

Deuteronomy 11:29, 12:7 NIV

MARCH 8

Moses knew that he was not going with the Israelites when they crossed the Jordan River to occupy the land promised to them. With great care he continued to address the assembly by telling them more specific instructions that would be vital for them to follow. *When the Lord your God has brought you into the land you are entering to possess, you are to proclaim on Mount Gerizim the blessings, and on Mount Ebal the curses.*

Then Moses detailed the importance of pure worship that pleases God. Again both negative and positive conclusions were explained. Moses desired those he lead for the past forty years to thrive in their new land.

So many benefits awaited those who choose to obey. *There, in the presence of the LORD your God, you and your families shall eat and shall rejoice in everything you have put your hand to, because the LORD your God has blessed you.* God was blessing them with a land promised to them. No more wandering, but meaningful work and life with their families was before them. Joy should be a part of work, of life, and it really can be as we live in the Presence of the Lord. I pray that as we live lives that are joyful, thankful and prayerful our times of personal worship as well as corporate worship would bless the Lord our God. Amen.

Blessed to Bless the Poor

Deuteronomy 15:4-6 NIV

MARCH 9

"However, there need be no poor people among you, for in the land the Lord your God is giving you to possess as your inheritance, he will richly bless you, if only you fully obey the Lord your God and are careful to follow all these commands I am giving you today. For the Lord your God will bless you as he has promised, and you will lend to many nations but will borrow from none. You will rule over many nations but none will rule over you."

To a newly established nation, this blessing from God must have seemed almost too good to be true. The Book of Deuteronomy is mostly one long message, and those initially hearing it had been listening for quite some time at this point. I have a feeling their ears perked up when Moses got to this part. Although sandals did not wear out from all the desert walking they did, presently they were not particularly rich.

When Russell and I started our married life together we encountered some challenging financial times. Every penny was stretched. We even sold a partial book of postage stamps to some friends so we could have enough change to buy a cold drink on one hot day. Even though we were poor, we decided to trust God and give at least a tenth of everything we earned toward God's work. As the years have passed and our blessings have grown, we have been able to help others and this has been one of our greatest joys.

When God's people remembered their history of being poor and enslaved in Egypt, and then reflected on all the years of living in the desert, the promise of wealth and power was a great contrast. This contrast offered hope in so many ways. The Israelites had an opportunity for a fresh start and it was due to God's faithfulness and blessings. And again we see that in the middle of it all was a big "if." The blessings are there if we are careful to obey.

Blessed to Give Generously

Deuteronomy 15:10 NLT

MARCH 10

We read in the New Testament that God loves a cheerful giver. This concept goes way back to the times of Moses. There will always be the poor among us, so those who have more should give more. *Give generously to the poor, not grudgingly, for the Lord your God will bless you in everything you do.* We are happier when we live life with an open hand rather than with a stingy heart. It is helpful to keep in mind that God has created all people, those who have and those who don't have. When we are given the opportunity to give, we should do so, for it is God who has blessed the work of our hands by providing us with the wealth to give. It is a delight to live as part of the solution, staying close to God to know His desires for the good of all. In the way of giving, we are blessed to be a blessing too. Giving generously is more than just giving financially. People need care, a listening ear, time. Do you have peace with God? If so, offer peace to others so they can know God and know peace too. Give generously, live generously; for we can trust that the Lord our God will bless us.

Blessed with Complete Joy

Deuteronomy 16:10; 15 NIV

MARCH 11

Would you like to live in complete joy? The people of Israel were told to give back to God. This giving was a celebration and in proportion to what He had provided and what He would continue to provide: blessings including success with work and abundant joy. Why would we not want to return blessing for blessing and to do so with a happy heart? *Then celebrate the Festival of Weeks to the LORD your God by giving a freewill offering in proportion to the blessings the LORD your God has given you.* Remember, life is not all about work and making a profit. Take time out from working to celebrate the Lord. *For seven days celebrate the festival to the LORD your God at the place the LORD will choose. For the LORD your God will bless you in all your harvest and in all the work of your hands, and your joy will be complete.* What price would you pay for complete joy? God has provided salvation, material blessings, His Word as a handbook for living a purposeful life, and so much more. Thank You God!

Curses into Blessings Due to Love

Deuteronomy 23:5 HCSB

MARCH 12

Moses retells a story found in Numbers 22-24 about a spiritualist name Balaam who was ordered by the king of Moab to curse the Israelites. In the end, the potential cursing turned to blessings, but why? Because again God showed His love toward His people. When Russell and I worked to start a fresh church for Spanish speakers in Texas, an outspoken man mocked us while doing door-to-door outreach. This man, Juan de Leon, made fun of the nervous way that Russell's disciple, Mario, was trying to share the good news. Russell took an opportunity to stand up to the challenge with a pun based on the man's last name "of the Lion".

He quoted a verse in Ecclesiastes and shared how it is better to be a live dog than a dead lion. Juan hesitated, nodded, and invited us in. Mario was encouraged, Juan became a Christian, and Juan's wife made us some great tamales. We were all blessed! There is no promise that we will go through life free of enemies who would like to see us cursed. So we, like the Israelites in their time, need to be reminded of God's love for us. *Yet the LORD your God would not listen to Balaam, but He turned the curse into a blessing for you because the LORD your God loves you.* Trust in the simple yet profound truth that God loves you.

Blessed Not to Be Greedy

Deuteronomy 23:20 NIV, 24:13 NLT, 24:19 NIV

MARCH 13

"In God we trust" appears on US coins and paper currency. The Israelites needed to decide if they were going to trust in God when it came to money matters and the following verse gave them guidance: *"You may charge a foreigner interest, but not a fellow Israelite, so that the LORD your God may bless you in everything you put your hand to in the land you are entering to possess."* Other laws were put in place to ensure that people were provided for: *"Return the cloak to its owner by sunset so he can stay warm through the night and bless you, and the Lord your God will count you as righteous."* Later on we will see how the following principle was lived out in Ruth's life to further God's Story: *"When you are harvesting in your field and you overlook a sheaf, do not go back to get it. Leave it for the foreigner, the fatherless and the widow, so that the LORD your God may bless you in all the work of your hands."* These specific examples helped establish the operating manual for life in the new land. God cares how we treat one another and blesses us for loving as He does.

Blessings Flowing like Milk and Honey

Deuteronomy 26:15 ESV

MARCH 14

God was concerned with the well being of the priests, the foreigners, the orphans, and widows, and to meet their needs, a special tithe was offered every third year. Those who presented the offering followed the commands of the Lord and then said to God, *"Look down from your holy habitation, from heaven, and bless your people Israel and the ground that you have given us, as you swore to our fathers, a land flowing with milk and honey."* When we give our "first fruits" to the Lord to help those who cannot help themselves, everyone is blessed!

We can bless people in a variety of ways today because many churches have foundations in place to help the poor, the widows, and the orphans in their communities. Even a tithe of time can bless us and those we share our time with. We can teach English as a Second Language, giving a much-needed life skill to people in our country who need to learn a new language. Time is a precious gift to those in retirement homes. Can we share a little of our time with them? We can make a difference for good by reaching out to foreign students in colleges near us. The impact we could have on other countries without even getting a passport is potentially incredible! By donating to and shopping at Salvation Army or other stores like it we can promote good. Recently I was helping a lady "shop" at our community benevolent center. It was as if a light bulb of hope came on for her when I said, "Sure, take as many of these shirts as you need, and when you don't need them anymore, bring them back or pass them on so then you can bless someone else." All of us can be a part of the blessing cycle. Be creative, be generous, be a blessing!

Overtaken with Blessings

Deuteronomy 28:1-4 HCSB

So many blessings come from the Lord when we are obedient. Some of the detailed blessings God offered to the Israelites were dependent on their obedience to Him. *"Now if you faithfully obey the Lord your God and are careful to follow all His commands I am giving you today, the Lord your God will put you far above all the nations of the earth. All these blessings will come and overtake you, because you obey the Lord your God: You will be blessed in the city and blessed in the country. Your descendants will be blessed, and your land's produce, and the offspring of your livestock, including the young of your herds and the newborn of your flocks."*

I love the phrase, "All these blessings will come and overtake you." Think about it: to be overtaken with blessings! And that is not all. The Israelites will experience even more specific blessings if they remain faithfully obedient to the Lord, so read on!

The Blessing of Food, Rain, and Children

Deuteronomy 28:5-6; 8, 11-12a NLT

Moses may not have used alliteration as he spoke, but I can imagine somewhere along the line a preacher saying, "Now if blessed cities, blessed countryside, blessed citizens, blessed cash crops and blessed cows are not enough to get a nation's attention, God continued speaking through Moses to tell of the additional blessings that await the Israelites." *"Your fruit baskets and breadboards will be blessed. Wherever you go and whatever you do, you will be blessed."*

God's plans also involved safety from their enemies. To a people in need of physical protection, this was a very big concern and God was offering to again defend and provide for His people. *"The Lord will* guarantee a blessing on everything you do and will fill your storehouses with grain. The Lord your God will bless you in the land he is giving you." Moses then recaps the message; "The Lord will give you prosperity in the land he swore to your ancestors to give you, blessing you with many children, numerous livestock, and abundant crops. The Lord will send rain at the proper time from his rich treasury in the heavens and will bless all the work you do."

It is as if God Almighty wrote His people a blank blessing check. And for them to cash it, all they needed to do was remain faithful to the God who cares for them and who has time and time again shown His covenant love. Will they love Him in return? Do we?

Stubborn Hearts Will Not Be Blessed

Deuteronomy 29:18-19a ESV

MARCH 17

I think I learn best with positive reinforcement, but God knows that not everyone is motivated by affirmation. Sometimes we also need to be aware of the negative consequences of a situation. After a detailed description of the blessings that would come from following God's ways, we read more than fifty verses that describe what will happen (in heart-wrenching detail) if God is not obeyed. It is tragically sad that these warnings foreshadow what will take place in years to come for the Israelites.

The Book of Proverbs, written later in history, wisely warn us to guard our hearts. That is what Moses seeks to convey as he retells the story of the Israelites, preparing them for their future. Everything we do flows from our hearts, where we decide and then act upon the options before us. I pray we would stay near to God and value His love and wisdom above all else. "Beware lest there be among you a man or woman or clan or tribe whose heart is turning away today from the Lord our God to go and serve the gods of those nations. Beware lest there be among you a root bearing poisonous and bitter fruit, one who, when he hears the words of this sworn covenant, blesses himself in his heart, saying, 'I shall be safe, though I walk in the stubbornness of my heart.'"

The consequence for a rebellious attitude is severe. No matter how much we might try to rationalize the situation, when we are separated from God we are far from safe. Beware, beware! Stubborn independence is not a virtue but a strong vice. Although we may feel free, God warns us that an obstinate mindset is a lethal trap.

Blessed to Be Restored

Deuteronomy 30:1-3 HCSB

MARCH 18

Even before we go our own way, God is fully aware of our propensity to stray. *"When all these things happen to you—the blessings and curses I have set before you—and you come to your senses while you are in all the nations where the Lord your God has driven you, and you and your children return to the Lord your God and obey Him with all your heart and all your soul by doing everything I am giving you today, then He will restore your fortunes, have compassion on you, and gather you again from all the peoples where the Lord your God has scattered you."*

Our God is famous for His mercy and compassion and He knows we are bound to wander. He lets us know just how great our restoration will be when true repentance takes place. Locations and time periods may vary, however, His Storyline loops back around to a recurring theme: there is goodness and blessing in God. Humanity fails, redemption takes place for the repentant, restoration comes from a compassionate God whose desire is to bless, and when all is said and done, there will be more blessings than we could ever imagine! We are blessed to go forth and love those who live in a world that is still upside-down. We can do this best when we reflect on how Jesus loved and look forward with joy in the hope that is yet before us.

Russell's explanation of a biblical worldview through Crown-HeartWorld, coupled with his insights from Jesus' Sermon on the Mount, has been an ongoing life transformation for me. God, as we grow in Christ-likeness, may we turn to You quickly when we do fail. Thank

You for gathering us into Your family, Your Story. Help us to come to our senses and live like life matters. Loving You with all we have should lead to loving people too. Fill us with compassion enough to care, then wisdom enough to act. Amen.

Blessed to Choose Life

Deuteronomy 30:16; 19 NLT

MARCH 19

God has blessed us to live abundantly and yet He still leaves it up to us to make the choice. Moses, as God's spokesman, pleaded to the Israelites that they would choose life. Today, the opportunity to live the abundant life is offered to us through Jesus Christ. Oh, that we would choose life!

"For I command you this day to love the Lord your God and to keep his commands, decrees, and regulations by walking in his ways. If you do this, you will live and multiply, and the Lord your God will bless you and the land you are about to enter and occupy." After describing what would happen if disobedience was chosen, which doesn't sound good at all, we read: *"Today I have given you the choice between life and death, between blessings and curses. Now I call on heaven and earth to witness the choice you make. Oh, that you would choose life, so that you and your descendants might live!"*

Blessed Tribes

Deuteronomy 33:1; 11; 13; 20; 23; 24 HCSB

MARCH 20

In a book filled with blessings, it is appropriate that the end of Deuteronomy would have another concentration of blessings. *This is the blessing that Moses, the man of God, gave the Israelites before his death.* Years before, these names were simply the names of Jacob's sons. Now we read that these same names have expanded into the tribes of Israel. We see how God's promises come true as each "son" is now a tribe and each tribe grows like stars in the sky.

About the tribe of Levi Moses said, *"LORD, bless his possessions, and accept the work of his hands."* Joseph's clan's blessings: *"May his land be blessed by the LORD..."* He said this about Gad's people: *"The one who enlarges Gad's territory will be blessed."* Picture Moses looking right into the eyes of those in Naphtali's tribe when he spoke the next blessing. *"Naphtali, enjoying approval, full of the LORD's blessing, take possession to the west and the south."* Do you remember how happy Leah was when her maid gave birth to Jacob's eighth son? The final blessing was for this eighth son, for Asher's descendants. The Hebrew meaning of his name is "happy, blessed, fortunate": *"May Asher be the most blessed of the sons..."*

Moses blessed each tribe and each blessing was a little different because each of God's people is a little different, yet God loves us all. The abounding blessing of redemption through His Son Jesus is now offered to every one of us. How will we respond to the blessings we are given?

Blessed to Live a Full and Interesting Life

Deuteronomy 33:29 NLT

MARCH 21

Mountaintop views are stunning! While Russell was at meetings for Asia Harvest, the board members' wives hiked each afternoon around the New Zealand countryside. Our time in this part of God's creation was rejuvenating. Beauty as far as the eye could see. One day we climbed the highest local hill, and I thought about Moses. Mountain climbing is not for the faint of heart, yet the view from the top is spectacular and oh so worth each step.

After blessing each tribe individually, God's righteous servant Moses shared one more verse of written words before he climbed alone up the mountain God told him to climb. He marveled at the vast land before him that the Lord promised His people, then he died after living 120 years. Final words are often words remembered and Moses did not want Israel to forget that they are a blessed people.

"How blessed you are, O Israel! Who else is like you, a people saved by the Lord? He is your protecting shield and your triumphant sword! Your enemies will cringe before you, and you will stomp on their backs!" Pretty strong and zesty final words from one of the greatest leaders the world has ever known. Moses led an incredibly diverse and exciting life. He may have begun the rescue mission with a speech impediment but Moses ended his life speaking strongly for the Lord he loved. He was a blessed man.

Blessed to Carry and Pass the Baton of Faith

Joshua 8:33b-34 HCSB

MARCH 22

It was time for the baton to be passed. Excitement builds when this is done during a middle school track meet or at the Olympic level for we know that the outcome of a good hard run race often comes down to a flawless passing of the baton. Our family had pioneered the mission work with an unreached tribe in China near the border of Burma. For many years prayer, language study, meeting people, sharing truth and a whole lot of life was lived as this group went from no known believers to young churches starting up to worship God in their own language. God's Kingdom expanded. We sensed we completed our contribution and those we trained were ready to grip the baton and run their leg of this great race.

Before he died, Moses passed on his ministry baton. Joshua was God's newly assigned leader for His people and several times God told Joshua to be strong and courageous. The first eight chapters of the book named after him, are packed with action. With the Promised Land before him, Joshua sent in two spies who were helped by Rahab. Then with the ark of the covenant leading the way, the Israelites crossed the dry Jordan River. The Israelites set up stones as a memorial, all the men were circumcised, and the Passover was celebrated. Finally, the fortified city of Jericho was captured with a march and a shout. Joshua erected an altar for offerings to the Lord and the entire nation of Israel gathered expectantly on both sides of the ark of the Lord's covenant. They faced the Levitical priests who carried it and waited for the priests *to bless the people of Israel. Afterward, Joshua read aloud all the words of the law—the blessings as well as the curses—according to all that is written in the book of the law.*

That is a lot of information to take in, and just imagine if we were there living it all out; our journals would be filled with one amazing act of God after the next! Yet in our own lives God intervenes, blesses, guides, provides and so much more, for us, His children. God, saying, "thanks" does not feel like enough for all that You do for us. The very air that we breathe is a gift, a blessing from You. Your nearness comforts, Your strength gives us strength, Your Presence guides us. Please accept our sacrifice of thanksgiving. With deep gratitude may we run strong and pass the baton of faith to those that will run after us. Amen.

A Forty Year Blessing Fulfilled

Joshua 14:13 NIV

MARCH 23

At this point in the Story, Caleb, a brave, honest man, was eighty-five years old and just as strong as ever. Back in the day, when Moses sent him and Joshua to Canaan as part of a twelve-man scouting party, Moses recognized Caleb's integrity and promised a specific portion of the Promised Land to him. Caleb was to receive this inheritance because he followed the Lord wholeheartedly. Now the time was right for Caleb to remind Joshua of the promise that Moses had made four decades earlier.

Both Joshua and Caleb must have felt the building excitement; the fulfilling of God's promise was here! They had waited an additional forty years since they first spied out that good, plentiful land that flowed with milk and honey. I can picture Joshua hugging his loyal friend, memories flooding through their minds of grape clusters so big it took two men to carry, of large fortified cities and of enemies big and strong. A younger Joshua and Caleb sought to rally the people when they returned from their forty-day exploration. "We can do this! God has promised the land to us! Don't be afraid, for God is with us and we will swallow those people up!" But sadly, the Israelites gave into fear and listened to the whiney report from the other ten leaders instead. It took forty years for all of the non-trusting people to die as they wandered in the desert. Now Joshua was leading with Caleb at his side and a new generation was about to see the promises of God fulfilled. Then *Joshua blessed Caleb son of Jephunneh and gave him Hebron as his inheritance.*

Some Blessings Need to Be Asked For

Joshua 15:19 HCSB

MARCH 24

Caleb was one mighty octogenarian. He received his portion of land and began to drive out the inhabitants who did not honor God. This took strength, bravery, wisdom and trust that God was on his side. Caleb offered his daughter in marriage to the man who was able to capture a certain city within his new domain. When she arrived to set up her new home her dad Caleb asked her what it was she wanted.

I picture a little feistiness as she makes her request. Maybe her hand was on her hip when she got off her traveling donkey and said, *"Give me a blessing. Since you have given me land in the Negev, give me the springs of water also."* So he gave her the upper and lower springs. This pioneer woman was then able to water her gardens, her herds, do laundry and have fresh water for making lemonade and for cooking. What a good blessing to ask for and to receive. Her husband and household would indeed be blessed!

Can you imagine how challenging simple day-to-day living would be without access to water? At times when we lived in various places there would be days without the convenience of electricity. Even in first-world countries when a major storm hits, power outages can be experienced and often the extended community steps in to offer help. But when there is not access to water, life takes on a whole new level of challenge. Caleb's daughter, Acsah, got the special favor she asked for: water.

Sometimes we go without because we do not ask. Other times we are like Caleb, the ones who are in the position to extend the blessing. Around the world today people still have the need to receive clean water. The good news is there are many opportunities to be involved with well digging projects. It is another good way we can be a part of blessing others!

The Blessing of Good Leaders

Joshua 17:14b NLT

MARCH 25

Joshua's main role at this point in history was to divide territories for all the tribes and clans of Israel. This division was accomplished by casting lots and recognizing which tribes were big enough to completely take over the new land. Dividing up the Promised Land was not always a clear-cut easy job for God's leader and, at times, Joshua's decisions were questioned.

The descendants of Joseph came to Joshua and asked, *"Why have you given us only one portion of land as our homeland when the Lord has blessed us with so many people?"* Joshua reassessed, gave more territory to Joseph's tribe and encouraged them that even though the Canaanites were strong and had chariots of iron, Joseph's descendants could drive them out.

Good, godly leadership is not easy to come by. God told Joshua often to be brave and I believe that this encouraged him. We can then see in the life of Joshua how he encouraged others to be brave too. God, we pray for our leaders today. May those that are in authority take the time to seek You for wisdom and to lead with integrity. I pray that when it is our time to lead (in big and little ways) we would do the same. Thank You God for being our good Leader. Amen.

Blessed to be Peacemakers

Joshua 22:6; 33b ESV

MARCH 26

After initial conquests had been made, Joshua commended those who had chosen to settle on the east side of the Jordan for their faithful service and told them they could return to their homes. Before they journeyed on, he urged them to continue to love the Lord, walk in His ways, obey His commands, hold fast to Him and to serve Him completely. *So Joshua blessed them and sent them away, and they went to their tents.*

Later a bit of a misunderstanding took place among the clans and when reconciliation was reached the tribes of Israel experience the joy of peace-filled unity. *And the people of Israel blessed God and spoke no more of making war against them to destroy the land where the people of Reuben and the people of Gad were settled.*

What a blessing it is for families to live at peace with each other! Even though it often takes work to understand and to be understood, it is so worth it to live in a restored relationship. Jesus expounds on this peace-making theme in His public teaching that took place on a mountain, saying that those who work for peace will be blessed. Years later a 13th-century Catholic saint named Francis begins his well-known prayer with: "Lord, make me an instrument of Your peace." Our greatest need is peace with God and perhaps the greatest gift we can give is peace in our relationships.

Rescued and Blessed

Joshua 24:10 NLT

A lot of good true stories are repeated. Ancient stories along with stories we hear today can be passed down to the next generation for teaching points, encouragement, and to be a reminder of the Lord's faithfulness. This is exactly what took place just before Joshua made a covenant with the Israelites and sent them away, each to his own piece of Promised Land.

Joshua retold God's Story starting with Abraham's father. He highlighted key elements of their unique history and reemphasized God's faithfulness, power and compassion. Joshua mentioned Balaam who had been sent to curse the Israelites. Quoting God, Joshua says, *"...but I would not listen to him. Instead, I made Balaam bless you, and so I rescued you from Balak."* God reminded the Israelites, through Joshua, that it was He who had provided victory after victory and in gratitude, the people responded saying they would serve and obey the Lord. Later the prophet Micah also encouraged the people of his lifetime by retelling the account of the Lord's blessings through Balaam and Balak.

One reason why I am writing this book is to remember God's blessings. By working through God's Story of blessings and retelling stories of how He blessed our family time after time, I am blessed all over again.

On our first Easter among an unreached people of China, the town's eight foreigners rode through the quiet pre-dawn with the desire to pray and worship the Redeemer on a mountaintop as the sun rose. Isaiah, five years old, excitedly raced past Sophie and slipping on a stone bridge, he gashed his head open when he fell backwards. Russ applied pressure to Isaiah's wound and used my jacket to absorb the bleeding, and we went on with worshipping our Lord. In time, and with the help of our neighbor, a nurse, Isaiah's head grew back together. He did not suffer any ongoing damage; his scar became a physical reminder to me of God's goodness. How good it is for us to reflect on God's faithful blessings and refresh our vow to honor Him.

Blessed among Tent-Dwelling Women

Judges 5:24 HCSB

MARCH 28

Summers in Michigan are best when they are spent by a lake and when I was growing up my family did a lot of lakeside camping. Meals around a campfire, waterskiing, and catching fireflies are all wonderful childhood memories. The experience of living from time-to-time in a tent blessed me to better connect with a tent-dwelling woman of the Old Testament.

After Joshua died, having served the Lord faithfully, there was still more of the Promised Land to conquer. Unfortunately, this conquest did not go well. By embracing pagan influences the Israelites allow themselves to be led astray and immediately the people of God found themselves far from Him. Time after time though, as they repented, God continued to provide for them. God told Deborah (the nation's judge at that time) that He would bring about the victory they needed. However, when Israel's commander Barak, heard the battle plan he balked. God was not thwarted and used a woman to achieve the goal in an intriguing manner.

Jael was very brave, strong and yet gentle. When Sisera the fleeing enemy commander approached her tent for a respite, Jael tended his needs by offering milk to drink and a blanket to make him feel cozy. When he fell asleep exhausted from battle, she softly entered the tent and drove a tent peg through his temple with a hammer. Jael accomplished what a mighty military army failed to do and Sisera lay dead at her feet. Deborah wrote a song praising Jael and giving the glory to God for the victory.

I re-pictured Jael's story while pitching a tent for a camping weekend with my sisters and their families in the summer of 2012. My reflection on this interesting part of God's Story, is to use the tools God provides us so we can faithfully serve Him. I hope my tools will not be hammers and tent pegs, but that is what they were for Jael and she was blessed for using them. *"Jael is most blessed of women, the wife of Heber the Kenite; she is most blessed among tent-dwelling women."*

Blessed for Victory

Judges 5:1-2; 9 ESV

MARCH 29

The courageous judge Deborah, who bravely took God's army into battle, led the troops home with a song of praise to the Lord when God provided the victory (and He saw fit to include Jael as well). Although Barak was slow to accept the plan, I like it that he joined in with the victory praise to God. *Then sang Deborah and Barak the son of Abinoam on that day: "That the leaders took the lead in Israel, that the people offered themselves willingly, bless the LORD!"* The song continues to tell of the Lord's praise-worthiness: *"My heart goes out to the commanders of Israel who offered themselves willingly among the people. Bless the LORD."* At times we may need to lead out courageously in order to take action and when God blesses us with the victory, let us not forget to offer praise right back to Him.

Set Apart and Blessed

Judges 13:24-25a NIV

MARCH 30

During this time in history, the Israelites wavered continually concerning their faithfulness to the Lord. Once more, after doing evil in the eyes of the Lord, they were delivered into the hands of their enemies, the Philistines; at this point for a period of forty years. Then someone who looked like an angel delivered life-changing news to a childless couple. *The woman gave birth to a boy and named him Samson. He grew and the LORD blessed him, and the Spirit of the LORD began to stir within him...*

Even those who may not know much about the Bible have probably heard of Samson, a man made supernaturally strong by God. Before birth Samson was set apart with a purpose from God: to begin to rescue the Israelites from the hands of their enemies. He may not have always made the best choices when it came to women, but when he lived according to his purpose, he did great things.

Five chapters of God's Story are reserved for telling Samson's movie-worthy story. Not everyone who is born has a starring role in the big Story, but each of us can be faithful with what God has called us to do. It is good for us to give some thought as to how God has created and gifted us individually, and how living out our calling can make a difference. Samson's uneven faithfulness in life was meaningful, but his wholehearted devotion at his death ended up being more effective than all he had done to that point.

The sooner we use our uniqueness to honor the Lord with our lives, living on purpose for Him, the better. But even if we have been uneven up to now, there is still time to trust Him.

Blessedness Should Not Lead to Corruption

Judges 17:2 NIV

MARCH 31

There was not a king in Israel at this time and everyone did as he saw fit. "Everyone did as he saw fit" could describe the driving practices of Burma (Myanmar). When I was thirty-five years old Russell cared for our kiddos in Thailand and for twelve days I traveled throughout Burma's Shan State with two younger ladies. National traffic flow had changed from the left to the right but several cars still operate for right side driving, which means a passenger sees oncoming traffic on a curve long before the driver does. Adding to the chaos, horns are preferred over turn signals, stop signs treated as optional and the roads that were maintained when the British occupied Burma had become a series of potholes. It was very natural to talk to God frequently about our safety as well as the human rights issues that affect so many in what should be a thriving country.

Israel also should have been a thriving nation, but instead of following God and His ways, they did as they saw fit and it led to head-on-collisions with sin. Micah was a man who lived during this time and told his mother, *"The eleven hundred shekels of silver that were taken from you and about which I heard you utter a curse—I have that silver with me; I took it."* *Then his mother said, "The LORD bless you, my son!"* This story goes on to illustrate the corrupt nature of the Israelites as some of them sought to live disconnected from God.

Now, just like then, a compromise with even the smallest things can lead to big deviations that affect more people than we might ever guess. In Burma the situation has gone from bad to horrendous. God, we pray for the people within Burma to have not only Your protection but to know You as their Savior. May the corruption end and Your justice go forth. Amen.

Reflections

As we march through the month of March, Moses paused with God's people to refocus them on the holiness and goodness of God. We too are reminded that blessings come when we love the Lord our God with all our heart, soul, mind, and strength. Before Moses died, he blessed the tribes of Israel and Joshua was appointed as the new leader. Joshua faithfully led the beginning conquest of the Promised Land. After his death, we get a sampling of what life was like during the period of the Judges.

April

From Bitter to Better to Blessed

Ruth 1:6 NLT

APRIL 1

Get ready! God's big Story is narrowing in on one particular family and this attention gives us a glimpse of how God's blessings make a difference in the lives of people like you and me. I really like Ruth's story, the four-chapter romantic mini-drama, although the beginning is tragic.

A famine in Bethlehem (a little town in Judah) forces a young family of four to migrate to Moab. In a short time, Naomi's husband dies leaving her with two sons to raise. Her sons both grow up and marry local Moabite women and then unexpectedly the brothers die as well. Naomi is left with only memories of what had been her family. Can you imagine losing your entire family while living in a foreign land? It would be easy to despair. Naomi is sad and even bitter about her situation.

But read on as the conclusion might just be the first recorded "and they all lived happily ever after" kind of ending. *Then Naomi heard in Moab that the LORD had blessed his people in Judah by giving them good crops again. So Naomi and her daughters-in-law got ready to leave Moab to return to her homeland.* The story is about to turn from bitter to better. Oh, for the times when the bitter to better transformation takes place in our lives, when we experience the journey with God, having faith that He leads us for our good.

Blessed with a Second Chance

Ruth 1:9 NLT

APRIL 2

Naomi did not expect her pagan daughters-in-law to actually leave all that was familiar to them and travel with her back to her hometown. With tears, Naomi prepared to go and said her farewells: *"May the LORD bless you with the security of another marriage."* Then she kissed them good-bye, *and they all broke down and wept.* But Ruth, one of her daughters-in-law surprised Naomi by saying, "I'm going with you and your people will be my people, and your God will be my God. I will even be buried wherever it is that you die and are buried."

I wonder what went through the minds of the two traveling companions as they made the fifty mile or so journey. As Naomi passed by familiar landmarks, did she remember the trip she and her husband and young sons made in her younger years? Was Ruth still grieving the husband she lost? Did each step toward Bethlehem give Ruth hope toward her future or fear that she might not be accepted? There is a lot to speculate, but what we do know is that Ruth was committed to Naomi and we will see how God blessed Ruth's commitment. True love and commitment go hand in hand. When we say, "May the Lord bless you with..." do we have faith that He will bless?

The Lord Bless You!

Ruth 2:4 NLT

APRIL 3

The two women, Naomi and Ruth, arrived in Bethlehem and were warmly greeted. How wonderful it feels to be welcomed after a long trip. They were, however, still without a male provider and they needed food, so Ruth went out to the barley fields to pick up whatever had been left after the harvesters had gone through the crops. *While she was there, Boaz arrived from Bethlehem and greeted the harvesters. "The LORD be with you!" he said. "The LORD bless you!" the harvesters replied.* At that time, Boaz had no idea just how the Lord was about to really bless him. If he was a socks-wearing man, we could say God blessed his socks off!

When he caught a glimpse of Ruth and heard of her faithful character, Boaz chose to offer her protection and provision while she worked in his fields. I picture their first meeting and I think it must have been love at first sight, but I'm getting a little ahead of the story. By-the-way, when Russell and I first met in the Gunnery Sergeant's office in Pensacola, Florida, he claims it was love at first sight. It makes me smile to go back to that time when we were two eighteen-year-old Marines and to think about all that God has brought us through since those days. That is a different story altogether, yet one still filled with God's blessings.

Blessed to Be Noticed

Ruth 2:19-20 NIV

APRIL 4

Ruth brought back a large bundle of grain and her mother-in-law asked, *"Where did you glean today? Where did you work? Blessed be the man who took notice of you!"* Ruth filled Naomi in on her good fortune concerning her work situation and then told her that the kind man that had helped her was named Boaz. The story gets even better when Naomi shares that Boaz is a respectable member of her deceased husband's family: *"The LORD bless him!" Naomi said to her daughter-in-law. "He has not stopped showing his kindness to the living and the dead." She added, "That man is our close relative; he is one of our guardian-redeemers."* This relationship tie meant that Boaz had a responsibility toward the two women.

In time, Naomi will put a little matchmaking plan into action so Ruth and Boaz can have a more intimate encounter. I have learned that matchmaking is not one of my God-given gifts. However, I love the joy and excitement that comes when a couple gets engaged and seeks God for their future. Ruth was blessed when Boaz noticed her and I sure was blessed the day that Russell took notice of me, a young Marine wearing combat boots and cammies. It is healthy to reflect on the truth that all goodness comes from God and He knows the plan way before we do.

Proper Pursuit Led to Blessings

Ruth 3:10 HCSB

Ruth met with Boaz at the threshing floor and he was pleased to see her. I envision him looking at her with adoration as he said, *"May the LORD bless you, my daughter. You have shown more kindness now than before, because you have not pursued younger men, whether rich or poor."* Wedding bells are going to ring for Ruth and Boaz! By following Naomi's guidance, Ruth has met a man who not only cares for her but is also able to provide her a place in the community. Boaz was offering Ruth a second chance at married love and by doing so he was blessed with a lovely wife.

It looks like God was answering the prayer that Naomi prayed when she was about to leave Moab. Back in Moab there were tears of sadness and even bitterness. Rather than taking matters into her own hands, Naomi took the situation to God and prayed for something specific for her daughters-in-law. Naomi asked that God would bless them with a second happy marriage. With God in the picture, bitter hearts can change making room for joy to come. Blessings can then flow. It happened then, and with God in charge, His blessings continue to flow today. Everyone was delighted with the arrangement but the story doesn't end here.

Blessed Be the Lord Who Redeems, Renews and Sustains

Ruth 4:14-15 ESV

God blessed their marriage and Boaz and Ruth gave birth to a son, Obed, who would become the grandfather to Israel's future king, David. We will see these names again as Matthew lists the genealogy of Jesus in the opening book of the New Testament. Ruth and Boaz's story concludes with the first chapter's main character: Naomi. *Then the women said* to Naomi, "Blessed be the LORD, who has not left you this day without a redeemer, and may his name be renowned in Israel! He will renew your life and sustain you in your old age. For your daughter-in-law, who loves you and who is better to you than seven sons, has given birth to him." And everyone lived happily ever after!

When you think about it, this is a miniature telling of God's Story. Before the famine, life was rich within the community. Then, loss caused sorrow and separation. Following this separation, God provided a way of redemption, and preparations were made for a wedding, just like the wedding God's people will celebrate with Jesus as the bridegroom. At last, we will all live with God in a community where there will be no more tears, worshipping happily through all eternity. I love God's Story!

The Childless Blessed to Have Children

1 Samuel 2:20 HCSB

APRIL 7

Just a few weeks before our first child was born in August 1990, I read from God's Story of a remarkable woman named Hannah who longed for a child. It touched me so deeply that when Russell returned from a mission trip I asked him if we could name our daughter Hannah. We prayed that our baby girl would grow to be like the Hannah of the Bible who was dedicated, faithful and trusting.

The ancient Hannah poured out her request and her tears before the Lord. When a son, Samuel, was born to her and Elkanah, she followed through with her promise to give him back to the Lord. Samuel grew up in the Temple where he served under the leadership of a priest named Eli. Hannah's prayer and praise to the Lord was a wonderful testimony of her faith. Each year she would make a new robe for her growing son and when they traveled to the Temple for worship she would give it to Samuel. *Before they returned home, Eli would bless Elkanah and his wife and say, "May the Lord give you other children to take the place of this one she gave to the Lord."* God answered that prayer too and blessed the couple with five additional children! The Lord used Samuel, the first born, in a great way and he was the last and greatest of Israel's judges, a mighty prophet, and he was chosen by God to anoint Israel's first and second kings.

May we be like Hannah and never underestimate the power of prayer and then faithfully live and model a healthy spiritual life of thanksgiving.

From Blessing a Sacrifice to Anointing a King
1 Samuel 9:13 NIV

APRIL 8

Samuel, who was once a small baby and then a boy in Eli's care, grew to be a man of faith and prayer, and at this point in God's Story is now an old man. Times are at a spiritual low for the Israelites and the people join together and clamor for an earthly king. God chooses a tall young man named Saul.

It might not make for the most exciting of coronation ceremonies but it is interesting how Samuel first met Saul. Saul's dad's donkeys had gone missing and Saul was sent out to find them. After three days he was about to give up but he heard that a man of God was in the next town. Maybe he could help. Some girls drawing water told Saul, *"As soon as you enter the town, you will find him before he goes up to the high place to eat. The people will not begin eating until he comes, because he must bless the sacrifice; afterward, those who are invited will eat. Go up now; you should find him about this time."* Saul found Samuel and Samuel went from blessing the sacrifice to anointing Israel's first king.

But the Israelites would soon realize that they should have never given up a theocracy by asking for a monarchy. We need to learn to be very wise with our requests.

A Cheerful "Blessing"
Does Not Cover Disobedience

1 Samuel 15:13 NLT

APRIL 9

"To obey is better than sacrifice." This is the truth that cost King Saul his crown. The basic story is that God gave a very specific message to Saul and sadly, Saul only partially followed God's command. Half-obedience is not obedience at all and Samuel was sent to let Saul know that the consequences of his choice would be grave.

When Samuel finally found him, Saul greeted him cheerfully. "May the LORD bless you," he said. "I have carried out the LORD's command!" Cheerfulness cannot cover sin and Samuel got right to the heart of the matter. Saul's glad greeting turned to rationalization which then turned to shifting the blame. Saul begged for forgiveness when he heard Samuel's words: "because you have rejected the word of the LORD, he has rejected you as king."

Unfortunately we are often like Saul. We rationalize here, or partially follow truth there. And then upon careful reflection we realize that our way of taking care of a situation is not obeying God's way at all. God does not want our "sacrifice" but our loyalty. Lord, have mercy on us. Amen.

Blessed to Be Close to God

1 Samuel 23:21 NIV

APRIL 10

God indeed will replace Saul with a man after God's own heart and Samuel anointed David but he does not become the new king right away. As a shepherd boy, David learned many valuable life skills. The close relationship he developed and maintained with God was perhaps his greatest asset. David, seeking to honor God, killed Goliath when he was still too young to fill out Saul's armor. Saul got to know David better when David came to play music to comfort him. Saul's own son Jonathan established a meaningful friendship with David and David even married Saul's daughter. By this time, David was an intricate part of Saul's family.

But because of David's growing popularity as a warrior, Saul became increasingly jealous of him and even wanted to take his life. One time in particular, Saul was out searching for David and got a lead on David's whereabouts. Saul replied to those who had helped him, *"The Lord bless you for your concern for me."* Even when it may have seemed to David that everyone was out to get him, God protected David from Saul's pursuits.

It was during this season that David poured out his heart to the Lord in songs. How we respond in times of unfair treatment can tell us a lot about ourselves. Closeness to God can make all the difference.

Bless the Lord at All Times

Psalm 34:1-2, 8 ESV

APRIL 11

David's praise and refuge were in the Lord even when Saul pursued him to take his life. *"I will bless the Lord at all times; his praise shall continually be in my mouth. My soul makes its boast in the Lord; let the humble hear and be glad."* It was easy to contemplate this psalm of praise in the spring of 2012 when I was at a weekend silent retreat and the nature surrounding me was majestic. Brilliant peacocks were climbing deep scented pine trees and it seemed natural to boast in the Lord who created such variety. But weeks later when I read the verse, copied into a friend's prayer letter, my head was throbbing with a headache in time with the computer's cursor. Yet the same God is Lord of all and like the psalmist I'm called to bless Him at all times.

In Hebrew, David's language, Psalm 34 is an acrostic poem and each verse begins with the letters of the alphabet in order like A, B, C, etc.

The poem is a wonderful lesson to always praise the Lord and it concludes in confidence that God's servants will be redeemed. On the good days and on the days that are harder, *"Oh, taste and see that the Lord is good! Blessed is the man who takes refuge in him!"*

David found this to be true so he shared it with us in song. Have we tasted the goodness of God for ourselves? Do those around us get a taste of His goodness from us? May His praise be in our mouth as we boast in Him alone. He is our place of retreat, of refuge, and we are blessed when we go to Him at all times.

Blessed to Be Freed

Psalm 124:6-8 ESV

APRIL 12

David is very aware of where his help comes from. He writes this song, Psalm 124, to remind God's people that if the Lord had not been on their side, it would have been a very different story! They would have been swallowed up alive. So all praise and blessing go to God! *Blessed be the Lord, who has not given us as prey to their teeth! We have escaped like a bird from the snare of the fowlers; the snare is broken and we have escaped! Our help is in the name of the Lord, who made heaven and earth.*

Where do we turn for help? Who is it that we call out to in times of need? God desires that our dependency is on Him alone. At times I feel He gives us a pop-test, a little glitch in our day, so that we can stop and assess just where it is that we place our trust. Father, You are the Creator of Heaven and earth and all that is in them and yet You hear us when we call out to You for help. Thank You, Lord, for helping us when we feel trapped and for freeing us from the sin that would like to keep us in bondage. May Your name be blessed. Amen.

Blessed with Peace

Psalm 29:10-11 NLT

David, a gifted poet and songwriter, wrote Psalm 29, a short song about the powerful, majestic and thunderous voice of the Lord. Many examples from nature illustrate God's voice. Imagine listening to the music of this song - loud instruments, drums beating and cymbals clashing, to drive home the point that God's voice is powerful. Slowly, one by one, the instruments stop playing and all that can be heard is a single strum of a guitar and the singer whispers the final line of the chorus: "God bless you with peace."

The Lord has a range from thunderstorms to a still small voice that whispers: peace. Jesus told his disciples that He leaves them with peace; it is His peace that He gives. *The Lord rules over the floodwaters. The Lord reigns as king forever. The Lord gives his people strength. The Lord blesses them with peace.*

Peace be with you. If I try, I can hear the reply from the congregation in the beautiful stained-glass Catholic Church of my youth, "and also with you." Peace with God comes through His Son. What wonderful joy to be at peace with the reigning King who offers His strength to those who are loyal to Him. When we are at peace with God, we can extend this peace to those around us as well. A heart filled with peace has little room for regret.

Your Hand of Blessing is on My Head

Psalm 139:3-5 NLT

Omnipresent is a word that when spoken about God, means that He is everywhere; all places at all times. God's own Son is called Immanuel, meaning God with us. This news is good, very good indeed. David does not write about God as some sort of stalker, but rather His Presence gives comfort, peace and protection. Oh, the joy of being led by the Lord, to be held by Him, to be blessed by Him.

When my kiddos were ten, eleven, and twelve years old, my dad came from Michigan for a visit to our home in China. After a great trip to Xian and Beijing and celebrating his birthday, my dad flew back to the US. Russell stayed in Beijing for meetings, so he put me and the kids on the train with a treasure of Subway sandwiches, and we saw some stunning countryside on our fifty-hour journey to Kunming.

The next stage of the trip home was an overnight bus that would twist through many mountains to our town near Burma. Exhausted from the trip the kiddos fell right to sleep. Throughout the long, bumpy ride I found myself checking on them and praying for safety, protection, and God's peace. On a stop just before dawn for breakfast noodles and makeshift restrooms, I saw a friend who was also returning to our town and he asked me if we still had our backpacks and money. Nearly everyone on the bus had been robbed that night and I, as a foreign woman with young children, would have been an easy target.

At that time, our friend Ken did not understand my explanation of God's protection, but I keep praying that one day he too will trust in God's goodness. May we daily know His nearness. *You see me when I travel and when I rest at home. You know everything I do. You know what I am going to say even before I say it, Lord. You go before me and follow me. You place your hand of blessing on my head.* I am not alone. You are not alone. We do not need to be afraid. God is with us, no matter where we go, when we walk with God we go with His blessing.

Blessed before a Watching World

Psalm 31:19 NLT

Psalm 31 is another vivid reminder of God's goodness. David reflects on this goodness not only when life is going great, but also when he is in need of protection from his enemies. *How great is the goodness you have stored up for those who fear you. You lavish it on those who come to you for protection, blessing them before the watching world.*

Sometimes we forget that we don't live in a vacuum, nor move through life in a darkly tinted bubble. Instead, people are watching to see just how we react to challenging situations in our lives. One gal waiting for help with food and clothing from a ministry of Houston's First Baptist Church, said she was curious to see how the Christian volunteers would respond when the computer holding critical information would not turn on. When we are squeezed by trials, what comes out? Praise, trust, and hope came out of David, and may that be what others see in us as well.

What about when blessings of various kinds come our way? Does a watching world see us praise God from whom all blessings flow? The woman at the Faith Center saw that instead of us getting flustered with the computer, we circled to pray and then when the computer began to work, thanksgiving to God was offered up. As God's children we can ask Him for all kinds of needs. At times His reply is right away and when we express our thanksgiving, people around us see His blessing too.

Blessed When We Do Right Because It Is Right

1 Samuel 25:32b-33, 39a ESV

We would never want Nabal to marry anyone we loved. Although he was rich, Nabal was also a selfish, harsh, evil, drinking fool. David and his men were traveling through Nabal's territory and the interaction went so poorly when Nabal rudely repaid evil for good that David wanted to kill him. It is a good thing that Abigail, Nabal's wife, was insightful and brave and when she heard of the situation she took matters into her own hands.

Immediately Abigail prepared gifts of food and drinks and with wise and humble words approached David and his troops to make peace. David received her message and gifts and thanked Abigail, *"Blessed be the LORD, the God of Israel, who sent you this day to meet me! Blessed be your discretion, and blessed be you, who have kept me this day from bloodguilt and from working salvation with my own hand!*

Nabal died about ten days later and when David heard this news David continued his thanksgiving to God, *"Blessed be the LORD who has avenged the insult I received at the hand of Nabal, and has kept back his servant from wrongdoing. The LORD has returned the evil of Nabal on his own head."*

David remembered Abigail who was now a widow, and asked her to become his wife. Abigail had no idea that the blessing she had offered would not only spare her life, but would also lead to a wedding proposal from Israel's next king! How good it is to do right because it is right. God knows our motives and in His good timing blessings will come.

Blessed with Peace
to Praise God All Day Long

Psalm 35:27-28 NLT

Although David had many life-long enemies who were out to get him, he also had many advocates. David was not yet the king but he was a well-followed leader and I have a feeling he had a special way of making those under his leadership know that they were all part of a big team. They worked together in awareness of God and gave Him the praise for His interactions that led to their good. And that is the way it should be today.

David sings out, *"But give great joy to those who came to my defense. Let them continually say, 'Great is the Lord, who delights in blessing his servant with peace!' Then I will proclaim your justice, and I will praise you all day long."* What is it that we find ourselves continually saying? Do we praise God all day long, or just on Sunday as we offer up a song? Let's make sure we are on God's team and let's be sure to come to the defense of others who wear His uniform too.

As Peacemakers We Are Blessed

1 Samuel 26:25 HCSB

Even though Saul was fixated on taking David's life, David modeled great restraint and respect toward Saul, honoring him as God's anointed king. David had an opportunity to put an end to the one who wanted to destroy him and the soldier with David was perplexed why he did not take that chance. Instead of killing Saul as he lay sleeping, David took Saul's spear and water jug. From the other side of the mountain, David called out to Saul.

Saul came to his senses and said to David, *"You are blessed, my son David. You will certainly do great things and will also prevail." Then David went on his way, and Saul returned home.* Saul and David had made peace, but life in general was far from peaceful. Not too long after this meeting with David, Saul's sons were killed during a great battle against Israel's enemy, the Philistines. Saul himself was critically injured by an archer and to avoid falling into the hands of the enemy, he took his own life.

David deeply lamented the deaths of these prominent men - Saul and his sons. After Saul's death, David became the king of Judah and he certainly did go on to do great things. I'm thankful for this passage in God's Story for it shows us how reconciliation really can take place. Let us be like David and actively seek peace while we can.

Kindness Returns Blessing for Blessing

2 Samuel 2:5-7 HCSB

APRIL 19

David became the king of Judah and continued to honor Saul even after his death. Men of Jabesh-Gilead carefully buried King Saul and David sent this message to them, *"The Lord bless you, because you have shown this kindness to Saul your lord when you buried him. Now, may the Lord show kindness and faithfulness to you, and I will also show the same goodness to you because you have done this deed. Therefore, be strong and courageous, for though Saul your lord is dead, the house of Judah has anointed me king over them."*

Many years later David was anointed king over all of Israel, fulfilling the promise the Lord made through Samuel. David would learn that with a very powerful position comes great responsibility. David went out of his way to bless those who had acted in kindness. Have we had some form of kindness shown to us recently? If so, how will we return that blessing with a blessing?

Blessed Is Everyone Who Fears the Lord

Psalm 128:1-6 ESV

King David wrote meaningful praise songs, from the heart, and over seventy of them can be found in the book of Psalms. These songs tell us the story of David's life and they include timeless themes of praise, rescue, provision and blessing. The songs were recorded so the whole nation of Israel could reflect upon the message sung during special times of the year. Psalm 128 describes those who walk in the ways of the Lord and it shows the various ways in which those who fear the Lord are blessed.

Blessed is everyone who fears the Lord, who walks in his ways! You shall eat the fruit of the labor of your hands; you shall be blessed, and it shall be well with you. Your wife will be like a fruitful vine within your house; your children will be like olive shoots around your table. Behold, thus shall the man be blessed who fears the Lord. The Lord bless you from Zion! May you see the prosperity of Jerusalem all the days of your life! May you see your children's children! Peace be upon Israel!

We are blessed when we choose to live life following God's blueprints. King David was blessed with children, but it was several long years after this song was written before Israel experienced great peace. Our choices can affect the peace that we experience. At times David's ungodly behavior robbed him of peace and blessings. We can also learn from David's desire for true repentance that we do not need to remain separated from God. Confession restores our relationship and we can return to walking in the ways of our Lord who is our greatest blessing.

When to Bless, When Not to Bless

Psalm 129:8 NLT

APRIL 21

In this song David writes about his enemies who continually attack him. Since his youth, David was acquainted with military campaigns. Over the years, men he knew and had great respect and compassion for, had been killed on the battlefields. And even now as king, there is no lack of adversaries who seek to assault him. It is about these enemies of Zion that David is referring to when he describes them as becoming like dried out grass planted on the rooftops. *And may those who pass by refuse to give them this blessing: "The Lord bless you; we bless you in the Lord's name."* Having God's blessing means everything. To not be blessed by God is reason to fear indeed, whether in battle or in day-to-day life. God, I pray that we would live loyally to You, our Lord, and in doing so receive Your blessing. May we be alive and growing, not dead, dried out grass. Amen.

Bless God's Name Forever and Ever!

Psalm 145:1-2, 10, 21 ESV

APRIL 22

About at the halfway mark during our engagement, Russell and I decided to prepare our hearts for the wedding by reading the Psalms. He was in Texas and I was in Michigan, and starting with Psalm 1 we began reading a psalm a day leading up to the reading of Psalm 150 on our wedding day in the summer of 1988. I was a new Christian and by pondering the many reasons God was praised, I learned so much about His faithful character in these ancient songs.

Six days before the Big Day, we read Psalm 145, a tremendous testimony of God's great acts. Here are a few of the blessing verses: *I will extol you, my God and King, and bless your name forever and ever. Every day I will bless you and praise your name forever and ever. All your works shall give thanks to you, O Lord, and all your saints shall bless you! My mouth will speak the praise of the Lord, and let all flesh bless his holy name forever and ever.* May we continue to meditate on the glory of His splendor and bless His holy name. Earth is our training ground and years of marriage have provided me opportunity again and again to grow in blessing God and loving people.

The Gift of Blessings

Psalm 16:5a, 7 NLT; Psalm 21:3, 6 HCSB

APRIL 23

Blessing is the theme of many of the psalms that David wrote. It is great to read these psalms and get a good taste of the Lord's blessings that David experienced, and then to choose to continue to sing God's praises today. *Lord, you alone are my inheritance, my cup of blessing. I will bless the Lord who guides me; even at night my heart instructs me.* David, as the king over all of Israel, rejoiced in the Lord's strength and blessings. *For You meet him with rich blessings; You place a crown of pure gold on his head. You give him blessings forever; You cheer him with joy in Your presence.* Inheritance, guidance, instruction, richness, cheerfulness and joy are all gifts from the Lord. When we experience these good fortunes we can count them as blessings, naming them one-by-one.

Blessed Be My Rock

Psalm 18:3, 46 KJV

APRIL 24

Psalm 18 has been sung throughout the ages, probably with a variety of musical styles. Michael O'Shields composed a recent tune to the ancient words in the 1970's as a young traveling minister. The original author however was King David. David wrote the song of thanksgiving after he was delivered from the hands of his enemies, again.

It may have been that even in David's day the men began the song with a catchy echo: *"I will call upon the Lord, who is worthy to be praised: so shall I be saved from mine enemies."* Did the women back then repeat each line after the men, like it is often done today? No matter what the style may have been, the song's conclusion is strong and triumphant: *"The Lord liveth; and blessed be my rock; and let the God of my salvation be exalted."* This good truth is worth repeating so let the chorus ring on and on!

The next time we hear this song, let's think back to David and the closeness he shared with the Lord who protected him from his enemies. We can ponder David's desire as a warrior to openly praise the Lord in song, then sing out loudly to God, our audience of One. May He be our blessed rock, our firm foundation and worthy of heartfelt praise and adoration.

Sing Blessings Back to the Lord

Psalm 84:4-6 AMP; Psalm 84:12 NIV;
Psalm 85:1, 12 NLT; Psalm 133:3 NLT

APRIL 25

As God's Story continues on David and other gifted songwriters pen many more blessings that are recorded in the Psalms.

Blessed (happy, fortunate, to be envied) are those who dwell in Your house and Your presence; they will be singing Your praises all the day long. Selah[pause, and calmly think of that]! Blessed (happy, fortunate, to be envied) is the man whose strength is in You, in whose heart are the highways to Zion. Passing through the Valley of Weeping (Baca), they make it a place of springs; the early rain also fills [the pools] with blessings. What a vibrant picture the psalmist paints of peace.

Lord Almighty, blessed is the one who trusts in you. Lord, you poured out blessings on your land! You restored the fortunes of Israel. Yes, the Lord pours down his blessings. Our land will yield its bountiful harvest.

Harmony is as refreshing as the dew from Mount Hermon that falls on the mountains of Zion. And there the Lord has pronounced his blessing, even life everlasting.

The blessings continue to flow because God is the giver of strength. He is our trustworthy Provider and He believes in restoration. He is the One who pours down blessings. The harvest He gives in our lives is a great testimony to His loving care. Harmony in song and harmony in life are both blessings that can stream from our grateful hearts to our gracious Lord.

Bless God with Great Rejoicing
2 Samuel 6:11b-12, 18 HCSB; 1 Chronicles 16:43 NLT

APRIL 26

Even kings need a time of transition to settle into the role and put things in order as they should be. Such was the case for David and the ark of God. After an unsuccessful attempt of transporting the ark of God to Jerusalem, it was left at the house of Obed-edom for three months, *and the Lord blessed Obed-edom and his whole family.* Then King David received this report: *"The Lord has blessed Obed-edom's family and all that belongs to him because of the ark of God." So David went and had the ark of God brought up from Obed-edom's house to the city of David with rejoicing.* It seemed everyone, except David's wife Michal, was extremely joyful. Great thankfulness was expressed as they celebrated the return of the ark. *When David had finished offering the burnt offering and the fellowship offerings, he blessed the people in the name of Yahweh of Hosts.*

1 Chronicles 16 records the same events and shares some additional interesting detail including a song that David wrote for the event. The passage ends with: *Then all the people returned to their homes, and David turned and went home to bless his own family.* I love how blessings and rejoicing go together. We can often feel a sense of being blessed after a meaningful time with God in church. Be blessed and happy, celebrate, then return home to be a blessing your family as you joyfully seek to meet

their needs. And even after the emotional mountaintop experience levels out into the valley of day-to-day living, bless on.

Blessed to Bless

1 Chronicles 14:2 NLT

APRIL 27

I believe we live life differently- maybe it's more thankfully, more aware, more abundantly- when there is a real realization that we are blessed. Confirmation from the Lord helps too when living purpose-filled lives. King David was indeed blessed by God. He recognized that the Lord's confirmation of his new job assignment as king was not for his good alone. *David realized that the LORD had confirmed him as king over Israel and had greatly blessed his kingdom for the sake of his people Israel.*

God, I pray we live in the reality that we are blessed by You and are blessed to bless others. May we wake up with the intentional purpose of blessing someone each day. As we resolutely do this, the world might actually become a little more like, "Thy kingdom come, Thy will be done, on earth as it is in Heaven." Amen.

My Cup Overflows with Blessings!

Psalm 23:5 NLT

APRIL 28

Perhaps the most familiar of all psalms is Psalm 23. I have fond memories of teaching this one to our kiddos when we lived in North Carolina in 1996 preparing to move to China. They were younger then than David was back when he was a shepherd boy caring for sheep. David grew into manhood and he learned that people and sheep have at least one thing in common: they go astray. They both have the need of a competent shepherd's guidance, protection and care.

Through many generations this psalm has been sung out as a prayer and a reminder of the Shepherd we have in God. When Jesus came to earth, John introduced Him as the Good Shepherd worthy of our trust and loyalty. Verse 5 of the twenty-third psalm in the New Living Translation caught my eye because most translations stop with "my cup overflows." Ever wonder, "overflows" with what? *You prepare a feast for me in the presence of my enemies. You honor me by anointing my head with oil. My cup overflows with blessings.* May the investments we make in children when they are young continue to bless them all their lives. As a parent, what could be a better blessing to receive, than seeing God's blessings overflowing in our children, when they are blessing others as they have been blessed?

Bless God in Private and in Public

Psalm 24:5 NLT; Psalm 89:14-15 NIV

APRIL 29

In Psalm 24, David writes how everything belongs to the Lord, but then he asks, "Who can go to the Lord's holy place?" The ones with clean hands, a pure heart and truthful lips will meet up with God. God blesses those who worship Him. *They will receive the Lord's blessing and have a right relationship with God their savior.* This idea of God's holy throne is carried further in Psalm 89. *Righteousness and justice are the foundation of your throne; love and faithfulness go before you. Blessed are those who have learned to acclaim you, who walk in the light of your presence, Lord.*

How can we acclaim God today? It can make a big difference when we learn to walk with Him daily and intentionally acknowledge, celebrate and rave about Him privately. Then, when the opportunity comes up, we can tell others how He is worthy of praise. This is "outside the sanctuary" kind of worship. When we live this way, we are more purposefully in tune with God in the little details (lost keys becoming found) and in the big (lost nations turning to God). As we mature, our awareness of the scope of life and understanding of God increases our ability to praise the Lord for all things.

Blessed to Sing a New Song

Psalm 96:1-2 ESV

APRIL 30

Declaring God's glory among the nations and His wonderful works among all peoples is a main theme of Christian missions. For about a decade and a half, from 1997-2011, our family met annually with many other families in a big group setting. For roughly a week we would focus on training which would increase our abilities to share God's love with those who did not yet know Him who were living in various Asian cultures. We gathered together to pray and to sing and often we were introduced to new songs expressing honor to our Creator and Redeemer.

This concept of singing new songs to God is at least as old as the Psalms. *Oh sing to the Lord a new song; sing to the Lord, all the earth! Sing to the Lord, bless his name; tell of his salvation from day to day.* The rhythm and melody may change over the years, but the profound need to sing praise to an unchanging God remains the same. May we wholeheartedly sing out God's praises and faithfully tell of His goodness to all nations, among all peoples, no matter where in God's world we live. Bless His name!

Reflections

April began as a romantic love story between Ruth and Boaz and we see how God blesses commitments. Samuel, Israel's last judge, a great prophet, and the one God used to anoint Israel's first and second kings enters the Story as a prayed-for little baby. We are introduced to King Saul as God's Story continues. Battles are frequent and life is turbulent. We read how David is a man after God's heart and get a glimpse of David's heart in the many psalms he pens that emphasize both being blessed by God and blessing God.

May

Forever Blessed

Psalm 107:38 NLT; 2 Samuel 7:29 HCSB (also in 1 Chronicles 17:27)

MAY 1

Psalm 107 is a long song about the Lord's acts of faithful love. God's character as our Redeemer, Provider and Protector is revealed as we read about His people in various situations. He is powerful yet merciful, and firmly establishes His people who love Him. God gives His people fertile soil to work into a fruitful harvest. *How he blesses them! They raise large families there, and their herds of livestock increase.* Things are going well for God's people and for the king that He has placed over them.

By this time in God's Story, King David is well established in Jerusalem, living in his fine house of cedar. David desires to build a house for God but Nathan the prophet informs David that he will not be be the builder of the Temple, but that his son will build it. When David heard this news, he shared his gratitude to God and ends his prayer with: *"Now, please bless Your servant's house so that it will continue before You forever. For You, Lord God, have spoken, and with Your blessing Your servant's house will be blessed forever."*

Forever blessed. Whether kings or paupers or somewhere in between when we serve the God of all blessings we are blessed forever. God is a loving Father who redeems, provides for, and protects His children.

Blessed to Be Fruitful, Fresh and Fulfilled

Psalm 1:1-2 NIV

MAY 2

I love listening to Russell teach Psalm 1 because he explains things in ways that make sense. After reading the first Psalm at a church north of Houston, Russell looked out at the assembled crowd and said, "Blessed is: Ahhhhhhh, things are right!" *Blessed is the one who does not walk in step with the wicked or stand in the way that sinners take or sit in the compa-*

ny of mockers, but whose delight is in the law of the Lord, and who meditates on his law day and night.

The psalm goes on to describe a tree that is planted by streams of water. If we want to grow fully into our God-given potential and live "ahhhhhhhh," then we need to stop mocking and scoffing and instead drink deeply from God's wisdom. Then we will be like a healthy tree: Fruitful when the season is right, knowing there is a time to work and a time for play. We will also be Fresh as we breathe out confessions of sin and breathe in God's peace. As well as being fruitful and fresh, we will be Fulfilled when we know that we are created to represent Jesus, whatever our individual role in society may be.

This first psalm introduces an ongoing theme that contrasts the concepts of living for God (the righteous) and living for self (the wicked). There is a difference between delighting in the Lord and living selfishly. God blesses the righteous and He watches, helps, and comforts them; not so for the wicked.

Drawing Near to God Blesses Me

Psalm 2:12c ESV; Psalm 33:12 NIV; Psalm 65:4a ESV

MAY 3

Various Bible translations choose different words to communicate the idea of "blessed" in English. Words like happy, joyful and fortunate are used to describe a person blessed by God. These scenarios show us a few examples of where blessings are found:

Blessed are all who take refuge in him. Think of a storm that suddenly appears and threatens to overtake you on your walk home. While fighting strong winds and hailing rain, relief comes as you approach your home and see a blazing fire in the hearth. In all of our storms, God is a warm, safe shelter. You are happy and fortunate to enter in.

Blessed is the nation whose God is the Lord, the people he chose for his inheritance. Imagine a nation that is so faithful that everyone within its political boundaries honors the Lord. Oh how joyful that place would be! See the daily goodness that would be experienced at the family level when love, joy, peace, patience, kindness, faithfulness and gentleness are lived out, like breathing clean, pure air. Blessed are all whose God is the Lord!

Blessed is the one you choose and bring near, to dwell in your courts! Draw near to God and He will draw near to you. In drawing near, you will experience a fortunate, happy, joyful, satisfied blessedness. It is His promise.

Blessed to Have My Sins Covered

Psalm 32:1-2 NIV

MAY 4

What if our sins, the obvious ones and the ones we rationalize, were not just covered up, but covered? Not buried or hidden but brought to light, and paid for in full? What if all that we've done wrong really could be forgiven? That is what Jesus made possible for us.

I praise God that He opened my eyes and then my heart on a rainy Michigan night back in 1988 when I was twenty-three. As I prayed to God, the Holy Spirit brought to my lips the sins that I had buried deep inside me, the ones that I had tried to cover up by stacking good works on top. He forgave me and made me whole. For Jesus this great exchange took place as He hung with the sin of all humanity on a cross; mine included. God showed that His good overcomes sin when He brought Jesus back to life again. My awareness of this exchange took place in a car parked along a dark road with windshield wipers swishing away the rain. Not my effort, but His grace. And then began what I like to think of as "the bonus": living a blessed life.

"Blessed is the one whose transgressions are forgiven, whose sins are covered. Blessed is the one whose sin the Lord does not count against him and in whose spirit is no deceit." When we experience forgiveness, we realize

we have the freedom to live blessed, happy, clean lives, and we get to share this simple yet profound goodness with others.

Blessed to Be an Upright Generation

Psalm 112:1-2 HCSB

MAY 5

"Hallelujah! Happy is the man who fears the Lord, taking great delight in His commands. His descendants will be powerful in the land; the generation of the upright will be blessed." Russell and I desired that the descendants who came after us would know that God does bless. So years ago our family developed a crest. Instead of seeking the origin of our name and then finding the coat of arms that may have corresponded to that name, we contemplated the values we hold and we drew from those.

This painted and framed crest, given to me by Russell on my forty-first birthday, has hung in five homes on three continents since I unwrapped it, and it is my hope it will continue to go where we go. The background of our crest is a tree with roots, which represent being rooted in God's teachings and trusting Him for all that we need. Think about the Psalm 1 tree that is thriving, growing uniquely, and drinking in deeply from the river of God's Story. That is how the wise person is blessed. The crest has been a good reminder to our family, as well as a visual teaching aid to others, when we share how those who fear the Lord can live happily and fulfilled.

God has created in His people through all generations, the ability to choose. Let's choose God. Let's choose to live upright even in a world that is upside-down. Our generation depends on it! Let's be eager to learn from God's good ways and then live out what we learn. There is great delight in living right. This idea can be enhanced significantly when we're part of a community that holds the same values. Ultimately, by advancing the Kingdom of God, good overcomes evil and communities of righteousness can grow. More and more people, out of gratitude of being rescued from worthless ways to meaningful life, can join in with the multitudes whose joy comes from the Lord. This can happen - one person at a time, one generation at a time. Be a part of the link with one hand holding on to God's blessings and the other hand reaching out to others who need to be blessed.

Jesus Is the Blessed Bread of My Life

Psalm 132:14-15 HCSB

MAY 6

David's reflection on challenging times begins the 132nd Psalm, but then he becomes hopeful and his writing reveals it. Faithfulness is God's desire for His people, and He tells David that his descendants would always be on the throne if they keep His decrees. God is a Promise Keeper and we can trace the genealogy of Jesus back to King David. Praise the Lord that King Jesus will forever be on the throne!

"This is My resting place forever; I will make My home here because I have desired it. I will abundantly bless its food; I will satisfy its needy with bread." Isn't it interesting that many years later Jesus says that He is the Bread of Life? Do we see ourselves as needy? A good perspective is when we recognize that our need for being fulfilled is met by God. When we feast on Jesus we will never go hungry. Jesus wants us to have blessed lives, full and satisfying.

God Does Not Reject Me – I'm Blessed!

Psalm 66:8-9, 20 ESV

MAY 7

Bless our God, O peoples; let the sound of his praise be heard, who has kept our soul among the living and has not let our feet slip... Blessed be God, because he has not rejected my prayer or removed his steadfast love from me! It is an incredible blessing to call out to God and to be heard by Him in prayer. Sometimes, although we *know* that God's love is steadfast and faithful, we may not *feel* it. Calling out to God does not always come easy, so what can we do when we get off track with Him? Go ahead and tell God the trouble you face. David did, and as he did he remembered God's past faithfulness, thought about why God is bless-worthy, and this lead to praising Him.

When we choose to be thankful for what God has most recently done for us or given to us, (how He has blessed us) somehow our feelings change - even if our situation does not, and we line up with the reality that God is near and He has not rejected us. Praise Him for one thing, then another. Don't let pride, pity, or any other ungodly act or feeling keep you off track, but take it to God. Near Him is the place where concerns and fears disappear, and goodness, acceptance and abiding peace remain.

David was not always on a mountaintop with a choir surrounding him, but like us, he was at times in the pit of despair. Why didn't despair win and hold him? David chose thankfulness. Gratitude opens the door to closeness with God. I pray that as God's children, we would be thankful kids. And from our core, we would let the sound of His praise be heard. Amen.

One Day All Nations Will Know God's Blessedness

Psalm 67:1-3, 6-7 HCSB

MAY 8

"May God be gracious to us and bless us; look on us with favor Selah so that Your way may be known on earth, Your salvation among all nations. Let the peoples praise You, God, let all the peoples praise You... The earth has produced its harvest; God, our God, blesses us. God will bless us, and all the ends of the earth will fear Him."

Be in awe of God. Said another way, fear Him. God is more than awesome; He is the ultimate and is worthy of all exhortation, honor, and blessing. He is gracious and shows us His favor. He cannot be controlled. But in a relationship with Him, we can ask Him anything. We can ask to be blessed, and when we are, may we be quick to thank Him and praise Him, the giver of every good and perfect gift. May His good ways be known to all, so all the nations may know the God who blesses.

Bless the Lord, O My Soul

Psalm 103:1-2, 20-22 ESV

MAY 9

Shortly after Russell and I joined Houston's First Baptist Church in the summer of 2012, the worship team introduced a new song based on an old psalm, and I was hooked. I often find myself praising God throughout the day by singing out the lyrics to Matt Redman's song, *10,000 Reasons (Bless the Lord)*. Read the original psalm with a focus on the blessing verses: *Bless the Lord, O my soul, and all that is within me, bless his holy name! Bless the Lord, O my soul. And forget not all his benefits... Bless the Lord, O you his angels, you mighty ones who do his word, obeying the voice of his word! Bless the Lord, all his hosts, his ministers, who do his will! Bless the Lord, all his works, in all places of his dominion. Bless the Lord, O my soul!*

The morning may start with singing on our lips, but it is only by intentionally reflecting on the many benefits of the Lord that praise can go forward in a non-delusional way, no matter what the day brings. May we still be joyfully singing God's praises into the evening and beyond!

Parents Are Blessed to Bless

2 Samuel 13:25 NLT

Among the responsibilities of running a kingdom, which required fighting many battles, the honor of writing psalms, and the desire to build a Temple for the Lord he loved, King David was surrounded by a challenging family life. At this point in his life, David had several concubines and a few wives including Bathsheba, who had been the wife of one of his great warriors. Bathsheba and David mourned the death of their first baby. Then Solomon was born and this little one was added to the great number of King David's children, many of whom were grown.

It is in this complex family tree that we find tragedy: Amnon, David's son by one of his wives, raped Tamar, David's daughter by another of his wives. Absalom, the brother of the defiled girl, planned to take revenge. Absalom invited King David and all of the king's sons to his home for a feast, as it was sheep sheering time. But David told Absalom, *"No, my son. If we all came, we would be too much of a burden on you." Absalom pressed him, but the king would not come, though he gave Absalom his blessing.* Although David did not go to Absalom's party, the others did, and that day Absalom took justice into his own hands, and killed his brother Amnon.

Even as king, David was not exempt from the deep pain caused by those closest to him. It is hard to really imagine the shock, anger, and grief that David and his various wives must have felt during this tragic time. Dysfunctional families are not a modern day phenomenon. And it is not a mystery that our actions come from our thoughts; and consequences, good and bad, will eventually follow what we choose to do. Circumstances can certainly get complicated.

When I think of David, the thoughts that come to my mind are a shepherd boy, a brave giant slayer, a gifted musician, a mighty warrior, a great king and a man after God's own heart. David was all of these things but maybe the role many of us can relate to most naturally is that of his role as a parent. David was the kind of father who wanted to bless his children, even the child intent on revenge.

Our Heavenly Father, no matter what role or position or title we may bear, I pray that as parents (or as aunts and uncles, brothers and sisters, friends) we would seek You and Your wisdom and we would invest wisely in those You have blessed us with. Help us, Lord God, to be part of the solution in a world that needs to see Your love in action. Justice and mercy can best be pursued when we choose to walk humbly with You. Lead us Father to love like You love. Amen.

Blessed by God to Bless the Lord

Psalm 3:8 NIV; Psalm 26:12 ESV

MAY 11

King David and his son Absalom eventually reconciled over the tragedy that left Amnon dead, but Absalom was bent on rebellion and conspired to overthrow his father and replace King David as king. David was torn: he did not want Absalom to be harmed yet he wanted to protect the rest of his family too. King David fled with his family to keep them safe and to focus on his responsibility of reigning over and leading Israel.

Psalm 3 is a prayer of desperation, and David called to God because many enemies had risen up against him. What begins in fear becomes a song of assurance as David proclaims that the Lord is his shield and the One who sustains. By the end, David is singing, *"From the LORD comes deliverance. May Your blessing be on Your people."*

Psalm 26 includes a similar theme of thankfulness for deliverance and ends with, *"My foot stands on level ground; in the great assembly I will bless the Lord."* In painful times of great uncertainty and betrayal, David found reassurance in the Lord who is faithful. Do we look for and find reassurance in Him? May God's blessing be on His people, and as His people, may we be faithful to bless the Lord.

A Blessed Heritage
Psalm 28:9 ESV; Psalm 62:4-6 ESV

Other deep, heart-felt psalms were written during this turbulent time in King David's life. A few excerpts that reflect not only the trouble that was presently at hand also include the blessings that come from a faithful God. *Oh, save your people and bless your heritage! Be their shepherd and carry them forever.* We need honest, strong care. Based on God's past faithfulness in his life, David had full assurance that God would continue to carry him and His people. We should remember the interaction that God has had with us personally and then rely on Him for the rescue yet to come.

God's enemies will try whatever it takes to throw God down, even causing harm to His children. *They only plan to thrust him down from his high position. They take pleasure in falsehood. They bless with their mouths, but inwardly they curse.* The complications of living in a fallen world originated in the time after Adam and Eve's rejection of God. If we are not fully for God, are we even for Him at all? David reminds us that we are to trust in God alone. When it comes to God, don't be wishy-washy. David continues this psalm like a prayer: "For God alone, O my soul, wait in silence, for my hope is from him. He alone is my rock and my salvation, my fortress; I shall not be shaken." My hope is in You, Lord. Amen.

Blessed into Everlasting!
Psalm 41:1-2, 13 ESV

In this psalm of David's, two elements stand out: the poor, and our enemies. In the New Testament, Jesus says we will always have the poor among us, and as we care for those who cannot care for themselves, it is as if we are caring for the needs of Jesus Himself. We are blessed so we can provide for others, and in providing, we receive blessing. This is a great win-win situation. *Blessed is the one who considers the poor! In the day of trouble the Lord delivers him; the Lord protects him and keeps him alive; he is called blessed in the land, you do not give him up to the will of his enemies.* We still have the poor, but do we have enemies in modern days?

Some in active military service will face real adversaries. For others, time - too much or the lack of it, can be considered a challenging foe. Disease and depression are both described as something we need to fight. Peter, as a follower of Jesus, reminds us that our enemy the devil prowls around like a roaring lion, seeking to devour us. We do have enemies. But we also have hope: God does not give us up to the will of our enemies. This is a great reason to praise!

The thing or situation the enemy might use to bring about fear can be the very thing that leads us closer to God, the One we can rely on at all times. I love being active. I thrive while running, walking, riding my bike, and truth be known, I even enjoy cleaning our home. All these things came to a screeching halt the day of my bike accident. At the time of this revision I'm into the third month of immobility. The enemy would win if I allowed my inability to physically walk rob me of my close "walk with the Lord." Discontentedness is a slippery slope to self-pity which can lead to all kinds of unhealthy attitudes. How thankful I am to God who draws me near. Praising Him for what I do have rather than dwelling on what I do not, keeps me from a pit and it will do the same for you.

No matter what the enemy may try, when we are in God's family we are blessed into everlasting - forever to live with the God of forever! Even with real enemies around him, David remained focused on God and concluded this psalm by praising Him. *Blessed be the Lord, the God of Israel, from everlasting to everlasting! Amen and Amen.*

Bless God When I am Blessed

1 Chronicles 18:9-10 NKJV

When David was victorious in battle, others also benefited. We read how blessings lead to more blessings: *Now when Tou king of Hamath heard that David had defeated all the army of Hadadezer king of Zobah, he sent Hadoram his son to King David, to greet him and bless him, because he had fought against Hadadezer and defeated him (for Hadadezer had been at war with Tou); and Hadoram brought with him all kinds of articles of gold, silver, and bronze.*

Although these names may be unfamiliar to us, I pray that the principle of extending blessings is more than just an idea but is a part of our lives. David received these valuable gifts and treasures from other nations, and he blessed the Lord by dedicating these items to Him. David recognized that he did not win the battle alone - God was with him, and so he gave back to God as different nations gave to him.

Church economics are similar: God blesses people within a church family (in various ways) and out of gratitude we give a portion back to Him through the church (in various ways). A healthy church will then bless people both near and far who have a variety of needs, and the blessings continue. It's not so much paying God back as it is applying the blessing He gives us to bless others. Being a part of the joy of His good blessings as they go forward sure can be a delight!

Blessed Is the One Who Trusts in the Lord

Psalm 40:3-4 NIV

God's Story involves ancient history, yet it lives on in every generation. In 1999 Hank became the first Christian among a minority people. Hank and his family live in a village in Southeast Asia. As a skilled artisan, he was very familiar with idols for he had carved quite a few in his day. Hank knew these idols could not save him; they were only made of stone or wood and their eyes could not see nor could their ears hear. Even though his generation, like the many generations before him, bowed before these false gods, deep inside Hank knew there needed to be something more.

When Hank heard of the Most High God, he placed his trust in Him and God gave Hank a new skill: Hank wrote the first worship chorus among his people and it is still sung today. Let us continue to pray for Hank, his family, his village and the people in surrounding areas.

Father, God, there are many who still need to hear that You are God. Idols cannot rescue us from death, or give us life - only You can. Open up eyes and draw people to You so many will see You and put their trust in You alone. Not You and idols or rituals, or traditions. But You alone. Amen. *"He put a new song in my mouth, a hymn of praise to our God. Many will see and fear the Lord and put their trust in him. Blessed is the one who trusts in the Lord, who does not look to the proud, to those who turn aside to false gods."*

Compassion, Mercy, and Generosity to Bless

2 Samuel 19:39 NLT

MAY 16

Even in the midst of turmoil, David seeks to bless. War continued and King David and his family were still in danger. In a move to protect the king, Joab, David's military commander kills Absalom, the king's rebellion-leading son. David bitterly mourned his son's death but with the opposition scattered, King David and the rest of his family were safe to return to Jerusalem.

At a crossing point on the Jordan River, King David forgave and spared the life of a servant named Shimei, he restored Saul's crippled grandson Mephibosheth back to a position at his table, and then a man named Barzillai greeted the group. This rich man had helped King David before and David wanted to generously honor him in Jerusalem. But Barzillai was now an old man so instead he offered Kimham as a servant to be honored in his place, and King David agreed to this exchange. *So all the people crossed the Jordan with the king. After David had blessed Barzillai and kissed him, Barzillai returned to his own home.* King David's compassion, mercy, kindness and generosity are indeed signs of a ruler after God's own heart.

Blessed Inheritance

2 Samuel 21:3 NIV

MAY 17

During King David's reign, the land suffered through a three-year famine. When David asked God about it, God said that it was because of the Gibeonites who had been killed by King Saul. So, David asked the Gibeonites, *"What shall I do for you? How shall I make atonement so that you will bless the Lord's inheritance?"* They gave him their answer, King David followed through with action, and afterward, God answered David's prayer for the land. Some Old Testament accounts are difficult to understand from our present day perspective. God's mercy and justice, however, are consistent with His character, even when we might not see the full picture.

This principle has not changed. It is a timeless truth that God is trustworthy so we can trust Him. At times we would love to know the full story; we want to see more clearly the step in front of us, and the step in front of that step. Walking by faith is what God calls His people to do. It's not like the blind leading the blind. He faithfully leads those who are faithful to Him. This kind of faith journey increases our dependency on the One who knows what is best for each of His children.

God Blesses the Godly
with a Shield of Love

Psalm 5:12 NLT

MAY 18

From the time David was a child, war was a part of his life. Against all odds, he killed the giant combatant Goliath with a slingshot and a stone, and as David reigned over God's people, he was personally involved in many battles. The Philistines remained an enemy, and many descendants of Goliath (all were giants themselves) fought against the Israelites. With this in mind, we can better understand his frame of reference when we read some of the psalms written by David when he was a warrior.

For you bless the godly, O Lord; you surround them with your shield of love. Warriors value shields. No matter what battle we find ourselves in, when we picture God's love as a protective shield surrounding us, we need not give up hope. His 360-degree surround-shield is what protects us, for our enemy is like a roaring hungry lion whose desire is to devour us. From which direction will the devil attack? Because it's different for each of us we are warned by Peter in the New Testament to be alert and to stand firm in our faith. We do not battle alone and there have been many throughout His Story who have battled before us. But God is with us and He continues to bless the godly.

Although Others May Curse Me,
Bless Me Lord!

Psalm 109:16-17, 26, 28 NLT

MAY 19

David continued to write songs including this one, Psalm 109, about his deceitful enemies. He asks God to deal with them in very harsh ways because they have repaid him evil for kindness, and hatred for love. Talking about one enemy in particular, David wrote, *"For he refused all kindness* to others; he persecuted the poor and needy, and he hounded the broken-hearted to death. He loved to curse others; now you curse him. He never blessed others; now don't you bless him."

Then, in the second half of the psalm, David calls out to God, *"Help me, O Lord my God! Save me because of your unfailing love... Then let them curse me if they like, but you will bless me! When they attack me, they will be disgraced! But I, your servant, will go right on rejoicing!"* Do we as God's servants go right on rejoicing regardless of our present situation and circumstance? Or do we give permission to the enemy to distract us from our goal of living to praise God? When we are undervalued instead of promoted, cursed at rather than praised, unfairly attacked due to the convictions we hold - do we lash back or take our hurt to God?

Help us, O Lord our God to keep right on praising You, for ultimately You will have the final say. When our mind shifts to this kind of thinking, we can have the compassion that Jesus talks about to actually pray for our enemies. When our lives are hidden in Christ we can go beyond the law of "an eye for an eye", to showing mercy in the same way that He showed mercy to us. Father, help us to live like Your Son lived. Amen.

Be Blessed and Bless!

Psalm 144:1-2, 15 ESV; Psalm 37:22, 26 NLT

MAY 20

Mentorship, apprenticeship, and life coaching are all present day practices that have been around since ancient times. Someone who has built a chair (or maybe a web-site) can teach someone who has never built a chair, etc. The same principle applies to spiritual disciplines we need to build. Being in this type of one-on-one teacher-novice relationship is a huge benefit when we seek to learn a variety of skills. But let us not overlook the guidance God gives to us through those in His Story. If we want to grow in our ability to authentically bless God, David is a wonderful teacher.

He never tires of singing God's praise. *"Blessed be the Lord, my rock, who trains my hands for war, and my fingers for battle; he is my steadfast love and my fortress, my stronghold and my deliverer, my shield and he in whom I take refuge, who subdues peoples under me."* David seems to suggest that God was his trainer as well as his refuge. David then lists several benefits of belonging to the Lord and says, *"Blessed are the people to whom such blessings fall! Blessed are the people whose God is the Lord!"*

In another psalm, David encourages us not to worry about the wicked, but instead to trust and take delight in the Lord. Focus on doing what is right. *"Those the Lord blesses will possess the land, but those he curses will die."* It is best to be on the team of the godly not the wicked. So what do the godly do? Honest and good things. They offer wise counsel and they put their hope in the Lord. *"The godly always give generous loans to others, and their children are a blessing."* Do good, practice generosity, be blessed, and bless. These are skills worth learning and living by, and in doing so we pass them on to others to learn as well.

Full Families Are a Blessing

Psalm 127:3-5a ESV

MAY 21

Families are fascinating. The same parents in the same environments can bring about very different and unique offspring. I am so grateful to God for the children He blessed Russell and me with. Isaiah's December birthday in 2012 completed our second decade of raising and enjoying three great kids. They keep growing into interesting and fun-to-be-around adults. I also love how families are not static. I'm continually blessed by Russell's family who took me in as one of their own on the day I became his wife. And I'm so thankful that my Michigan family loves my Texan husband and extends warm welcomes to us whenever we return for visits. Presently we have one son-in-law, (and a little grand baby on the way) and the joy increases as our family merges with Andrew's.

Psalm 127 is a psalm I believe that David wrote to his son Solomon. *"Behold, children are a heritage from the Lord, the fruit of the womb a reward. Like arrows in the hand of a warrior are the children of one's youth. Blessed is the man who fills his quiver with them!"* A man may hold an arrow but it requires dedicated training to make that arrow valuable in the hands of a warrior. Parents too require training. In order to effectively teach discipline that is needed to hit godly bull's eyes in life, it is best if parents are actually living out healthy spiritual disciplines.

It is incredible that although a father wrote this psalm many generations ago, the same sentiment of blessedness is felt today concerning the gift of children. God, thank You for the heritage of family. I pray that the children of my youth will always delight You. May those of us who are parents rejoice in Your good blessings. God please give us patience and strength and the ability to make wise choices in every season of training children up in the way that each of them should go. And as You grow our family tree, may it be our desire to actively choose to love each branch You add to it. Amen.

Blessed Be God - He Adopts Us into His Family
Psalm 68:19, 26, 35 ESV

MAY 22

The poetry of David keeps flowing like a living river from God's royal throne. In some Bibles, Psalm 68 is sub-titled, "God is the Father of the Fatherless". This lengthy poem was sung to a tune written by the Chief Musician. Verse 6 says, "God sets the lonely in families; he leads the prisoners with singing." May this song give hope to many in our generation; to those who are slaves to human trafficking, to orphans in great need for loving families, and to the lonely and the elderly who long for meaningful connection.

"Blessed be the Lord, who daily bears us up; God is our salvation. Selah." I picture those faithful believers with tambourines, singing out, *"Bless God in the great congregation, the Lord, O you who are of Israel's fountain!"* With a strong finale the song concludes with, *"Awesome is God from his sanctuary; the God of Israel—he is the one who gives power and strength to his people. Blessed be God!"* The entire psalm is a powerful masterpiece! All praise and blessing go to God, for He cares for the needs of the fatherless, the oppressed, and the lonely. We can unload all of our anxieties upon Him for He cares for us and He uses us to be the blessing for others.

Way beyond the normal age for adopting children, two Christ-centered teachers who taught our kiddos in northern Thailand, traveled to Cambodia and began a long and laborious process to adopt not just one, but two young girls. Their story is one of hope and trust, and their lives, as well as the lives of their new daughters, will never be the same.

And the good examples continue: Colleagues who focused on getting God's goodness to those in Vietnam adopted a girl from China, and then three years later were able to return to the same overcrowded orphanage to adopt the childhood friend of their new daughter.

A young, single woman who served in a Guatemalan orphanage continues to have meaningful impact. When a baby was abandoned and not expected to survive, she adopted him, and all praise to God, he is now a thriving teen!

Friends we mentored in China traveled to India to bring a neglected baby boy into their home, making them a happy family of six.

And, long time friends from North Carolina are faithfully parenting their son with fetal alcohol syndrome whom they adopted from Russia in 2001. Glory to God for this young man's recent baptism!

One day all who place their faith in God will be united as one big family. Let us not miss out on living like a family here and now, blessing others as we have been generously blessed by God. In order to really do this well, we need what the psalmist joyfully sings about: power and strength from God.

Pronounce Blessings in His Name Forever

1 Chronicles 23:13b HCSB

David was at the end of his life so he got his affairs in order and obtained many of the supplies needed so his now grown son Solomon could build the Temple. The Temple was a symbol of the nation's commitment to God. At a large assembly, David enlisted the help of Israel's leaders to work in unity on the upcoming Temple project; responsibilities were assigned and genealogies were chronicled.

It was a time to ponder their heritage. David read the names of Levi's sons, and then said this about Aaron, Levi's grandson and the firstborn to Amram, *"Aaron, along with his descendants, was set apart forever to consecrate the most holy things, to burn incense in the presence of Yahweh, to minister to Him, and to pronounce blessings in His name forever."* Although blessings in the name of the Lord would go on forever, it was the beginning of the end for King David. Reflection is a good thing, especially when looking back upon a godly heritage. I hope that as he thought about his life, David's mind was full of meaningful memories, for he was a hero to many.

One of my heroes is Ted Hope. By the time we got to know him in the initial stages of Bible translation for the people group we served in Asia, he had already been involved with over fifty Bible translation projects. He and his dear wife Nell helped the Lisu tribe in Thailand become Christians. When Dr. Hope and Russell traveled together in China, they sought out the grave of yet another godly man, a British missionary named J.O. Fraser who brought the Good News of Jesus to the Chinese Lisu. Inscribed on his gravestone are Jesus' words from John 12:24, "unless a grain of wheat falls into the earth and dies, it remains alone; but if it dies, it bears much fruit."

Aaron and his descendants were set apart to pronounce God's blessings. God used James Fraser in incredible ways to bless the Lisu of China. Ted Hope carried on that good work with the Lisu in Thailand. We are all given one life to live. Will those who come after us remember us for our love for God and His people? Are we bearing fruit as people who die to self to live for God?

A Blessing within a Parenthesis

1 Chronicles 26:5b NIV

MAY 24

Duties were divvied up in preparation to build the Temple. Priests were needed as well as singers, musicians, gatekeepers, treasurers, judges, and the military, not to mention the manpower it took in skilled and manual labor to actually build the Temple. On one of the lists of names of gatekeepers, Obed-Edem and his eight capable sons were acknowledged. And then a little parenthesis: *(For God had blessed Obed-Edom.)* Do you remember this family? They were the ones entrusted with the ark of God before King David moved it to Jerusalem. They had a job to do, they faithfully followed through, and they were blessed. It took all kinds to live for God back then, and it takes all kinds now.

I'm grateful that Dr. Cutrer followed God and used his medical training to save my life, deliver Hannah with an emergency C-section and then fourteen months later, he brought Sophie from purple to healthy when she was born. The following year, Isaiah was born and Dr. Bill was recovering from heart surgery. Then about twenty years later, on a Saturday morning, Dr. Bill began the day on a bike ride and ended it in the presence of the God he loved.

Russell and I met Dr. Bill Cutrer and his wife Jane in the Sunday school class he taught for newly married couples. Back in those days many of these young husbands were students at Bible colleges in Dallas. The godly influence of the Cutrer family continues to point people to live for Jesus, to study diligently, to overcome by God's grace and to joyfully serve through the job they've been given. This morning I awoke with a line from Dr. Bill's favorite praise hymn on my mind. The song, *And Can it Be that I Should Gain,* is rich in theology and asks the question, "How can it be that thou, my God shouldst die for me?" Like the song goes on to point out, this kind of love is amazing. And it gives us plenty to ponder.

God blessed Obed-Edom. He blessed the eighteenth century songwriter Charles Wesley. He blessed Bill Curter. Each of these men, and many more throughout His Story, have lived and have now passed from this life. Let's live doing good today, for today is what we have been given.

Bow Low and Bless the Lord

1 Chronicles 29:10, 20 NKJV

MAY 25

With all the leaders still gathered around King David in the great assembly, David made it clear that it is God Himself who chose Solomon to be the next king. He told his son Solomon the importance of serving God with a whole heart and a willing mind. Then David led by example and joyfully gave from his personal treasures for the building of the Temple, and then all the leaders present also gave willingly.

Therefore David blessed the LORD before all the assembly; and David said: "Blessed are You, LORD God of Israel, our Father, forever and ever"... Then David said to all the assembly, "Now bless the LORD your God." So all the assembly blessed the LORD God of their fathers, and bowed their heads and prostrated themselves before the LORD and the king.

The Most High God united them; a common goal to bless the Lord kept them focused on the task and in due time the Temple was completed. King David was a model in both words and action for the new king, his son Solomon. From one generation to the next, may we lead by example to bless the Lord.

Blessed Be the Lord

1 Kings 1:47-48 NKJV

MAY 26

Could it be that David would have eliminated a whole lot of family strife if he had had fewer wives? Now another of his sons, Adonijah, positioned himself to be the new king and he had quite a committed following. Adonijah and his men were huddled for a pow-wow when they heard a noise so great that the earth split open from the sound. A messenger arrived to give them the news that Adonijah's father, King David, had just made Solomon the new king.

"And moreover the king's servants have gone to bless our lord King David, saying, 'May God make the name of Solomon better than your name, and may He make his throne greater than your throne.' Then the king bowed himself on the bed. Also the king said thus, 'Blessed be the Lord God of Israel, who has given one to sit on my throne this day, while my eyes see it!'"

David lived a full life, and one of the consistent things about him was his thankfulness to God. He did not have a trouble-free life, but David did live to bless the Lord. Maybe that is what it means to have a heart after God.

God Remembers and Blesses Us

Psalm 115:12-15 NLT; 1 Kings 2:45 HCSB

MAY 27

It is not clear who authored Psalm 115, but I like to think that David wrote it at the very end of his life. It begins by saying that glory does not belong to people, but to God alone. I envision David looking back on his life and thinking about history, all the way back to the creation of the world. I imagine that David breathed in and out the assurance of God's goodness and trustworthiness.

The song rings of hope for generations yet to come - including us, and calls all to trust in God's love and faithfulness. *The Lord remembers us and will bless us. He will bless the people of Israel and bless the priests, the descendants of Aaron. He will bless those who fear the Lord, both great and lowly. May the Lord richly bless both you and your children. May you be blessed by the Lord, who made heaven and earth.*

God, who originated the whole blessing concept by creating all things good, will continue to bestow blessings on those who live to honor Him. David reigned over Israel for forty years, then Solomon became the king. God's Story records in 1 Kings 2:45, *"...King Solomon will be blessed, and David's throne will remain established before the Lord forever."*

Blessed to Sing God's Praise Songs

Psalm 118:26 NIV

MAY 28

Through the years, many meaningful choruses, hymns, and praise songs have moved me. Now when I sing them decades later, in a different setting, a flood of memories come to mind, when yet again these songs are used to lift up praises and thanksgiving to our King. Although Psalm 118 was written many generations before the birth of Jesus, it is very likely that Jesus sang it during the Last Supper with his disciples. One stanza of this song is, *"Blessed is he who comes in the name of the Lord. From the house of the Lord we bless you."* We can read a similar refrain in all four of the Gospel accounts when Jesus entered Jerusalem, riding on a colt.

Another part of this song says, "This is the day that the Lord has made, I will rejoice and be glad in it." Jesus sang this knowing what was before Him. He endured our sin and overcame His death. He was able to rejoice and be glad, trusting that God's good purposes would not be thwarted. Good songs are meant to be sung forever. Singing God's praises is one thing we know we will do through all eternity, so let's keep on singing now, or as in my case, keep making a joyful noise unto the Lord!

Godly Discipline Blesses Us

Psalm 100:4-5 ESV; Psalm 94:12 NIV

MAY 29

Why are we to "Enter his gates with thanksgiving, and his courts with praise"? Why should we, *"Give thanks to him; bless his name"*? Because "the Lord is good; his steadfast love endures forever, and his faithfulness to all generations." We know His goodness, and yet sometimes we choose to go our own way. God loves us too much not to pursue us. *Blessed is the one you discipline, Lord, the one you teach from your law...*

Thank You, God, for correction so we can with clean hands and pure hearts again enter Your courts with thanksgiving and bless Your name. Thank You, Lord Jesus, for forgiveness and for the story You told of the prodigal son who went his own way, far from his father's home, but never too far from his father's love. Our Father in Heaven, thanks for welcoming us back with Your steadfast love. Amen.

From the Rising to the Setting Sun, Bless You Lord!

Psalm 113:2-4 ESV

MAY 30

"Blessed be the name of the Lord from this time forth and forevermore! From the rising of the sun to its setting, the name of the Lord is to be praised!" After living more than a dozen years of her life in Asia, our oldest child, Hannah, began university in the US. We celebrated her eighteenth birthday together, we toured her college campus, prayed, cried, and took one last photo under the trees that would be her new "home". Then our family, now minus one, flew away.

Life in London was a big transition for me. Our family dynamics had changed, we went from tropical weather in Thailand to the cold wetness of England and from a town surrounded by mountains to a city we accessed by the Underground. There was a noticeable difference in culture too, including how people interacted. But I have learned from experience that in the midst of change, there is great comfort in the God of the Bible who not only does not change, but is here, wherever "here" is.

Listening to the London rain, I read this praise song to God in Psalm 113, and thought about how there was once a time when the sun did not set on the British Empire. Yet, no matter where in the world we go, and no matter where the sun is in its rotation (from its rising to its setting), the Lord is to be praised. Let's pray hard for London, now home to people from almost every nation. May the city hear and rejoice in the good news of Jesus, and in many languages, bless the name of the Lord forevermore! "The Lord is high above all nations, and his glory above the heavens!"

Blessed to Walk in God's Ways

Psalm 119:1-3, 12, 56 ESV; Psalm 119:122 NLT

MAY 31

The intricate acrostic poem of praise we know as Psalm 119 is, in many ways, an expansion of Psalm 1. *Blessed are those whose way is blameless, who walk in the law of the Lord! Blessed are those who keep his testimonies, who seek him with their whole heart, who also do no wrong, but walk in his ways!... Blessed are you, O Lord; teach me your statutes!... This blessing has fallen to me, that I have kept your precepts... Please guarantee a blessing for me. Don't let the arrogant oppress me!*

Back in 1992 when our second daughter Sophie was just a toddler, she wanted to add her own notes to my copy of Psalm 119. To this day I smile every time I see her scribbles in my Bible, not just in one but two colors of ink. Sophie has grown into a beautiful young lady and she has an interest in learning languages. During a semester abroad her junior year at Rice University, she had the adventure of going to Kenya where she learned Swahili.

I'm thrilled that each of our children embraces a love for learning. I pray they would continue to grow like the Psalm 1 tree, drinking in the goodness of God's Word. May this generation be challenged and strengthened by God's teachings, walk in His ways, and seek Him with their whole hearts. May they be blessed to bless. Amen.

Reflections

As David grows older his songs and poetry reveal more and more of what it means to be blessed as we journey on in God's Story. The month of May also provides additional information of who David is as Israel's second king and reveals his interactions as a father. Life is challenging and it is often in hard times that we recognize afresh the need to depend upon God. David did not live a perfect life, but his life was lived to bless God and people. Solomon, David's son with Bathsheba, became the new king at the end of David's life.

June

Bless the Lord, You Who Fear Him

Psalm 135:19-21 NKJV

JUNE 1

Bless the Lord, O house of Israel! Bless the Lord, O house of Aaron! Bless the Lord, O house of Levi! This makes sense in a Jewish culture. Due to their personal connection with God Jews are to praise Him. But what about those who do not have a Jewish genealogy? The original blessing given to Abraham promised that all nations on earth would be blessed to be a blessing. The world is blessed to praise God. I believe that the psalmist indicated with the next verse that non-Jewish people too are included in the praising: *You who fear the Lord, bless the Lord!* Do we fear the Lord? That is good.

We can join in praising the Lord, like the psalmist, for His greatness in creation. We can sing of His power over the weather and His ability to defeat His enemies throughout time. God is all-powerful and we are reminded that He has no patience for idols or for those who trust in them. The sooner mankind understands this the better! *Blessed be the Lord out of Zion, Who dwells in Jerusalem!* Jesus came from Heaven to Jerusalem as the fulfillment of Jewish prophesy. He was God from the beginning and throughout the New Testament we see His greatness and His goodness. So what is a healthy response to our Lord? To praise Him! We were made to know Him, to bless Him, to love Him and to make Him known. Bless the Lord!

Blessed to See the Light of Life

Psalm 49:16-20 NIV

JUNE 2

This song by the Sons of Korah is a serious dirge about the need to trust spiritual insight even more than wealth. *Do not be overawed when others grow rich, when the splendor of their houses increases; for they will take nothing with them when they die, their splendor will not descend with them. Though while they live they count themselves blessed—and people praise you when you prosper—they will join those who have gone before them, who will never again see the light of life. People who have wealth but lack understanding are like the beasts that perish.*

Is this song about you, about me? Do we trust wealth rather than God who desires to bless us even beyond the here and now? Years after this song was written Jesus was teaching in the Temple in Jerusalem. I love how John recorded Jesus' words, "I am the light of the world, He who follows Me shall not walk in darkness, but have the light of life." Life with Jesus is not stumbling around in the dark, for His words light our path. He is the only way to see the light of life that Psalm 49 alludes to. We may have the means to buy tickets for most events on earth, but riches cannot redeem our souls.

Bless God by Seeking, Praising, Meditating on and Following Him

Psalm 63:1, 3-4, 6, 8 NKJV

JUNE 3

When we were newlyweds in 1989, Russell studied at a Bible college in Dallas, Texas and worked at a Christian bookstore. One day he surprised me with a *New King James Version Bible*, my new married name etched in silver on the pink leather. It was my first leather Bible and I loved the way it felt in my hands, and when I wrote in the margin my handwriting was extra neat. My notes from a sermon on Psalm 63 read, "Passion for God: Seek Him, Bless Him, Meditate on Him, Follow Him." *O God, You are my God; Early will I seek You... Because Your lovingkindness is better than life, My lips shall praise You. Thus I will bless You while I live... When I remember You on my bed, I meditate on You in the night watches... My soul follows close behind You; Your right hand upholds me.*

These timeless truths continue to be a trustworthy compass. God's Word is a foundation for marriage and I thank God for the many lessons that I learned at Audelia Road Baptist Church during that formative time in our lives. Over two decades later, even though the miles separate us, it is a joy to be connected to those from our newly-married Sunday school class, and we continue to learn about new stages of life and closeness to God. May God be blessed with each day He gives as we seek Him, praise Him, meditate on Him, and follow our good and faithful Guide. Passion for a spouse and passion for God can grow deeper as the years grow longer, especially as we live aware of God's lovingkindness in each day.

All Nations Call Him Blessed

Psalm 72:15b, 17-19 ESV

JUNE 4

Solomon was known for his wisdom, a gift he received when the Lord said He would give Solomon anything he chose. Israel's new king put this wisdom to great use as he strengthened the kingdom. Along with great wisdom God blessed him with great wealth. Psalm 72 was written about King Solomon, and it foreshadows Jesus, the King of all kings. The psalm begins as a prayer that God would give justice and righteousness to the king so the king will reign fairly. *May prayer be made for him continually, and blessings invoked for him all the day!* After a prayer for the land and the people of the cities, we get a foretaste of Jesus: *May his name endure forever, his fame continue as long as the sun! May people be blessed in him, all nations call him blessed!*

There is a day coming when every knee will bow to King Jesus and every tongue will proclaim that He is Lord of all. What a blessed day that will be! The world has never seen a king as good as Jesus. The world's best diplomats, the wisest fairytale kings, leaders who have brought about the most needed reforms - Jesus is so much better than all these put together. *Blessed be the Lord, the God of Israel, who alone does wondrous things. Blessed be his glorious name forever; may the whole earth be filled with his glory! Amen and Amen!*

144

Blessed to Have a Beloved

Song of Solomon 6:9 ESV

Since I'm a bit of a romantic, I am glad that there is at least one blessing in the wonderful love song, the Song of Solomon. After listing several physical attributes of the one he loves (including that none of her teeth are missing), the writer continues to sing the praises of his beloved's virtues: *"My dove, my perfect one, is the only one, the only one of her mother, pure to her who bore her. The young women saw her and called her blessed; the queens and concubines also, and they praised her."*

She is fortunate indeed to be chosen, treasured, and loved so deeply. These are desires that run deep within the heart of most women. Men too have desires and need to know that they are valued, loved, and respected. For those of us whom God has blessed with a spouse, I pray that we take the time to sing a love song to our beloved. Go ahead and read through Solomon's Song if a little inspiration is needed, then sing out. Married love is a wonderful gift from God, and a blessing that is meant to last a lifetime.

All Praise to Jesus Whom God Has Blessed Forever

Psalm 45:2 NIV

One of the explanations of this poetic psalm is that it was written in the time of King Solomon about the Messiah yet to come. Jesus the mighty Warrior, victorious in truth, humility and justice, will be established on a throne that will never be shaken. His position and authority are solid. And one day there will be a great wedding as Jesus is united with His bride, the church.

The time leading up to our oldest daughter, Hannah, and her fiancée Andrew's wedding was full of happy preparations. Lists were compiled and double-checked to be sure that all of the meaningful details were adequately cared for as we kept a joyful wedding day in our sights. The morning of the wedding, we gathered in the renovated neighborhood fire station to decorate it for the reception. I love remembering how Hannah and her bridesmaids laughed as they practiced the line dance they would do together later that night. Evening came, the church filled with guests, and Hannah was a joyful, stunning, composed bride. Her mind was free to focus on their marriage vows and to savor the festivities of their wedding.

Are we, as the church, the Body of Christ, mindfully preparing for the wedding yet to come? Do we live in happy anticipation, waiting for Jesus our Bridegroom? The psalmist writes, *"You are the most excellent of men and your lips have been anointed with grace, since God has blessed you forever."* God's blessing mentioned here is to His Son and the poem continues on to show His strength and justice. The words form a picture of a wedding in which beauty and honor are elevated and joyful praise is the outcome. May the excitement build as each day brings the wedding celebration closer.

Blessed to Find Wisdom

Proverbs 3:13-14, 18, 33 ESV

JUNE 7

Proverbs are succinct statements that can bring about a change in thinking. Frequently, opposing views are presented so the informed reader can make decisions with more awareness of potential outcomes. Who other than Solomon could be better suited to be the primary author of the Book of Proverbs? I love how, at this point, God's Story is divided into thirty-one chapters, a whole month's worth of daily wisdom just waiting for us! *Blessed is the one who finds wisdom, and the one who gets understanding, for the gain from her is better than gain from silver and her profit better than gold...She is a tree of life to those who lay hold of her; those who hold her fast are called blessed...The Lord's curse is on the house of the wicked, but he blesses the dwelling of the righteous.*

It is interesting that blessing often comes after wisdom is applied. God, Your Word is rich and You are so generous to give us truth that remains stable no matter if the economy rises or falls. Rather than anxiously looking at the stock market every day, we can look to Your Word and live a life that is profitable, alive like a healthy tree, and blessed. Wisdom and blessings go hand-in-hand. May we seek both like we are hunting for treasure. Amen.

May Your Wife Be a Fountain of Blessing

Proverbs 5:18 NLT

JUNE 8

By comparing immoral relationships and healthy marriage, a lot of good practical advice is revealed in the fifth chapter of Proverbs. When it all gets boiled down, what comes up is one negative command - Do not commit adultery, and one positive command - Be faithful to your spouse. *Let your wife be a fountain of blessing for you. Rejoice in the wife of your youth.* Faithfulness leads to blessing, and blessing leads to rejoicing. God's plan for fidelity within the husband and wife union is even better than we can imagine.

One of the most complex relationships is marriage, and a good marriage takes attention, effort, thought, time, and consideration - what some would call hard work. For a healthy, happy, and growing Christian marriage, mutual commitment to God and to each other is essential. Love like this is patient and kind. There is no room for rudeness and selfishness. If we add stubborn pride to the unhealthy mix of self-centeredness, we can create damaging barriers that can block the fountain of blessing from flowing. Respect and forgiveness are key factors in a blessed marriage. But even in the best relationship, misunderstandings will come, so it is wise to get good at making peace. Proverbs 5 suggests that there is no better gift than to grow old with the marriage partner of our youth. We can't help but rejoice with a gift like this.

Blessed Are Those Who Keep God's Ways

Proverbs 8:32-36 NIV

JUNE 9

Wisdom calls out to all who will heed her counsel. *"Now then, my children, listen to me; blessed are those who keep my ways. Listen to my instruction and be wise; do not disregard it. Blessed are those who listen to me, watching daily at my doors, waiting at my doorway. For those who find me find life and receive favor* (another word for blessing) *from the Lord. But those who fail to find me harm themselves; all who hate me love death."*

That is pretty straightforward. If we choose to hate wisdom by going our own way, we hurt ourselves, and often those who care about us. One of the saddest things is the death of a relationship. God desires for our relationships to be restored and whole, including our relationship with Him. When we seek to live outside of God, the paths take us from full life and lead us to death. To live beyond the world's wisdom, we need God's wisdom. When we intentionally listen to instruction and actively apply it, we can live blessed. The Book of Proverbs is full of useful, relevant information that can guide us in God's ways. We can be blessed physically, relationally, and spiritually. Healthy truths are not hidden from us, but are made available to us when we look. God wants our lives to succeed.

Blessings Are on the Head of the Righteous

Proverbs 10:6-7; Proverbs 11:11, 26 HCSB

Solomon does not waste time by making the distinctions between the righteous and the wicked sound poetic; rather he tells it like it is: *"Blessings are on the head of the righteous, but the mouth of the wicked conceals violence. The remembrance of the righteous is a blessing, but the name of the wicked will rot... A city is built up by the blessing of the upright, but it is torn down by the mouth of the wicked...People will curse anyone who hoards grain, but a blessing will come to the one who sells it."* "But" is a little word that reveals a big difference. The contrasts between the righteous and the wicked also include the consequences that follow. God has given us free will to choose to be wicked; why would we want to when being blessed is so much better?

Blessed to Share with Neighbors and the Poor

Proverbs 14:21 NLT; Proverbs 22:9 HCSB

Jesus says that whenever we feed those who are hungry it is as if we are feeding Him. When we are hungry and someone gives us some of their food then blessings flow. When we see someone who is hungry and we share with them, we both are blessed. The early church shared their meals with each other and the Book of Proverbs indicates that this is a good way to live life. Proverbs 14:21 encourages us to ask and identify, "Who is my neighbor?" *It is a sin to belittle one's neighbor; blessed are those who help the poor.* Another way to say it is, *"A generous person will be blessed, for he shares his food with the poor."* Want to be blessed? Share.

This simple concept can become a joyful way of life and all it takes is a little awareness of the needs of those around us in our local community and the needs of people all over the world. That is step one. Step two is to intentionally practice generosity. By trusting in the Lord, listening and obeying what He says, we are better equipped to know how and what to give. This life-style pattern can help us remain focused on the One who blesses us with the desire, the ability, and the means by which we can share.

Blessings Linked to Good Choices
Proverbs 16:20-22 NIV

JUNE 12

Seeking good instruction, practicing trust in God, valuing discernment, are all healthy choices - decisions that lead to blessings and to living a blessed life. There is another way for us to choose but it is the path of folly (recklessness, senselessness, stupidity) and in the end there will be punishment. Fools go down that road. Sometimes we need to see the opposite to realize that going God's way really is best. *Whoever gives heed to instruction prospers, and blessed is the one who trusts in the Lord. The wise in heart are called discerning, and gracious words promote instruction. Prudence is a fountain of life to the prudent, but folly brings punishment to fools.* God does not preprogram us; we get to choose. It is good to know not only what the choices are but also the consequences of those choices. Wisdom is a good teacher and the diligent student will often have an overflow of blessings.

As a new driver I made a lot of mistakes and our family car showed it with several dents and scratches. But I have never been more scared than on a Thursday night in 1982 when my friend and I were driving home from volunteering at Saginaw General Hospital. Midway across a large bridge we realized that I was driving the wrong way, against traffic. Although I had received a lot of driving instruction, I still needed more opportunities for practical application, and thanks be to God, He spared us that night from a serious accident. Experience is a very good teacher and in the more than thirty years of driving since then, I have not made that mistake again. I was an immature driver, but that night I grew up and matured real fast. In other non-driving areas of my life, I've learned from the same types of middle-of-the-bridge experiences. Jesus wants us to learn from our errors, not to relive them over and over. He offers us a way to go forward through God's mercy. Let's be wise to trust God's ways.

Integrity and Blessings;
Now and for Generations to Come

Proverbs 20:7, 20-21 NLT

JUNE 13

Several of the blessings found in God's Story pertain to a specific person, like Abraham, or a certain nation, like Israel. But in the Book of Proverbs we read of how blessings follow choices and these have an impact on our lives and those of future generations. God desires right relationships. His insight is helpful and His ways can be learned. May we see things the way God does and live with uprightness of heart, making good choices, especially when it comes to the interactions within our families. *The godly walk with integrity; blessed are their children who follow them... If you insult your father or mother, your light will be snuffed out in total darkness. An inheritance obtained too early in life is not a blessing in the end.* Understanding healthy family structures, including the importance of respect and honesty, can go a long way if one desires peaceful relationships. God-centered building blocks found in healthy families are much needed foundations for the growth of future generations. May our children be blessed as they follow in our ways as we walk humbly with God and honorably before them.

Blessed to Have God as Our Judge

Proverbs 24:25 NLT

JUNE 14

Every four years in the US it is a big election year. 2012 was one of those years, so whether I wanted it or not, the talk was of politics. Signs were posted for months, bumper stickers promoted or demoted nominees in clever ways, and speeches were written, evaluated and then debated. There were many candidates for various offices including the position of judge. Proverbs 24 has this to say about the person who holds that office: *"A judge who says to the wicked, "You are innocent," will be cursed by many people and denounced by the nations. But it will go well for those who convict the guilty; rich blessings will be showered on them."* May God give wisdom to those who hold political power to serve responsibly. And may our nation's judges keep in mind that one day everything will be evaluated by the Judge who rules over all. God will not be bribed. He is not on any rung of the ladder of success, and He is not in need of anyone's help to climb up. His judgment is right, and He will have the final say.

Blessed Heritage

1 Kings 5:7b NKJV

JUNE 15

Not only was Solomon a prolific writer of wisdom literature, he also built a Temple. King David, Solomon's influential father, was a big help to Solomon as he worked on this monumental building project. When Hiram, a friend of the late King David, heard that Solomon was the new king, he was really happy about the situation and said, *"Blessed be the Lord this day, for He has given David a wise son over this great people!"* Hiram also agreed to Solomon's request for shipments of much needed cedar and cypress timber. It was a win-win situation. With Hiram's help and support, many men throughout the land were employed and the required supplies were gathered to build the Temple. God blessed the Temple building process from start to finish.

I can't help but think that David would have been proud of his son Solomon, like parents are when their children's wise choices make the world a better place to live. Living an upright life is a blessing for us now and for our children who come after us.

Blessed to Do What Is Right

Psalm 106:3 NIV

JUNE 16

Under the reign of King Solomon the magnificent Temple was completed and everything was ready for its dedication to God's glory. Before Solomon addressed the masses, the people celebrated with trumpets and cymbals, and raised their voices together to sing out praises to God, "He is good; His love endures forever." This familiar chorus shows up in about a half dozen other psalms and is still sung by God's people today. Reading a little further in Psalm 106 we discover yet another blessing. *Blessed are those who act justly, who always do what is right.*

Justice is important to God. The Temple was a reminder to the people of their covenant relationship with a just God. God is faithful, that is without a doubt. The question is: are we faithful to Him? Do we value justice, love mercy, and walk humbly with God each day? If so, we are blessed. Do we practice patience, exercise gentleness, overflow with gratitude? If not, why not?

Like so many things in life, desired results require disciplined resolve. We won't become physically fit overnight. No matter how much one might dream of being in shape, if we want to see a change in the outcome, we most likely need to change our input. Imagine this cycle: treasure wisely, put off the bad, put on the good, live this out. Treasuring wisely, in this case a strong fit body, leads us to put off the habits that keep us from achieving that goal, maybe laziness and poor food choices. We then add exercise, get proper rest and nutrition and repeat the pattern until it becomes the new norm. In time we enjoy the benefits that come from our disciplined resolve to have a healthy body.

We follow this same cycle to train our minds to master a new language or a musical instrument or a computer program, but what about our most important endeavor, the maturity of our souls? Are we putting on justice and mercy or are we ignoring those qualities? Our soul's health can improve as we put off such things as contempt and pride, and practice living peaceable, pure, humble lives. God, help us to see that it is a blessing to consistently do what is right. Help us to treasure this blessing enough to joyfully endure our workouts. When we get resistance may we see it for what it is, and press on into You. Amen.

God's Glory Filled the Temple; All Were Blessed!

1 Kings 8:14, 54-56 HCSB (also in 2 Chronicles 6:3)

JUNE 17

The dedication and blessing of the Temple continued, and the glory of the Lord began filling the Temple. Pause here for just a minute to take that in. What exactly was it like to experience the Lord's glory filling the Temple? Then Solomon, *the king, turned around and blessed the entire congregation of Israel while they were standing... When Solomon finished praying this entire prayer and petition to the Lord, he got up from kneeling before the altar of the Lord, with his hands spread out toward heaven, and he stood and blessed the whole congregation of Israel with a loud voice: "May the Lord be praised! He has given rest to His people Israel according to all He has said. Not one of all the good promises He made through His servant Moses has failed."*

This great day was full of celebration and dedication and it reminded everyone that God keeps His promises. Life in the time of Solomon and life now has a lot of layers of differences. It helps us to better understand life then if we can try and put ourselves into the Story. Can you picture yourself as a builder who helped to construct the Temple, or as one who offered needed materials or special skills? Would you have been leading up the singing, or maybe joining in with the thankful ones who had been given a rest from war? Those present that day saw God's glory with their own eyes! What would that have been like? The outcome was certainly joyful and both their king and their God blessed all who were assembled.

Blessed to Celebrate!

1 Kings 8:66b MSG

JUNE 18

During the Temple dedication, the people were urged to fully commit to the Lord, live by His decrees, and obey His commands. The festivities included a lot of sacrifices, and the celebration, lead by Solomon, went on for two weeks. Everyone who attended *blessed the king and went home, exuberant with heartfelt gratitude for all the good God had done for his servant David and for his people Israel.*

God likes a good celebration! Let's get good at it for a whole lot of celebrating will take place in Heaven. Heaven is the future home for all who believe. How real is Heaven to you? Are we preparing now for that final move? If you knew you were going to move from the US to Germany, studying German as soon as you could would be a great investment. When our family was relocated to London, England I learned about linguistic differences between US English and British English in a little phrase book Russell gave me. Another book, *Watching the English*, clued me in on many cultural distinctions that helped me relate more effectively with our new neighbors.

I smile when I hear a flight attendant say, "If such-and-such city is your final destination, weather upon landing is so-and-so." My final destination is Heaven. Long ago Jesus not only paid for my ticket with His life on a cross, he bought my permanent citizenship. There is no need to worry about turbulence or missing a connection, and it thrills me that I will travel light; I won't even need a carry-on! Only God knows when that flight will take place, but I love preparing for life in the home He is preparing for me by celebrating life and fully living it now.

God Bless You

Psalm 134:1-3 ESV

JUNE 19

Psalm 134 is a three-verse song that is dedicated to one major theme: to bless. *Come, bless the Lord, all you servants of the Lord, who stand by night in the house of the Lord! Lift up your hands to the holy place and bless the Lord! May the Lord bless you from Zion, he who made heaven and earth!*

Our family lived in Thailand on and off between 1999 and 2011. During those years there were many opportunities to use the Thai phrase, "Khaw Phra-jaow Huay Phawn Khoon Kha" which means, "May God bless you." This blessing has been verbalized throughout the ages and in many different languages, and it concludes this ancient song. Please pray with me for the many people in Thailand who still do not know that the God and Maker of Heaven and earth desires to bless them. God, Your Word lets us know that You love all people, and we pray that one-by-one all will have the opportunity to bless You back. May those who leave offerings in Buddhist temples trying to make merit for past sins rejoice when they hear the truth that Jesus is the final sacrificial offering for a life of peace between You and humanity. Amen.

Bless God Who Is Our Hope

Psalm 146:5-6 ESV; Psalm 147:12-13 HCSB

Here are a few more praise choruses from the writer of the Psalms to the Maker of it all. *Blessed is he whose help is the God of Jacob, whose hope is in the Lord his God, who made heaven and earth, the sea, and all that is in them, who keeps faith forever... Exalt the Lord, Jerusalem; praise your God, Zion! For He strengthens the bars of your gates and blesses your children within you.* God blesses His people because that is the kind of God He is! We praise God with all that we have; God blesses His people, which then leads to more praising. This is a good cycle. Even if He never gives us one more blessing, He is so worthy of our praise. Exalt Him. Let's let our children and grandchildren know that He is Heaven's Maker and all good things are from Him. We often sing songs about what we believe; may the music from our mouths honor our God.

Do Not Bless Too Early or Too Loudly

Proverbs 27:14 NIV

Have you ever heard the saying, "too much of a good thing is not a good thing"? Well, Proverbs 27 says that too loud of a good thing (especially before noon) is not a good thing. *If anyone loudly blesses their neighbor early in the morning, it will be taken as a curse.* I learned this wise saying when we began our married life in an apartment in 1989 in Dallas. Our upstairs neighbor played the drums and even though he was part of a Christian band, when we heard the creative sounds from his drums too early in the morning (or late at night) it did not fall upon us like a blessing! A few years later we moved into our next apartment with three babies under three years old. I have a feeling that our "little blessings" who cried at various times of the day and night might not have always been a sweet sound to our new neighbors' ears. But still, it is good to share goodness, so go ahead and bless your neighbors, just not too early or too loudly!

Blessed When We Choose to Live Wisely

Proverbs 28:14 NLT; Proverbs 28:20 NIV; Proverbs 29:18 NIV

JUNE 22

A faithful, wisdom-heeding, do-righter is a blessed person. We can choose however, to be a stubborn, money-grubber who throws off restraint. If we do, we then also choose not to be blessed by God. Choices (good or bad) form our habits, and consequences (good or bad) follow our habits. *Blessed are those who fear to do wrong, but the stubborn are headed for serious trouble... A faithful person will be richly blessed, but one eager to get rich will not go unpunished... Where there is no revelation, people cast off restraint; but blessed is the one who heeds wisdom's instruction.* Solomon was a very wise man and he chose to share his wisdom by writing many proverbs. God, may we too be wise people, learning from what Solomon wrote under Your inspiration. Amen.

Sin Can Remove Blessings

1 Kings 10:9 ESV (also in 2 Chronicles 9:8)

JUNE 23

Solomon's fame spread far and wide. The queen of Sheba heard how Yahweh had blessed Solomon with wisdom and wealth and she came to see for herself if it was true. She was overwhelmed and impressed with everything she saw. Real life was even greater than the rumors she had heard. She was also amazed that Solomon was able to answer all her questions so wisely. The queen said, *"Blessed be the Lord your God, who has delighted in you and set you on the throne of Israel! Because the Lord loved Israel forever, he has made you king, that you may execute justice and righteousness."*

Did this kind of praise and Solomon's many accomplishments go to his head? Did Solomon believe he was invincible? Was his turning to sin gradual, just a little here, a little there? We read one chapter later in Solomon's portion of God's Story, of how Solomon's love for pagan women and then his worship of their false gods was a deep offense to God. His refusal to faithfully love and obey God cost him the kingdom. Solomon was richly blessed by God but tragically turned his back on the One who gave him everything. What a lesson for us today. How slippery is the slope of sin and disobedience.

Bless Rather Than Curse Your Parents

Proverbs 30:11-14 ESV

JUNE 24

Even though some people are like those described in Proverbs 30:11-14, it is wise not to be like them. *There are those who curse their fathers and do not bless their mothers. There are those who are clean in their own eyes but are not washed of their filth. There are those—how lofty are their eyes, how high their eyelids lift! There are those whose teeth are swords, whose fangs are knives, to devour the poor from off the earth, the needy from among mankind.*

It is better for us to be wise and to bless instead of curse the loving parents and others who care for us throughout life. We can think that we are doing okay, living life according to our own standards, but it is what God thinks that really matters. Are we "clean" on the outside but inside do we have a big mess? Do we seek to raise ourselves up by cutting others down? Agur, the author of Proverbs 30, shares these valuable lessons by using contrasts, and he leaves the choice up to us. Let's not trick ourselves into believing that everything is all right. Instead let's take our needs to Jesus who is faithful to cleanse us from everything in our lives that is not right. With fresh joy of being clean we can live to bless and encourage rather than go with the world's flow of faultfinding and cursing.

Children, Rise up and Call Mom Blessed!

Proverbs 31:27-29 ESV

JUNE 25

On Mother's Day in 1995, when our kiddos were young and we were serving at Antioch Baptist Church in North Carolina, all the moms at church received a beautiful scroll inscribed with the last few verses from the thirty-first Proverb. The godly woman that we encounter in the last proverb recorded in God's Story intimidates many women. *She looks well to the ways of her household and does not eat the bread of idleness. Her children rise up and call her blessed; her husband also, and he praises her: "Many women have done excellently, but you surpass them all."* This godly woman could have disheartened, overwhelmed, and intimidated me. She appears to be somewhat of a Christian Superwoman. But instead she encouraged me, and she should encourage you too because it is wonderful to learn from a role model like this.

Back then, my kiddos were too young to know or use the word "blessed" but I certainly felt blessed by their hugs and hand-drawn cards. God does not call mothers to be super-women but daughters of the King, and He wants us to know our true identity in Him. In the joy and strength that God supplies, we serve our family faithfully, loving our Lord without reserve. How thankful I am to the women in my life, including my own mom, who continually model this kind of beauty.

Blessed to Know
Mankind's Duty is to Bless God

Ecclesiastes 10:17 NIV

JUNE 26

King Solomon surpassed all the kings of the world in riches and in wisdom and he did not hold back on living life fully. And like those in the Garden of Eden, he loved the good God gave, but sadly he felt it was not enough. He wrote about many of life's experiences in a book called Ecclesiastes and captures the attention of many with his opening statement: everything is meaningless, vanity, absolutely futile. Toward the end of the book Solomon makes a proverb-like comment: *Blessed is the land whose king is of noble birth and whose princes eat at a proper time—for strength and not for drunkenness.* I think this is an interesting thing for King Solomon to write. Was he reflecting on the present situation, or simply stating something that is true in principle? Generally when leaders make wise choices those living under their leadership also reap the benefits. We will see that the reverse is also true and those in Solomon's kingdom will reap the consequences that came from him following idols and foreign gods.

After a careful evaluation of all he had experienced, Solomon concluded Ecclesiastes with hope. Are we searching for more than vanity and futility? Do we want a life of meaning? A very good starting point is to realize that life is a gift from God; so eat, drink, enjoy your labor, but in all you do, keep a proper perspective. Instead of being self-seeking as one only living "under the sun", remember the One who is over the sun and above all else. Solomon asked a good question, "What is the whole duty of man?" The answer: to fear God and keep His commandments. When we learn this and really live by it, the more meaningful our lives become.

The Valley of Blessing

2 Chronicles 20:26a NLT

JUNE 27

We have discovered that somewhere along the journey of leading Israel as their third king, Solomon took his eyes off God. One thousand marriage partners was not enough, and tragically Solomon's disobedient choices had grave consequences for himself and for Israel after him. The large nation that began with Abraham was now divided in two: the Northern Kingdom, which was still called Israel; and the Southern Kingdom, Judah. Peace became a rare thing; outside kingdoms attacked the newly divided kingdom with a vengeance, and even Israel and Judah fought against each other.

Fear, instability and destruction continued for generations. When Judah's fourth king, Jehoshaphat, heard that three mighty armies had joined to fight Judah, he knew his people were in grave danger. He also knew idols could not save them; they needed God. King Jehoshaphat begged for the Lord's guidance and called his people to fast. After the king's prayer, the Lord spoke and the people of Judah obeyed. The enemies would have won if not for God's intervention. The Lord fought this battle and not one enemy escaped. With singing and great praise to God, it took Judah over three days to collect all of the valuable plunder. *On the fourth day they gathered in the Valley of Blessing, which got its name that day because the people praised and thanked the Lord there.* All glory went to the Lord, and news of this event spread. And for a while everyone, God's enemies as well as those who trusted Him, were in awe of God.

Taking Someone Else's Blessing Will Not End Well

2 Kings 5:15b KJV

JUNE 28

Judah continued more or less in God's ways and more than less its people received God's blessings. However, many kings who rejected God ruled over Israel. It is good to keep in mind that no matter who is in charge on earth, there are always some people faithful to God who is in charge of it all. Once there was a raid on Israel and a young girl was taken captive. She became the maid to the wife of Naaman the commander for the Aramean army. This girl knew God and was not afraid to share what she knew with her mistress.

Naaman's story is intriguing. He had a skin disease cured by dipping seven times in the Jordan River according to the direction of the godly prophet Elisha. Miracles in countless forms pointed people back to God, for it is His desire that all would know, follow, and be blessed by Him. Naaman was at first angry about the medical procedure that Elisha prescribed but after he was persuaded to give it a try, he was thrilled with the outcome! He praised God and he and all his men returned to Elisha and said, *"Behold, now I know that there is no God in all the earth, but in Israel: now therefore, I pray thee, take a blessing of thy servant."* What was the blessing that Naaman offered to Elisha? Did Elisha take the gift? The story has an interesting twist, so go ahead and read it in its entirety. Clue: do not take a blessing that does not belong to you.

Will God Give Us a Blessing or a Curse?

Joel 2:14a NLT

JUNE 29

A prophet speaks the truth concerning present or future events. In the Bible a prophet is often called a man of God, and the prophet Joel was certainly a man of God used by God, to point people back to God. We need to remember that although prophets are prophets, they are also people, and like all people they live in time and space. At this point in God's Story, Joel's time and space was in the middle of great destruction. An army, not of men but of locusts, devastated Judah. Every aspect of life was changed. I have a feeling Joel got the people's attention when he went on to explain that an even greater devastation would come at the hand of the Lord if the people did not return to Him with all their heart; with fasting, weeping and mourning. *"Who knows? Perhaps he will give you a reprieve, sending you a blessing instead of this curse."*

The passage continues with encouragement of how the Lord is compassionate, and present, and everyone who calls on the name of Yahweh will be saved. Centuries later, both Peter and Paul quoted the prophet Joel as they preached to people and offered God's good news.

Some days it may feel as if we too are living in a time of great devastation. It may be on a nation-wide level, or maybe the hardship is personal. God offers us the same promise He gave those living in Old

Testament times. Will we properly assess our situation and realize that without Him we have no lasting rescue? Will we call on Him?

Come Trembling to the Lord and to His Blessing

Hosea 3:5 NIV

JUNE 30

Hosea's ministry spanned the reigns of four of Judah's kings and began during the reign of Israel's ninth king, Jeroboam. At various times the Northern Kingdom of Israel, and the Southern Kingdom of Judah would repent and God would faithfully forgive His people and even delivered them from their enemies. Sadly, Judah and Israel were bent on worshiping stone carvings and wooden poles. God's people became like an adulterous wife, betraying the One who loved them. Hosea knew all too well what an unfaithful wife was like; he was married to one, and like God, he mercifully extended hope.

Afterward the Israelites will return and seek the LORD their God and David their king. They will come trembling to the LORD and to his blessings in the last days. It had been years since David was alive, but he was known as a man who was after God's own heart and I think Hosea wanted to stir that deep level of commitment within God's un-committed people. The word-picture of a nation trembling back to God and to the blessing He gives is interesting. It reminds me of the advice Paul gave many years later about working out our salvation with fear and trembling. What frightens us? A healthy realization of our sin should bring about fear and mourning. When we take our sin to God in Christ with repentance, we receive forgiveness, and real comfort and blessing from God can return. God does not want for us to continue in estranged arrangements, but to live wholly connected to Him. He is our faithful Example.

Reflections

June focused on the life of King Solomon, known for his wisdom, a gift from the Lord. Solomon shared this wisdom with us by writing proverbs and insightful poetry. When Solomon built the Temple, God's fame spread as the One who blesses. Unfortunately, Solomon's choices to turn from God affect the whole community and the Israelites become a divided kingdom. Obedience and blessings are often linked and God used prophets to try to get the attention of His disobedient people.

July

Please God, Bless Our Children

Hosea 4:6 NLT

JULY 1

Hosea's ministry lasted over sixty years as God's people lived in and out of faithfulness. National leaders were not strong for the Lord, and even the priests did not faithfully follow Him or teach others to do so. God said through Hosea, *"My people are being destroyed because they don't know me. Since you priests refuse to know me, I refuse to recognize you as my priests. Since you have forgotten the laws of your God, I will forget to bless your children."* God said that the destruction that was taking place was related to His people not knowing Him. Knowing God changes everything.

Geographically speaking, China is closer to the land that Jesus walked than America is yet when we arrived in China in 1996, the number of people I met who had never even heard of Him was phenomenal. News of Jesus reached those in China in the seventh century, so why didn't more Chinese people, centuries later, know Him? The basic answer is the sad truth for all of mankind: we turn from our Creator to worship creation instead. We choose to refuse to know God.

It is natural to pass on good news about someone we really know and love. If our children and their children after them don't hear about the greatness of our God from us, maybe it is because we do not think God is that great. If we all knew and loved God and really lived out that love in the way we treated people, would there still be a need for missionaries to go to China or to the US? If we really know God, we will want to make Him known. If I really love God, and God and I have a great relationship, how can that not come out in conversations with my children, my friends, and even strangers? We may or may not be priests, but we can certainly heed the message that Hosea sought to make clear during his lifetime. For our own sake and for the sake of our children, I pray we do not get all caught up in "life" and forget God who blesses us with breath.

Wrestle and Plead for God's Blessing

Hosea 12:4-6 NLT

JULY 2

Because of rampant immorality, violence, lies, and all sorts of idolatry, both Israel and Judah will fall as their rebellions continue. Hosea's reference to God's Story is a reminder that the Israelites came from a heritage that knew and loved the Lord. Then Hosea mentioned Jacob. *Yes, he wrestled with the angel and won. He wept and pleaded for a blessing from him. There at Bethel he met God face to face, and God spoke to him—the Lord God of Heaven's Armies, the Lord is his name! So now, come back to your God. Act with love and justice, and always depend on him.*

I wrestle every day - my will or God's will? We again need to hear what Hosea clearly said: "Come back to your God!" May our hearts beat for the things that God is for: justice, mercy, love, and humility. God, we need to depend on You. And when we do have deep dependency on You, You empower us not to give in to immorality, violence, cheating and other vices that tempt us. Help us not to fall for substitutions but to find our satisfaction in You. God, we plead for Your blessing. Amen.

What Good is the Blessing of a Goddess?

Amos 8:13-14 MSG

JULY 3

God called a shepherd named Amos to speak to His people, to warn those who needed to hear it. Amos lived at the same time as Hosea so we know that at least two people were seeking to help God's people get back on track with the Lord. Through Amos, God's message about the judgment to come was directed at those who appeared religious, but in their actual day-to-day lives they oppressed the poor and the needy. *"On Judgment Day, lovely young girls will faint of Word-thirst, robust young men will faint of God-thirst, along with those who take oaths at the Samaria Sin-and-Sex Center, saying, 'As the lord god of Dan is my witness!' and 'The lady goddess* of Beer-sheba bless you!' Their lives will fall to pieces. They'll never put it together again."

Although this message was spoken long ago, do we need to pay attention to the warnings today? Yes. There is a day of judgment coming, and looking "religious" is not going to cut it with God. If the alternative to looking religious is that we could really enjoy life and live for God now, what changes would we need to make? Asking "who is God?" is a very good starting point. If God is God, and we are not, let us drink in His teaching with great expectations! But if we live like we are God, then good luck; judgment day may find us very thirsty.

Restored for Blessings
Amos 9:13 AMP

JULY 4

God's wrath on unrepentant rebellious people is real. And so is His forgiveness, restoration, and blessings for those who return to Him with all that they have. Only a holy God has the perfect way to give mercy and justice, and He is trustworthy. If we choose to live as if He does not exist we are choosing to be His enemy and He will faithfully honor that decision. A time is coming when those disloyal to God will no longer have access to Him or the good that He graciously provides. I pray we seek His face while we still can.

Behold, the days are coming, says the Lord, that the plowman shall overtake the reaper, and the treader of grapes him who sows the seed; and the mountains shall drop sweet wine and all the hills shall melt [that is, everything heretofore barren and unfruitful shall overflow with spiritual blessing]. That is a picture of restoration. But it is not for everyone, it is for those who call out to God for help. What do we value more, our pride which will eventually lead to barren lives or humility that comes before overflowing blessing? Oh how good life can be when we connect to the Giver of all things good. God, please continue to extend Your mercy and fill us afresh today with spiritual blessings as we seek Your Presence. Amen.

Bless Our Children, Lord

Micah 2:9 HCSB

JULY 5

History is long and complicated and sometimes I wonder if people really ever make lasting personal changes from studying the past. God's people have had good examples, bad examples, warnings, punishment, restoration, and I marvel at God's loving patience and mankind's stubborn rebellion. I also marvel at God's continued patience in my own life and I am daily thankful. As a prophet to the people of Judah, Micah observed that although leaders should know what is right and what is just, they instead love evil and hate good. How sad it is that the enemy of God is His very own people.

Micah speaks for God when he says, *"You force the women of My people out of their comfortable homes, and you take My blessing from their children forever."* No one wants to hear the news that judgment is coming, or that captivity is a result of our own selfish, evil, repetitive crimes of injustice. When we live fat and comfortable in our sin, why would we want to change? Micah's warnings are mixed with the blessings that are for the remnant who remain faithful to God. Are we in the camp of the rebels, or are we living loyally to the Lord? In this situation there is no Switzerland.

God Desires to Bless and to Lead

Micah 6:5 NLT

JULY 6

God tells the rebellious to plead their case against Him, and then He gives them a quick reminder of His faithfulness throughout His Story. He says, *"Don't you remember, my people, how King Balak of Moab tried to have you cursed and how Balaam son of Beor blessed you instead? And remember your journey from Acacia Grove to Gilgal, when I, the LORD, did everything I could to teach you about my faithfulness."* God tells us to be just, merciful and humble and too often we think that living in our own "wisdom" is all we need.

Yet as humanity we go astray like sheep, as if we had no Good Shepherd. God, please continue to have mercy, all the while knowing judgment is coming. Thank You God, that even in the dark times You give a glimmer of hope with prophecies fulfilled through Jesus. Amen.

God knows the direction of His Story and we as His people can have hope in our future, even on days when our present feels uncertain. What can help us is to intentionally remember God's past faithfulness and in doing so, be thankful. The faithful shepherds, teachers, preachers and prophets continue to seek to assist people so all can see and experience the blessings that God has in store for those who hear His voice and choose to follow.

Align to the Lord and to His Blessings

Isaiah 19:24-25 ESV

JULY 7

The most evangelistic prophet of all times was perhaps the prophet Isaiah. Used by God for over forty years, Isaiah spoke truthfully about the sins of the people Judah, and the severe punishment that will follow those choices. He offered hope that people would realize they can change and return to the Lord. Isaiah lived during the times of many kings and he witnessed first-hand the need that all have for a Savior. After nineteen chapters of warnings, Isaiah talks of a day of blessing. *In that day Israel will be the third with Egypt and Assyria, a blessing in the midst of the earth, whom the LORD of hosts has blessed, saying, "Blessed be Egypt my people, and Assyria the work of my hands, and Israel my inheritance."* This is an interesting alliance but we will find that true peace comes only when we are aligned to the Lord.

I love how in the minority area of China, where we lived, there was a man who became like the prophet Isaiah. This "Tai Isaiah" knew there needed to be more than idols and he was thrilled to learn about God's plan for abundant life through Jesus. But why had the Christians in the area neglected to share this good news with his tribe? The answer is much like how it was in the time of Isaiah: God's people had turned inward and they did not offer His blessings to others so more could be blessed. Russell and the Tai Isaiah pressed on, reaching out to others who had never heard God's Story and challenging those who knew God to share His goodness. As more people align to God, His hope and peace can change hearts and nations.

Blessed to Bless the Lord

2 Chronicles 30:27 HCSB

JULY 8

At this point in history, God's people lived in a sinful state no matter which nation they were in. Injustice, idolatry, pride, greed, immoral self-indulgence and arrogance ruled the day. And then there was the sin that all of this behavior could be rationalized as they went through the religious motions even though their hearts were far from God. Did they think that God is blind? Do we? The prophets continued to warn the people and they experienced God's holy anger. Some people repented and were rescued, and praise was offered to God for His deliverance.

The reforming King Hezekiah offered hope, and spiritual renewal began to take place, as the Temple was again used to honor God. Invitations to celebrate the Passover were extended beyond Jerusalem to all of Israel. *Then the priests and the Levites stood to bless the people, and God heard their voice, and their prayer came into His holy dwelling place in heaven.* Oh, what joy there is when individuals and whole nations return to the Lord! Back then some people lived as if they could handle life just fine on their own. They were wrong. All people at all times have needs that cannot be fully satisfied apart from God.

We need right relationships not rationalization. Let's not be deceived and kept from life that is full and abundant and dependent upon God. When we realize God is the One who can, and will, meet our needs and we humbly turn to Him, joy and deep peace like never before can be ours.

Blessed Heaps

2 Chronicles 31:8-9, 10b ESV

JULY 9

In order for priests and Levites to devote their energy to the law of the Lord, King Hezekiah told the others to give a tenth of their blessings to bless those set apart by God to serve in these distinct ways. Look what happened. *When Hezekiah and the princes came and saw the heaps, they blessed the Lord and his people Israel. And Hezekiah questioned the priests and the Levites about the heaps.* Here's the answer King Hezekiah received: *"Since they began to bring the contributions into the house of the Lord, we have eaten and had enough and have plenty left, for the Lord has blessed his people, so that we have this large amount left."*

Have you ever received a heap of blessings? Sometimes our eyes are not even open to see the heap. Other times we see God's goodness and blessings all over the situation. Let's keep our eyes open and focused, and offer up the blessing of thanksgiving to God when our heaps are before us. And from our blessings let us bless others. Joy overflowing!

174

The Lord's Hand of Blessing

Isaiah 25:9-10a NLT

When Russell and I first got married and before the babies came, we read the book of Isaiah aloud together. It was my first exposure to this book. Isaiah's writings cover many warnings and blessings over a wide span of years and he wrote of prophecies that have now been fulfilled and of prophecies that offer future expectations. He remains Russell's favorite prophet and it was easy for the two of us to agree on "Isaiah" as the name of our only son, an early Christmas gift given to our family in 1992. I love remembering how his two older sisters, who were quite young themselves, held their baby brother with great care. In order to keep up with them, Isaiah was walking on his first birthday and since then, I have prayed that he would walk with integrity.

A man of great integrity, Isaiah the prophet, told it the way it was during the dark times for God's people. Isaiah also offered hope for that period as well as hope for the future. Isaiah said that God would destroy death forever and that He would wipe away the tears from every face. *In that day people will proclaim, "This is our God! We trusted in him and he saved us! This is the Lord, in whom we trusted. Let us rejoice in the salvation he brings! For the Lord's hand of blessing will rest on Jerusalem."*

Sometimes the blessings we read about are for the future and our anticipation grows when we think about what is yet to come. Justice will prevail. God indeed has a hand of blessing. And this is not the only time we will read about His hand wiping away all tears. There is a lot of good yet before us! Bless God!

Blessed to Wait for God's Help

Isaiah 29:22b-23 NLT; Isaiah 30:18 NLT

JULY 11

Israel, the nation, was not healthy. Her founding fathers held to godly principles but they were not valued in Isaiah's time and this abandonment was having its due effect. Scoffing, arrogant evil plotting, and outright lying dominated the times and people of authority perverted righteousness. God said to the people of Israel, hold on. In God's timing justice will come. *"My people will no longer be ashamed or turn pale with fear. For when they see their many children and all the blessings I have given them, they will recognize the holiness of the Holy One of Israel. They will stand in awe of the God of Jacob."* God extends hope that the wayward and the confused and the complainers will gain instruction and understanding.

Is He still waiting all these years later for humanity to humbly come to Him? *So the Lord must wait for you to come to him so he can show you his love and compassion. For the Lord is a faithful God. Blessed are all those who wait for his help.* God waits for us. We are not fully grown spiritually. We often demand immediate justice; we do not want to wait for God to administer it. But when we wait, trusting Him, we are blessed. Stand in awe and recognize God for His many blessings; wait for Him to deliver justice and with open hands and hearts receive His compassion.

This is easier to write than to do, but life is great when individuals and groups are restored to a vibrant and healthy relationship with Holy God. Because growth is a process, restoration takes place on one level, and that new rebuild then prepares us to see where more renovation is needed. Our hearts are complex and our faithful God is compassionate. Let's keep growing, for He is willing to help us.

God Blesses with What We Need

Isaiah 30:23 NLT; Isaiah 32:20 NIV; Isaiah 44:3 ESV

Let me list a few more blessings from the prophet Isaiah allowing the blessings to flow and to show God's faithfulness. *Then the LORD will bless you with rain at planting time. There will be wonderful harvests and plenty of pastureland for your livestock... how blessed you will be, sowing your seed by every stream, and letting your cattle and donkeys range free... For I will pour water on the thirsty land, and streams on the dry ground; I will pour my Spirit upon your offspring, and my blessing on your descendants.* God cares about the things we need and He wonderfully provides.

Chiang Mai, the city our children call home, is nestled in the mountains of northern Thailand. For about nine months out of the year I find the weather to be perfect, but then comes the extremely hot, dry, smoky season. Pollution from burning the remains of the harvested crops lingers in the valley, making it challenging to breathe, and a thick haze blocks the mountains from view. Vegetation wilts and browns, and all of God's creation anticipates the coming rains. Distant thunder brings hope, as year after year God faithfully provides what is needed.

We do need rain in due season (or whatever equivalent is relevant to our present day livelihood) and we need the Holy Spirit poured out. God, please pour out Your blessings upon us, the Thai people and those all over the earth, just like rain clouds pour the rain. I pray that we would take in Your Word the way a thirsty land absorbs the showers. Amen.

Blessed to Experience God's Mercy

Isaiah 51:2 HCSB; Isaiah 54:10 NLT

Looking back on the faithfulness of the Lord increases our faith; as we reflect on God's goodness, we gain courage to live in the present and have real hope to face the future. Isaiah encouraged King Hezekiah as he sought the Lord and reminded the king of God's promise of a nation that was to come out of one couple. *"Look to Abraham your father, and to Sarah who gave birth to you in pain. When I called him, he was only one; I blessed him and made him many."*

God made a nation for Himself out of one man and woman, and through the years led this nation into the land He promised. But again, God's people were in hard times brought on by their own rebellion and sin; they needed a wake-up call to God's mercy. *"For the mountains may move and the hills disappear, but even then my faithful love for you will remain. My covenant of blessing will never be broken," says the LORD, who has mercy on you.* Because of God's benevolent faithful love we have hope. This is a call worth answering with thanksgiving.

God Blesses the Foreigners

Isaiah 56:1-2, 4, 6 NLT

JULY 14

God's blessings are extended beyond His people Israel to even foreigners! I have lived more than half of my adult life as a foreigner and now that I'm back in the US, it is not a surprise that I seem to be drawn to people from other countries. Sophie's plane from Africa was several hours delayed. So while waiting in the international terminal I watched weary people arrive from around the world. I wanted to have a cooler filled with bottled water and a big sign and a hug to welcome everyone coming to Houston for the first time. I think it would make God smile, for He too wants to bless and rescue the foreigner.

This is what the Lord says: "Be just and fair to all. Do what is right and good, for I am coming soon to rescue you and to display my righteousness among you. Blessed are all those who are careful to do this. Blessed are those who honor my Sabbath days of rest and keep themselves from doing wrong... For this is what the Lord says: "I will bless those eunuchs who keep my Sabbath days holy and who choose to do what pleases me and commit their lives

178

to me"... "I will also bless the foreigners who commit themselves to the Lord, who serve him and love his name, who worship him and do not desecrate the Sabbath day of rest, and who hold fast to my covenant."

God, bless the foreigners among us. May we honor You by how we treat others, those that are similar to us and those that are different. Your desire is for all to know and love Your name and to wholeheartedly worship You, for in doing so we are blessed. Amen.

Joyous Blessing Instead of Mourning

Isaiah 61:3, 9 NLT

JULY 15

Years later when Jesus was in Nazareth teaching in a synagogue, He read a portion of the scroll from the prophet Isaiah: "The Spirit of the Lord is upon me, for he has anointed me to bring good news to the poor. He has sent me to proclaim that captives will be released, that the blind will see, that the oppressed will be set free, and that the time of the Lord's favor has come." I picture Jesus pausing and lowering the scroll to look out at those He had been reading to with eyes of deep compassion. He then said, "Today this Scripture has been fulfilled in your hearing."

Isaiah's prophecy goes on to say, *"To all who mourn in Israel, he will give a crown of beauty for ashes, a joyous blessing instead of mourning, festive praise instead of despair. In their righteousness, they will be like great oaks that the LORD has planted for his own glory."* May God's glory shine in our lives. Yahweh the faithful One, loves justice. He will reward His servants, His ministers with garments of salvation and robes of righteousness. *"Their descendants will be recognized and honored among the nations. Everyone will realize that they are a people the LORD has blessed."* God's Story has amazing continuity. His theme to bless excites and encourages and energizes all at once! Fill me Lord, so I can go forward as a blessing. Amen.

Blessed by the God of Truth

Isaiah 65:8, 16, 23 ESV

JULY 16

Isaiah's prophecies are coming to an end, and as in earlier chapters in God's Story, we see that His desire for redemption continues. Listen to the hope that Isaiah recorded as the Lord spoke: *"As the new wine is found in the cluster, and they say, 'Do not destroy it, for there is a blessing in it,' so I will do for my servants' sake, and not destroy them all... So that he who blesses himself in the land shall bless himself by the God of truth, and he who takes an oath in the land shall swear by the God of truth; because the former troubles are forgotten and are hidden from my eyes... They shall not labor in vain or bear children for calamity, for they shall be the offspring of the blessed of the LORD, and their descendants with them."*

Those of us who are the Lord's servants are the descendants of the Lord's blessings. We're blessed because the people who came before us were blessed. We are blessed to be a blessing. And the blessings don't stop! There is no reason to fill our days mindlessly doing busy work when we can actively live and move and work in the God of truth. Jesus tells us to know the truth for the truth will set us free. Real freedom comes only through Him.

Please continue to pray for the young women in the Thai juvenile detention center. Great freedom has been given to teach God's good news to them and hearts are changing. Some of the girls have begun a probation period and are starting fresh lives as nannies at an orphanage run by Christians. As these young ladies embrace God's forgiveness and see how their lives can be different, may they forget their former troubles and thrive in the blessings of the Lord of second chances.

God Blesses Those with Humble Hearts

Isaiah 66:2-3, 14b NLT

In the last chapter of Isaiah's book, we read what God has been saying since the beginning of time: *"My hands have made both heaven and earth; they and everything in them are mine. I, the LORD, have spoken! I will bless those who have humble and contrite hearts, who tremble at my word. But those who choose their own ways— delighting in their detestable sins— will not have their offerings accepted... When they burn frankincense, it's as if they had blessed an idol."* Again we see that God acknowledges our ability to make choices. He will also be faithful and deliver the consequences of our choices.

He is the One who rewards, and He is the One who executes judgment; a time is coming when this will all be clear. *Everyone will see the LORD's hand of blessing on his servants— and his anger against his enemies.* So far, that final judgment time has not yet come. That means we have today to choose to humble our hearts and serve the God who created everything. We can seek Him and be blessed, or we can choose to delight in the detestable and meet God as an enemy. The end of the Story tells us that God's enemies do not stand a chance against Him. Isaiah was a brave prophet and we would be wise to learn all that God wrote through this man of integrity. Isaiah himself announced early on that he was a man of unclean lips. God cleansed him and used him mightily. God can do the same for us.

Actively Seek God's Blessings

Zephaniah 1:4-6 NLT

Prophets had been crying out to the people about their rebellion against God, but very few listened. The Assyrian empire was a major military power and after they invaded Israel (the Northern Kingdom), they took many people captive from those ten northern tribes. The prophets continued to cry out against rebellion and against the cruelty of the Assyrians toward the captives, and God's wrath came down on His enemies no matter who they were, where they lived or where they were from.

The Southern Kingdom, Judah, had a new and godly king but he was young so God called his relative, Zephaniah, to be His spokesman. Judah is shocked by the message: *"I will crush Judah and Jerusalem with my fist and destroy every last trace of their Baal worship. I will put an end to all the idolatrous priests, so that even the memory of them will disappear. For they go up to their roofs and bow down to the sun, moon, and stars. They claim to follow the Lord, but then they worship Molech, too. And I will destroy those who used to worship me but now no longer do. They no longer ask for the Lord's guidance or seek my blessings."*

Let's be wise and not fall for trendy false worship no matter which Hollywood star or philosophical intellectual makes it seem appealing. Let's be wise and not let "seeking God" become something we used to do. Let's keep asking God to lead us. It is good to seek His blessings, and God does not mumble when He says that He is to be our exclusive choice. God, please guide all of us who seek to follow You. No matter what is taking place around us, may we desire to focus on You, invite You into the situation, and listen for Your wise counsel. Day-by-day, step-by-step, may we obediently follow You. Amen.

Blessed to Be a Blessing to the Nations of the World
Jeremiah 4:1-2b NLT

JULY 19

Jeremiah was the next prophet God used to try to get the attention of His straying people. It is interesting that along with strong admonitions, Jeremiah's conversations with the Lord are also recorded in God's Story. Jeremiah's ministry lasted nearly half a century and he is known as the weeping prophet.

"O Israel," says the Lord, "if you wanted to return to me, you could. You could throw away your detestable idols and stray away no more... Then you would be a blessing to the nations of the world, and all people would come and praise my name." Our Heavenly Father pleads like a loving parent yet His children ignored Him and in doing so they missed the opportunity to be a blessing to the nations of the world! They passed on their turn to bless. And not only did they miss out on being a blessing, but things go from bad to worse as chapter after chapter, year after year, hard stubborn hearts refused to return fully to God who loves them.

Contrary to Buddhist thought, we only get to live once; let's take our chance to bless while we can. How will we be used by God to be a blessing to the nations of the world? He can only use us when we yield to Him and when we let go of the things we value more than God. In our day and time, idols are not necessarily carved from stone or wood, but boy do we have things that are important in our eyes that may distract us from seeing the Lord clearly.

Sin Can Rob Me of Blessings

Jeremiah 5:25 NLT

JULY 20

Rather than living in awe of an awesome God, God's people not only neglected to thank Him for His blessings, but they pursued evil as if wickedness were a treasure. As they broke all of the Ten Commandments and then some, their sins left them hungry for more sin. Goodness from a good God is not at all what they were experiencing at this point in the Story. *Your wickedness has deprived you of these wonderful blessings. Your sin has robbed you of all these good things.* Throughout history, mankind has not been content with good alone, as was established in the Garden of Eden, but has added evil to it. May God help us break this cycle of treasuring sin in our own lives and in our communities, so once again we can thank Him for His generous blessings to us.

As I edit this portion of *The Blessing Book* it is November and I'm reflecting on the Lord's goodness. I'm so thankful for forgiveness of my sins and I'm so grateful for the bonus of living in God's wonderful blessings - too many to count. My sin could have robbed me of all the joy of being in God's family but thanks to Jesus, I am forgiven. And I'm blessed as my family is extended and includes Hannah's new married family too. Our kitchen was filled with the smells of Thanksgiving. I had time before the Minicks met up at the Roberts' to enjoy good food together, so I rode my bike to Houston's Memorial Park and locked it to a pole. The crisp autumn air was perfect for running laps. My eyes and ears focused on people from a variety of countries who were spending their holiday morning at the park. I thought back to the first Thanksgiving when Pilgrims and Native Americans thanked God together. Praying for those on the running trail increased my gratitude. I asked God to bless everyone I saw with good food to share with family, and more than that, to know the God of every good blessing.

Getting back to Jeremiah's admonition, may we trade wickedness (if that is too strong of a word we could use selfishness, or a number of other words that mean sin) for wholesomeness, and live in awe of God with gratitude. As God's people we can celebrate Thanksgiving in July too!

God Can Say "Times up" No More Blessings

Jeremiah 16:5b NIV

JULY 21

Jeremiah's role of being a prophet was a thankless job. God's people, Israel (called "faithless") and her sister Judah (called "unfaithful") rebelled all the more and refused to return to the Lord. As their disobedience heightened, and Jeremiah's plea for their re-thinking intensified, some even tried to kill Jeremiah for giving a "negative" prophecy. It was a very low point in God's recorded Story. Those He created in His image, those He loved and rescued and designed a covenant with, were far away from Him and far away from living out any of His virtues and values.

Then, God said it was too late, that Jeremiah shouldn't even bother praying for them anymore since destruction was coming. The Lord gave clear instructions: *"Do not enter a house where there is a funeral meal; do not go to mourn or show sympathy, because I have withdrawn my blessing, my love and my pity from this people,"* declares the LORD.

How disheartening that the people did not take God's warnings to heart or His rebukes through Jeremiah seriously, and they completely rejected His loving kindness. Will we learn from history? I pray that our nation, our world, has not pushed God too far. Please, God, do not withdraw Your love from us. May we fully return to You while there is still time. Amen.

Trust in the Lord, Be Blessed

Jeremiah 17:5, 7 HCSB

JULY 22

The summer of 2011 was a blessed season of reunions. It had been three years since we had been together with our extended families in the US. Our family of five arrived in Michigan from Thailand on different days and after a lot of travel we enjoyed a wonderful party hosted by my mom to celebrate Sophie and Isaiah's high school graduations. Before meeting up with the Minick family in Branson, Missouri for another meaningful family reunion, Isaiah attended a pre-college retreat for missionary kids in Illinois. Resting from the drive, Hannah and I laughed through a quirky movie in our rented room. The main character was seeking to rescue a gal but she was not so sure that he was the good guy. So he tried to persuade her of her need to trust him by raising and lowering his hand. Her chances for survival were better with him (hand raised) than without him (hand lowered). Maybe because the young lady in the scene was under some stress, the rescuing man needed to repeat his illustration.

Without meaning to be irreverent, I can picture God lowering and raising His hand when He says: *"The man who trusts in mankind, who makes human flesh his strength and turns his heart from the Lord is cursed. The man who trusts in the LORD, whose confidence indeed is the LORD, is blessed."* We are oh so much better off with God than without Him. With God we are blessed; without Him we are cursed. Do we not see our total need for Him to rescue us? Thank You, Father God, for showing us in so many ways how You are trustworthy. With You we not only survive but we have the ability to thrive as Your Holy Spirit lives within us. May we sing with joy about the joy that is for those whose confidence is in the Lord. Amen.

Obey and Be Blessed

Jeremiah 18:9-11 NLT; Jeremiah 20:14 NIV

JULY 23

Jeremiah used an illustration from a potter's shop for his next sermon. The same way a potter, when forming a bowl, can reshape the clay if it is not going the way he wants, so God can reshape a nation. He is the Potter; nations are the clay. God says, *"...if I announce that I will plant and build up a certain nation or kingdom, but then that nation turns to evil and refuses to obey me, I will not bless it as I said I would. Therefore, Jeremiah, go and warn all Judah and Jerusalem. Say to them, 'This is what the Lord says: I am planning disaster for you instead of good. So turn from your evil ways, each of you, and do what is right.'"*

The leaders did not want to hear news like this! They brought so much ridicule and punishment for Jeremiah that he says, *"Cursed be the day I was born! May the day my mother bore me not be blessed!"* Hang in there, Jeremiah, God is on your side! He is on the side of all who turn to Him and His right ways. When God is for us, what are those who are against us but mere humans, clay in the hands of a great Potter.

Be Just, Do Right, Be Blessed

Jeremiah 22:15 NLT

JULY 24

King Josiah listened to Jeremiah's wise counsel and brought about some spiritual reforms during his reign. But what about the next generation? Would Josiah's son follow in his footsteps? When Josiah died, God told Jeremiah to go right up to the palace in Jerusalem and address the new king. What are the signs that make a king a good leader? Jeremiah boldly proclaimed, *"But a beautiful cedar palace does not make a great king! Your father, Josiah, also had plenty to eat and drink. But he was just and right in all his dealings. That is why God blessed him."*

Tragedy would strike because Josiah's son was wholeheartedly set on dishonest profit. He did not provide care for people who could not care for themselves. He and those who followed his evil ways faced captivity by Nebuchadnezzar the king of Babylon, and Judah was about to find out that life was not going to be lived in luxury for much longer. The beautiful cedar palace did not protect them. The only thing that will ultimately protect us is a right relationship with God. He blesses those who deal with situations in right and just ways.

Bless the God of Heaven

Daniel 2:19-20 ESV

JULY 25

King Nebuchadnezzar, as we will find out, is an interesting character in God's Story. At first glimpse we might stereotype him as the bad guy for he powerfully ruled an enemy kingdom. Nebuchadnezzar ordered that the smart and handsome young men of Judah's royal family be taken captive and trained to serve in his palace in Babylon. Daniel was one of the Southern Kingdom's elite and he was selected for this role. Early on he resolved not to defile himself in this new environment and instead remain faithful to God.

Daniel was given an opportunity to declare the power, wisdom and goodness of God when he volunteered to interpret a disturbing dream that bothered King Nebuchadnezzar. *Then the mystery was revealed to Daniel in a vision of the night. Then Daniel blessed the God of heaven. Daniel answered and said: "Blessed be the name of God forever and ever, to whom belong wisdom and might."* Daniel did not take the credit himself but gave credit where credit was due: to God.

What we resolve to do, or not to do, says so much about us. Living faithfully in that steadfast resolve builds character, and God uses people of character to communicate to others that they too can know God and grow in His good character. That is the way He does it; don't we need human examples of godly living? Healthy teaching coupled with learners who desire to mature, is like seeds falling on suitable soil; growth will happen.

During the end our last year of living in Thailand, Russell taught the book of Daniel at our house church. Each Tuesday the ladies of our church gathered to discuss the lesson and study more verses from Daniel. We prayed together and helped each other with individual applications. Like Daniel, we wanted to live out our resolves. Because I knew the year before us would be filled with lots of transition and lots of uncertainty, my resolve was to live presently and thankfully each day. To make this resolve more concrete, I chose to take at least one photo a day and then journal why I was thankful. God gave Daniel the ability to interpret dreams for the king. He gave me peace and gratitude as I lived trusting in Him with resolve through a very unresolved year.

Blessed Be the Glory of the Lord

Ezekiel 3:12-13 ESV

JULY 26

As a good priest serving in Jerusalem (where Jeremiah continued to prophesy) Ezekiel was another man who was brought into Babylonian captivity. These were dark years in Judah's history and God's Story does not shirk from showing them to us. Ezekiel and Daniel were about the same age and by this time, Daniel was established within the government, and Ezekiel's new job was to be a missionary to his fellow captives. The language barrier was not a problematic issue as it often is on the mission field. What Ezekiel faced in Babylon was similar to what he encountered in Jerusalem: hard, stubborn hearts that refused to respond to God's love and lordship and His offer for restoration.

God gave dramatic signs to Ezekiel, to strengthen him during the two decades of challenging service before him. Ezekiel wrote, *"Then the Spirit lifted me up, and I heard behind me the voice of a great earthquake: "Blessed be the glory of the Lord from its place!" It was the sound of the wings of the living creatures as they touched one another, and the sound of the wheels beside them, and the sound of a great earthquake."*

Ezekiel recorded over sixty interactions with God and each conversation ended with God saying, "Then they will know that I am the LORD." Do we live today knowing that He is the Lord? If so, we will seek to obey our Lord and when we get off track, we will be quick to turn our way back to Jesus who is the Way. A restored relationship with God gives us hope. Being filled with His love helps us as well as those we seek to communicate His love with. Blessed be the glory of the Lord! May we be like Ezekiel, a magnifying glass of God's goodness wherever God seeks to move us.

Blessings Will Come Back

Jeremiah 31:2, 23 NLT

JULY 27

Meanwhile, 500 miles away from Babylon (if you marched in a straight and direct line) back in Jerusalem, as the city was about to be totally devastated by the Babylonians, Jeremiah was still faithfully proclaiming the Word of the Lord. God's people needed encouragement but they would face the ramifications of their sin before they would experience the rescue from God. *This is what the LORD says: "Those who survive the coming destruction will find blessings even in the barren land, for I will give rest to the people of Israel." ...This is what the LORD of Heaven's Armies, the God of Israel, says: "When I bring them back from captivity, the people of Judah and its towns will again say, 'The LORD bless you, O righteous home, O holy mountain!'*

This promise became reality, but first the people experienced sin's consequence: seventy years of captivity. Make no mistake, sin is a trap, a deadly snare and only God can save us from it. And oh, how we rejoice when the Lord of Heaven's Armies comes in to rescue us. Are we calling out for Him to hear us? Be wise to know that we cannot handle sin's net on our own.

Our Good Shepherd Blesses

Ezekiel 34:25-27 HCSB

JULY 28

Themes are found throughout God's Story. Love, redemption, justice, mercy, peace, freedom, and responsibility are just a few. One of the responsibilities God gave Ezekiel was to let the leaders of Israel know that they were bad shepherds, and that they would be held responsible because they did not care for their flocks. God says that He himself will look after the lost sheep. *"I will make a covenant of peace with them and eliminate dangerous animals in the land, so that they may live securely in the wilderness and sleep in the forest. I will make them and the area around My hill a blessing: I will send down showers in their season—showers of blessing. The trees of the field will give their fruit, and the land will yield its produce; My flock will be secure in their land. They will know that I am Yahweh when I break the bars of their yoke and rescue them from the hands of those who enslave them."*

God's loving care never stops. Through all generations He shows justice and mercy far beyond what humanity deserves. He even gave Jesus, His dearly loved Son, to mankind to offer us life instead of sin and death. Jesus is the Good Shepherd for all of us who are still like sheep and go astray. He cares for us. Thank You, Lord, for Your shower of blessings! Thank You, Lord Jesus, for washing us clean! Thank You for breaking us free from our habitual shortcomings and giving us true peace in You. Amen.

Blessed Be the God of...

Daniel 3:28b NKJV

JULY 29

As you have probably guessed by now, this was not a peaceful time in history. Battles raged and on-going struggles for power shaped each reign as kings were killed and new ones were set up. God continued to send prophets to warn unfaithful people but they continued to do what seemed right in their own eyes - neglect God.

Back in Babylon, jealous leaders in King Nebuchadnezzar's regime made arrangements for Daniel's friends to be thrown in a fiery furnace. When the three men were not burned, King Nebuchadnezzar, who liked Daniel, rejoiced, saying, *"Blessed be the God of Shadrach, Meshach, and Abed-Nego, who sent His Angel and delivered His servants who trusted in Him, and they have frustrated the king's word, and yielded their bodies, that they should not serve nor worship any god except their own God!"*

Nebuchadnezzar went on to say that only the God of Daniel and his friends could rescue like this, and if others did not follow Him, they would be cut to pieces and their houses burned down. He was not exactly the father of friendship evangelism. It may have taken many years for King Nebuchadnezzar to fully understand God's love and power and to trust in Him alone. We will see later in his life how his pride eclipsed his loyalty to God.

Although this part of God's Story mainly reveals the failure of His people as a nation to see how they had been blessed so that they could be a blessing, I love the glimpse we get of God's love for individuals as well. Nebuchadnezzar is an encouraging example as I look at my own life (I have never been a political leader but I do struggle at times with control) and God shows how He is the One who is ultimately in control of it all. This portion of Daniel's story also encourages us to keep on praying for belief and trust in God to come to those we love. Do others know of our allegiance to the King? There is no blessing in being a secret saint, but with a clear conscience we need to do what we do so that others can be blessed, and then everyone will give glory to our Father in Heaven. Can it be said of us, "Blessed be the God of…"?

Blessed to Give Firstly to God

Ezekiel 44:30 NLT

JULY 30

Over a dozen years after Jerusalem's fall, and while still in exile, Ezekiel received another vision from God. This new vision was for a new Temple. Along with many precise details of its measurements and what materials to use, God also explained the duties and the privileges of the faithful Levite priests. *The first of the ripe fruits and all the gifts brought to the Lord will go to the priests. The first samples of each grain harvest and the first of your flour must also be given to the priests so the Lord will bless your homes.*

This blessing from God contained conditions for God's people. As a real reminder to them that all blessings come from Him, they were to give the first of their harvest back to the Lord. In this case the gift was given to the priests who had been set apart to serve God. Once this was done, God would bless their homes. Ezekiel's devoted ministry prepared many people to return to the Lord, and to see afresh that He is the Giver of all things good. Centuries after Ezekiel faithfully served, godly leaders continue to teach that the blessings received from God are not to be hoarded but given.

With much prayer and informational build-up, Houston's First Baptist Church launched an incredible giving opportunity in February 2013 called Mission 1:8. Funds given would support numerous ministries in our city, country, and world. Russell and I were committed as a couple to embrace the incentive by contributing financially as well as with our service. But I wanted to give money individually too. The challenge was that I did not have a job. So as I prayed, I wrote on my pledge card that my desire was to offer my first paycheck. What blessing was mine as within a month, I was able to give my "first fruits" check, for God provided me with a wonderful job! He continues to bless our home, our family and the work of our hands. It is a joy to give back to God and give forward to people.

Bless the Most High and Praise Him Forever

Daniel 4:34 ESV

JULY 31

An interesting thing happened to King Nebuchadnezzar near the end of his reign. He had another dream. It was a very scary dream and when he called for Daniel's interpretation, he chose not to heed Daniel's warning. So about a year later, as the king was proudly boasting about his own majesty, the nightmare came true. He descended into madness and became like a wild animal. King Nebuchadnezzar stayed this way until he acknowledged that the Most High God is sovereign over all kingdoms.

When he yielded to God he came to his senses and said, *"At the end of the days I, Nebuchadnezzar, lifted my eyes to heaven, and my reason returned to me, and I blessed the Most High, and praised and honored him who lives forever, for his dominion is an everlasting dominion, and his kingdom endures from generation to generation..."* The insanity was temporary and his mind was changed, and joyfully he honored God and wanted everyone to know the greatness of the Most High.

King Nebuchadnezzar had spent most of his life oppressing God's people and then he himself became a true believer. In a way he had a conversion much like Saul to Paul in the New Testament, but this man had lived many years earlier. God's power and His grace are still alive and active in our days. I pray we live fully embracing our role in His Story.

Reflections

The Israelites, now the Northern and Southern Kingdoms, grew in their ungratefulness and rebellion. Fighting, hotter than Texas in July, took place on multiple levels and increased the instability. God's spokespersons, (Hosea, Amos, Micah and Isaiah) faithfully urged both Kingdoms to return to Him, but to no avail. Then the unthinkable happened: captivity of God's people by God's enemy. Daniel, Ezekiel, Zephaniah and Jeremiah entered the Story yet the stubborn refusal of God's blessings meant life got worse before it got any better.

August

How Do I Respond
When Blessings Are Removed?

Job 1:9-11 HCSB

The background of the story of Job is difficult to determine. His was a life of incredible suffering, tried faith, and restored blessings but the timeframe for when the book was written is hard to pinpoint. Job lived even before Abraham and it is possible that the account of his life had been passed down orally from generation to generation, each father telling his family. If ever God's people needed a reminder of God's faithfulness in the midst of tremendous suffering, now was that time. Due to on-going national sin, the faithless, the unfaithful as well as those loyal to God were oppressed in Babylon and stripped of familiarity and of comfort. Turning bitter would have been easy, returning to God offered hope and the blessing of restoration.

Being reminded of Job's life still spurs us on to much needed hope. Job's story begins with a dialogue between God and Satan, and Satan posed this question: *"Does Job fear God for nothing? Haven't You placed a hedge around him, his household, and everything he owns? You have blessed the work of his hands, and his possessions have increased in the land. But stretch out Your hand and strike everything he owns, and he will surely curse You to Your face."* This sets the stage for what was a sobering and life-changing time for Job and for those in his sphere of influence. What did Job do when the hedge of protection around him was removed? We can learn so much from his integrity during hard times.

No Matter What, Blessed Be the Name of the Lord

Job 1:20-22 ESV

Life became very challenging for Job. Within a few paragraphs we read that he had lost his livelihood, his servants, and each of his grown children had been killed. He was totally devastated. What would you do? How would I respond if I were Job? *Then Job arose and tore his robe and shaved his head and fell on the ground and worshiped. And he said, "Naked I came from my mother's womb, and naked shall I return. The Lord gave, and the Lord has taken away; blessed be the name of the Lord." In all this Job did not sin or charge God with wrong.* Great suffering just hit and what did Job do? He worshipped!

Job was full of sadness but his faith was strong. This is just the beginning of over forty more chapters of Job's suffering. Until real tragedy strikes us it is hard to know how we will respond. It is wise to contemplate the truth that we live in an upside-down world and even as God's children, we are not exempt from suffering. In fact, the New Testament teaches us that it is through our trials that maturity comes. When Job said, "The Lord gave and the Lord has taken away" can you picture along with me all that Job had lost? It is challenging to imagine his great loss and yet his faith is going to continue to be tested.

Blessed to Be Corrected

Job 5:17 NIV

Job's suffering grew more intense and more personal. Painful boils covered his entire body and even his wife told him that he should curse God and die. But Job did not lose his integrity. Three scholarly friends came to visit Job and offered their theological understanding. They concluded that Job had sinned and that God was punishing him. One friend said, *"Blessed is the one whom God corrects; so do not despise the discipline of the Almighty."* There is truth in this statement; it just does not apply to Job's situation. And later, God will let Job's friends know that they were off track when it came to their accusations about Job's life.

God's people living in Babylonian captivity (and all who suffer unjustly now and throughout time) certainly could relate to the extreme adversity that Job faced. When suffering is upon us, each of us must choose how we will respond. If our suffering is a form of punishment, we are wise and even blessed to accept the Lord's discipline and change. If we suffer through what we feel to be unwarranted, may God give us the courage to suffer bravely. May we keep in mind that our affliction will not last forever and that God is with us during our suffering. It is interesting that I find myself today, doing edits on the entries of Job, on the heels of a three-day migraine. At times we can be very thankful that the Lord takes away. His grace saw me through another headache series, and it is during these times that I rely upon Him in more intimate ways. When the migraine is behind me, once again I'm blessed to enjoy sunlight, and noise and fully engage in the life He gives.

Blessed by God's Intimate Friendship

Job 29:4-5 NIV; Job 29:11-14 HCSB

AUGUST 4

Job looked back on his good life, the time before his intense suffering. *"Oh, for the days when I was in my prime, when God's intimate friendship blessed my house, when the Almighty was still with me and my children were around me..."* Job lived a righteous life and he used his wealth and influence to care for his family and care for the needy people in his community. He recalled how he was highly respected among people of authority. *"When they heard me, they blessed me, and when they saw me, they spoke well of me. For I rescued the poor man who cried out for help, and the fatherless child who had no one to support him. The dying man blessed me, and I made the widow's heart rejoice. I clothed myself in righteousness, and it enveloped me; my just decisions were like a robe and a turban."* Job will learn that God had not left him, but certainly those long days of testing were very hard. Remember, God is with us always. In all times, in all places, He is there. Remain faithful. If it helps, think about Job.

Blessed to Live for God's Majesty

Job 31:19-22 HCSB

Because of God's majesty, Job chose to live his life to please God. His friends could not fathom Job's great loss and suffering unless it was connected to sin; that was how they were able to make sense of what they knew. Job tried to tell them again that he was innocent. *"...if I have seen anyone dying for lack of clothing or a needy person without a cloak, if he did not bless me while warming himself with the fleece from my sheep...then let my shoulder blade fall from my back, and my arm be pulled from its socket."* Job acted on his faith, cared for others, and was loyal to God. So why was he suffering?

It was at an Unreached Peoples conference in 2002 where Russell and I first met Simon and his sweet wife, Ai Ling. Native Singaporeans, they were passionate about God's love and Kingdom going forth. Simon has had lupus since he was nineteen years old and he suffers bravely while continuing to live joyfully and sacrificially in spite of severe pain and medical uncertainty. Whether setting up a school to teach English in rural China, leading his house church in Singapore, or sharing God's love in meaningful ways during his lengthy hospital stays, Simon and his family offer praise to God.

May you be as blessed as I was from reading excerpts of a correspondence he wrote at the end of 2011. "Ai Ling and I believe and want this illness for the glory of God... We do not want to waste my sickness but to make much of Him in it...We see Jesus more clearly for Who He really is since my lupus relapse... He cares about my lupus, cellulitis, high blood pressure, high cholesterol and every pain that I feel in my body. He cares about my anxieties and emotional stress and even how I look... Oh, how I pray that many more will know that Jesus did not come to give us an easy life, but eternal life!"

Simon is perhaps the most Job-like person that I know. His wife remains cheerful despite their many challenges. Their young daughter wants to grow up to help orphans. We often are left unsure of "why" we suffer, but we are assured of how to suffer. Simon's response to life's circumstances and his faithfulness to God offer perspective and hope. He lives for God's majesty, like Job did.

Job's Friends' Advice:
Repent and Be Blessed

Job 36:11-12 NLT

AUGUST 6

A fourth scholarly friend is a younger one named Elihu who chimes in to try to make sense of Job's circumstance. He reflects and then claims, *"If they listen and obey God, they will be blessed with prosperity throughout their lives. All their years will be pleasant. But if they refuse to listen to him, they will be killed by the sword and die from lack of understanding."* This response follows a familiar line of reasoning: people sin, and God's mercy is that He shows them their sins (even if it takes a drastic situation) so that they can repent and be blessed. This is not untrue.

However, not all suffering comes directly from sin. Job is an example of a righteous person suffering. The world is a place of deep affliction and anguish for many people and suffering is not always related to choices within the control of any one individual. Jesus tells us that we will have trials and tribulations but to take heart, for He has overcome the world. Hold tight to Him in the pain. Through Jesus we too can overcome the hindrances of even deep suffering.

Blessed to See God

Job 42:12-13 ESV

Job is not a make-believe story that happened once upon a time. He was a real man with a real family who encountered real affliction. Later in history, several prophets will quote from Job's life as they address the needs of the people during their own difficulties. God did not remain silent at the time of Job's suffering. At the end of the written account He questioned Job, and then in front of his friends, God validated Job for his pure heart and steadfast faithfulness. Job prayed for his friends, like the Lord told him to do, and everyone celebrated gathering at Job's home.

And the Lord blessed the latter days of Job more than his beginning. And he had 14,000 sheep, 6,000 camels, 1,000 yoke of oxen, and 1,000 female donkeys. He had also seven sons and three daughters. Job lived for another 140 years, seeing even his great-great grandchildren. Job's time of trial was severe but he remained loyal to God and was incredibly blessed. I think his biggest blessing was seeing God. I love this little verse tucked in at the conclusion of Job's story. Job said, "I had heard rumors about You, but now my eyes have seen You." How marvelously blessed we will be when it is our turn to see God with our own eyes! Jesus tells His followers that the pure in heart are blessed for they will see God.

An Appalling Blessing

Psalm 137:8-9 ESV

Even with the hopeful conclusion of Job's story to encourage those who reflected upon it while in captivity, there was a whole lot of lamenting among God's people in Babylon, and for good reason. We may have been taunted at a sports event by the opposing team but God's people were being more than taunted; their lives were radically turned upside-down by their oppressors. The Israelites shed tears of pain, hurt, frustration, and great loss. Some of them wept along a river where their tormentors demanded songs of joy. In the later years of his short life Jamaican reggae singer Bob Marley sang about what many of the Jewish captives experienced. The song *By the Rivers of Babylon* describes weeping along a river as those in exile remembered their dearly loved Zion.

Oppression is appalling; it has to be in order to consider the last verses of Psalm 137: *O daughter of Babylon, doomed to be destroyed, blessed shall he be who repays you with what you have done to us! Blessed shall he be who takes your little ones and dashes them against the rock!* This imagery is too much for me to take in. I almost did not include this "blessing" in the book, but maybe we need to be reminded of the awful consequences of evil. People can really hurt other people. Sometimes it's us being hurt, or those we love, or the weak who cannot defend themselves. And the damage done can cause us to want to take matters into our own hands. God, help us to hate sin of all kinds and yet love our enemies. This is not an easy prayer but a needed one. We are blessed, God, to have You as our righteous Judge and Defender. Vengeance is not ours, it is Yours. Amen.

Blessed Be Our God Who Saves

Psalm 106:47-48 ESV

AUGUST 9

Here is another psalm, and although it was written years before, it was sung during the time of the captivity. It describes Israel's history and it's also a prayer for rescue. *Save us, O Lord our God, and gather us from among the nations, that we may give thanks to your holy name and glory in your praise. Blessed be the Lord, the God of Israel, from everlasting to everlasting! And let all the people say, "Amen!" Praise the Lord!* When times are tragic, people call out to the Lord.

The House of Hope Orphanage is an answer to the prayers of crying children left as orphans by the on-going civil war in Burma. Founded in 1999 in the hills of Mae Hong Son, Thailand, House of Hope is home to many children elementary age up through high school. Christmas of 2004 I joined my Thai language teacher for a nearly seven-hour mountainous drive to spend our holiday at House of Hope. I was blessed beyond measure by the love this "family" had for one another. Their hardship brought them together and their reliance on God keeps them together.

With joy, the children and young adults put on a Christmas party for the community complete with hand-made decorations, traditional dancing, and special food. We experienced God's adoptive love through song, the Christmas Story was read, and several people shared their own personal stories of His goodness too. There was a lot of thanksgiving going on that Christmas. Everyone who gathered, from the community to the newest member of the orphanage, was offered the opportunity to know God in His greatness, God who saves in so many ways. God, we pause to thank You, to bless You our great Rescuer. O Lord, in the little things, in the massive things, You gather us to You. You are our Father who adopts us into Your family to live a life of hope. Thanks be to God! Halleluiah! Amen.

Daniel's Last "Blessing"

Daniel 12:12 NLT

AUGUST 10

Daniel was getting old and he had lived his role in God's Story well. He had served alongside several kings through his many years in Babylon. His life had been full of visions, dreams, interpretations, and a visit to a den of lions. He rallied God's people in prayer. He stood up for good and for God. He purposed early on to be faithful to God, and God blessed him.

Cyrus, king of Persia, is now in charge and he decreed that the Israelites, now called Jews, could return to Jerusalem to rebuild the Temple and re-establish the desolate post-war land. We hear from Daniel one last time, a series of challenging end-time prophesies which include an interesting statement: *And blessed are those who wait and remain until the end of the 1,335 days!* I will not pretend to know what that means, but Daniel was blessed and received a final promise of rest and an allotted inheritance.

He was a good man and lived a good life. Thank You God for Daniel and for his life that continues to inspire. May we make resolutions about things that really matter and then be faithful to keep them our whole lives through. Help us to remember that life is not over until it is over, and then for those who love You, life really begins! Amen.

Make God Our Priority; Blessings Will Come

Haggai 2:19b HCSB

AUGUST 11

With the okay from the Persian king Cyrus, over 42,000 Jews made the long trip back to Jerusalem. Can you image such a caravan? After all those years of living outside of their homeland, emotions must have been high as they walked day after day, mile after mile. Did the tired travelers sing songs of joy as they neared their beloved land after four months of walking? Provisions had been made to rebuild the Temple in Jerusalem and a Jewish teacher and scribe named Ezra (still living in Babylon) recorded correspondence about the progress as well as the opposition.

Prophets Haggai (an older man) and Zechariah (a younger man) tag-teamed to get the attention of God's people who had now returned from exile. God said, "Give careful thought to your ways" and He pointed out how the people were busy making their own homes luxurious while the Temple still remained in ruins. Something needed to change. What changed was the attitude of the people, and they began in earnest to start the Temple restoration project.

Prosperity would come from their commitment to go forward with building the Temple. Up until this time, crops had not produced their yields. God then said, *"But from this day on I will bless you."* And

He did. And He still does! It is not that big of a leap for us to picture our lives and our priorities today. Are we spinning in circles thinking that the next new thing is going to bring lasting satisfaction? Let us be content with what we have, being sure to give attention to what draws us closer to God. There is always blessedness in the peace we have when we are near Him, when we give careful thought to our ways.

May God Bless the Temple Again

Zechariah 4:7 NLT

AUGUST 12

The Jews needed assurance reestablishing their lives based on following God. God gave Zechariah eight visions that provided affirmation and affected areas of their lives as a community. During this point in God's Story, Zerubbabel was the governor of Judea and he is mentioned in the fifth vision that involved the completion of the Temple. *"Nothing, not even a mighty mountain, will stand in Zerubbabel's way; it will become a level plain before him! And when Zerubbabel sets the final stone of the Temple in place, the people will shout: 'May God bless it! May God bless it!'"*

They blessed God with their obedience and asked Him to bless the work of their hands as they built the second Temple. Today God's people are not building an edifice to show loyalty to Him, but with the Holy Spirit living within us, we are the Temple of God. We do not belong to ourselves. God paid a high price for each of us. We have the high calling of honoring God with our bodies, minds and our action. Thinking about our identity and joyfully realizing that we really do belong to Him, gives us hope. From a sense of belonging we can then pursue a good direction for our actions. May God bless us as we grow in His ways, building our character on the foundation of His love, forgiveness and peace. As in the days of Zechariah, may God's people shout: May God bless His Temple!

Be a Symbol and Source of Blessing

Zechariah 8:12-16 NLT

AUGUST 13

The prophet Zechariah is blessed by God to deliver an awesome "do-over" for God's people. Zechariah boldly proclaimed what God had told him to share and God's people listened. The Lord of Heaven's Army said: *"For I am planting seeds of peace and prosperity among you. The grapevines will be heavy with fruit. The earth will produce its crops, and the heavens will release the dew. Once more I will cause the remnant in Judah and Israel to inherit these blessings. Among the other nations, Judah and Israel became symbols of a cursed nation. But no longer! Now I will rescue you and make you both a symbol and a source of blessing. So don't be afraid. Be strong, and get on with rebuilding the Temple! ... I was determined to punish you when your ancestors angered me, and I did not change my mind. But now I am determined to bless Jerusalem and the people of Judah. So don't be afraid. But this is what you must do: Tell the truth to each other. Render verdicts in your courts that are just and that lead to peace..."*

They were allowed to start over, to have a clean slate. They were blessed to be a blessing, to be a symbol of receiving God's blessing and then to be a source from which others would be blessed. This is a familiar theme; let's live it out as well. God says His people should not to be afraid to work hard, be truthful, and to look for ways to be peacemakers. It is His character that He longs to see shining through us.

Ask the Lord to Bless

Zechariah 8:20-22 NLT

AUGUST 14

The barren and desolate land of Jerusalem was about to be revived! Judah and Israel had a bad reputation from the neighboring countries. But God was about to change that around by giving His people what they would need to succeed as they valued justice and mercy. This was good news.

And good news has a way of traveling. *"This is what the Lord of Heaven's Armies says: People from nations and cities around the world will travel to Jerusalem. The people of one city will say to the people of another, 'Come with us to Jerusalem to ask the Lord to bless us. Let's worship the Lord of Heaven's Armies. I'm determined to go.' Many peoples and powerful nations will come to Jerusalem to seek the Lord of Heaven's Armies and to ask for his blessing."*

People today are still blessed by a visit to Jerusalem. Back in 1985 as an atheistic existentialist in the Marine Corps, Russell walked the Via Dolorosa in Jerusalem. And as he walked this road of Jesus' suffering, he began to think about the man Jesus. This reflection led to questions, reading, searching, and more questions. About a year later in the Pacific Northwest, Russell became a follower of Jesus. Although Russell has not spent much of his life in Washington, I think it's interesting that both his physical birth and his spiritual birth both took place in that state.

Jesus changed Russell's life. Knowing Jesus revolutionizes everything. He is the Lord of Heaven's Armies. He is the Prince of Peace. He is worthy of our praise. Wherever we are, let us worship the Lord and search out His good blessings in our lives. Maybe even write them down, if that helps us. May the good news of His blessings continue to travel around the world to people of every nation. Russell is one of my favorite good news teachers and I love learning about the teachings of Jesus from him.

Two Blessings for Each Trouble

Zechariah 9:9-12 NLT

AUGUST 15

With vivid detail, the last of Zechariah's prophecies points to the Messiah yet to come. *Rejoice, O people of Zion! Shout in triumph, O people of Jerusalem! Look, your king is coming to you. He is righteous and victorious, yet he is humble, riding on a donkey—riding on a donkey's colt... your king will bring peace to the nations. His realm will stretch from sea to sea... Because of the covenant I made with you, sealed with blood, I will free your prisoners from death in a waterless dungeon. Come back to the place of safety, all you prisoners who still have hope! I promise this very day that I will repay two blessings for each of your troubles.*

What a promise! What an awesome King is Jesus! I love how we are blessed to have the New Testament and can read in wonderful detail of the life of Jesus. He really knows how to bless because He does what He sees His Father do. Jesus lived to restore whatever needed to be restored in the lives of those who trusted Him. He died to bring us into a holy relationship with Him and His Father whom He loves. It has always been and always will be, that whoever calls on the name of the Lord will be saved, rescued, redeemed, restored. Thank You, Lord Jesus!

Heed the Lord's Warning; Cursed Blessings Are Not Good

Malachi 2:1-2a NKJV

AUGUST 16

Although the word "bless" is not found in the story of Esther, she herself was certainly blessed by God and by man. The beautiful chosen queen did not selfishly enjoy her elevated position but she humbly used it to bless others. In fact, she saved the lives of the Jews who were scattered across 127 provinces. Esther lived during a pivotal time in Israel's history: the Temple had been rebuilt (the same Temple that Jesus would visit during His time on earth) yet many of God's people living in Esther's time had grown tired of doing good. It is hard to believe that again after all God had rescued them from that they dishonored God and ignored His covenant promises, and "going to church" became a meaningless and routine task.

God warned the unethical priests through the prophet Malachi: *"And now, O priests, this commandment is for you. If you will not hear, and if you will not take it to heart, to give glory to My name," says the Lord of hosts, "I will send a curse upon you, and I will curse your blessings."* God's warnings are not idle words. If rewards did not woo the leaders back, then punishment would certainly come.

It is the same now as it was then: those in leadership positions hold a great responsibility. Peace is what God offers but evil is what many of His people seek. Wise people honor God and listen to His Words. If we need to make changes in our attitude toward God, His Story, and church, I pray we would do so. He is not like some college professors who give credit to students just for attending; God desires for us to actually know Him by spending time with Him. It is true that He expects us to learn and apply what He teaches so that our lives will be lived in better, blessed ways. When we are living blessed, may we, like Esther, live to bless others.

Open the Floodgates of Blessing

Malachi 3:9-10, 12 NIV

AUGUST 17

Return to God what belongs to Him and He will return a blessing to you. It is not too late. Listen to what He says: *"You are under a curse—the whole nation of you—because you are robbing me. Bring the whole tithe into the storehouse, that there may be food in my house. Test me in this and see if I will not throw open the floodgates of heaven and pour out so much blessing that you will not have room enough for it. Then all the nations will call you blessed, for yours will be a delightful land," says the Lord Almighty.* A blessed nation is a nation that acts on its faith in Almighty God. God doesn't desire mere lip service; He wants the real deal. Even though we cannot fully see or comprehend Him now, there is nothing more real than God. How we obey His Word is a reflection of our values and it has always been that way.

This warning about robbing God reminds me of a story that did not end well for a king in New Testament times. Herod the Great's grandson was the new leader on the throne and he caused much trouble for the early church. Although I do not know of his tithing practices, King Herod robbed God of the praise and glory due Him and was immediately eaten by worms and then he died. There may be a number of reasons that motivate us to give to God. I love giving back to Him because all good blessings come from Him.

God Blessed the Journey Back to Jerusalem
Ezra 7:27-28 ESV

AUGUST 18

Ezra was a priest, a committed teacher of God's law, a faithful scribe, and a successful diplomat. He and 1,500 of his fellow Jews made up the second assembly to return to Jerusalem from Babylon and they did so with the blessings, as well as the provisions, of the new Persian king. Ezra shared his gratitude as he took his teaching ministry on the road; the road back home. *Blessed be the Lord, the God of our fathers, who put such a thing as this into the heart of the king, to beautify the house of the Lord that is in Jerusalem, and who extended to me his steadfast love before the king and his counselors, and before all the king's mighty officers. I took courage, for the hand of the Lord my God was on me, and I gathered leading men from Israel to go up with me.*

This journey took Ezra and his companions five months but the final restoration of the city would take much longer. Ezra was a man of godly action and that was a good thing. The city walls were not the only things in need of rebuilding. Ezra was also used by God to rebuild the lives of the disloyal people who lived within those city walls. He was God's man for the job and his teachings and example can encourage and influence us even today. May we too take courage for whatever God puts before us. If God is for us, who can be against us?

God Blessed Jabez by Answering Prayer

1 Chronicles 4:10 HCSB

Genealogies and national archives are an important part of any nation's history and it is possible that Ezra may have been the one who took the time to record name upon name for the official records of the nation of Israel. Tucked in a list of names of those from the tribe of Judah is a request of blessing made to God by an individual. *Jabez called out to the God of Israel: "If only You would bless me, extend my border, let Your hand be with me, and keep me from harm, so that I will not cause any pain." And God granted his request.*

That's about all we know about Jabez, a man who God's Story says was more honorable than his brothers. Are we bold to call out to God in prayer like Jabez did? God, I pray that Your hand of protection would be on us and that we would not cause others pain as we go through our days. But because we live in a fallen world, we will not always be free from giving or receiving pain. We need to focus on You no matter what the situation holds. This life is a training ground for how we relate to You. Bless us Lord, yes, bless us and may we live faithfully in the realm of influence that You give to us. Amen.

Ask for Blessings

Nehemiah 5:19 NLT

It had been fourteen years since Ezra returned to Jerusalem. Word got back to Nehemiah, a Jew serving in the Persian palace, that Jerusalem's city walls were still in disarray. As the newly appointed governor to Jerusalem, Nehemiah received a commission from the Persian king to make the journey to Jerusalem to help revitalize the city. Nehemiah was faithful and put into motion the task before him as he rallied the work force to focus on rebuilding the city walls. Nehemiah was a man who cared for

God's people and talked to the Lord in prayer. *Remember, O my God, all that I have done for these people, and bless me for it.* God did bless him: the wall was completed in fifty-two days! Even Israel's enemies had acknowledged that God had accomplished the task!

We had been living in our supervisor's home in London while they were on an extended stay in the US, and my Bible reading for the year had me at this point in God's Story. Although a lot of good was coming from our living situation, I was anxious to move into our own place and begin to establish our identity in that new area. For fifty-two days in a row I prayed, and house after house that we sought to rent fell through. I remember thinking how Nehemiah rebuilt the walls of a whole city with God's help. Certainly God could help us find a home. And He did. And I grew closer to God in the anticipation of His provision.

His desire was to give us more than just a house; He provided this home at just the right time so we could host a house-warming Christmas party as the conclusion of a counseling class I attended at the local university. So, my classmates - students of various ages from a variety of countries, heard more good news of Jesus while we gathered in our new 110-year-old home. What great (or small) thing does the Lord want to accomplish through you? Are you talking to Him about it? Prayer brings us closer to the One who desires to give to us the desires of our hearts.

Bless the Lord; Amen!

Nehemiah 8:6 ESV

AUGUST 21

There was a lot to be sorted out for the newly re-established city with its completed walls. Ezra and Nehemiah were a great team. With Jerusalem now stable again, some of God's people chose to live within her walls and were blessed to do so, and the rest returned to their towns throughout Israel. The most important thing in the lives of those who had traveled from exile was the re-institution of the holidays, and for God's law to be read again in public.

They needed God's wisdom and were ready to hear it. The time was right and all of the Israelites who were old enough to understand gathered. God's law was read. There was mass confession of sins, then great joy and celebration followed. *And Ezra blessed the LORD, the great God, and all the people answered, "Amen, Amen," lifting up their hands. And they bowed their heads and worshiped the LORD with their faces to the ground.*

The joy of the Lord truly was their strength as they lived in blessedness, and for a time, close to Him. Lord, You indeed are the great God of all, and worthy of praise and worship. As we Your people read Your Story and see how You have called us as a people to worship You, may we honor You with obedience and thankfulness. May we often celebrate Your goodness to us. May we see Your blessings as gifts we love to unwrap and delight in and share. Amen.

Bless the Lord
from Everlasting to Everlasting

Nehemiah 9:5b-6 NIV

AUGUST 22

Celebrate with me one more time, lifting high our great God as we bless His holy name! This was a meaningful time for all who were present as God's Story continued to unfold. Levites joined together and prayed: *"Stand up and praise the Lord your God, who is from everlasting to everlasting. Blessed be your glorious name, and may it be exalted above all blessing and praise. You alone are the Lord. You made the heavens, even the highest heavens, and all their starry host, the earth and all that is on it, the seas and all that is in them. You give life to everything, and the multitudes of heaven worship you."* People recited pages of God's faithfulness throughout history and everyone at the gathering swore an oath to commit themselves to follow God.

Oh how I wanted this time of dedicated celebration to be what His people focused on during the four hundred-year silence between the Old and New Testaments. But sadly, God's dearly loved and chosen people drifted into neglecting Him and in time they were again living in their self-centered rebellious ways. This tragic shift did not happen overnight but it happened. How easy it would have been, and justified too, for God to have let mankind go on down the road to destruction. Praise be to God; He does not leave us in our sin, but through His Son Jesus He offers hope upon hope when we turn to Him.

Mary Received a Shocking Blessing
Luke 1:28b AMP

AUGUST 23

We are introduced to the lead character in God's Story, and Jesus changes everything! The time for God's promised One to live on earth had come. God chose His holy messenger Gabriel to bring the first blessing of the New Testament, and it was delivered to a young maiden named Mary. Mary was a simple, country girl from a small town called Galilee in Nazareth and she was engaged to a hard working carpenter. I wonder what she was doing when the holy visitor arrived. Was she pondering her upcoming wedding as she went about her daily chores?

Gabriel's appearance may have startled her as he proclaimed, *"Hail, O favored one [endued with grace]! The Lord is with you! Blessed (favored of God) are you before all other women!"* Then seeing her shock, Gabriel told her not to be afraid. How would Mary respond to the news he was sent to give? Would she receive this blessing and assignment from God? How would it affect the rest of her life?

Sometimes a blessing can confuse and even disturb us, like this news did for Mary. We also receive invitations that require faith to go forward and we then choose to either disregard the message or to accept the blessing (that often will require change). What we decide can affect not only our future but also the future of many others. Mary's news included the phrase, "the Lord is with you." Great joy can be experienced as we live knowing that the Lord is always with us. May we focus on His Presence when faced with decisions that are far too big for us to handle on our own.

Double Blessing for Mary and Jesus

Luke 1:42b NLT

AUGUST 24

Gabriel told Mary that she was going to be the mother of the Son of the Most High. Mary asked the announcing angel a question, "How can this be since I am a virgin?" She got her answer and humbly took in all this new information. Young Mary's wedding plans could have come to a screeching halt when Joseph heard that she was pregnant. But Joseph, after receiving some confirming news in a dream, went forward with the wedding arrangements.

Mary left her hometown, traveled to a town in Judea's hill country and spent her first trimester with her older cousin Elizabeth who was thrilled to see her. When Mary entered Elizabeth's home, Elizabeth excitedly greeted Mary, *"God has blessed you above all women, and your child is blessed."* What a greeting! Mary was glowing with happiness as she shared the intriguingly good news with her relative and received from Elizabeth an encouraging double blessing. Mary was blessed and so was her Child. Good news is even better when it is shared.

Blessed Because of Belief

Luke 1:45 NLT

AUGUST 25

Both Mary and Elizabeth were refreshed and encouraged by the special time they shared together. Their bellies were growing and so were the hopes for the child each would bear. These boys would grow up as cousins. Picture Mary so young and not even married and then Elizabeth so old that her husband Zechariah doubted the angel when he was told that a son would be born to him. Perhaps Elizabeth embraced Mary again as she looked deep in her eyes and said, *"You are blessed because you believed that the Lord would do what he said."* This blessing was linked to belief, belief in the faithfulness of God. How blessed we are indeed when we believe the Lord.

It did not make logical sense to me that God would call us back to Asia within a year of leaving Thailand. This was some of my reasoning: Our China team was well prepared to go forward with the ministry and we were excitedly engaged in new ministry opportunities in England. With Hannah, our oldest daughter in her first semester of college in Texas, my heart was thankful that we lived in London, just one plane ride away, rather than halfway around the globe. Sophie and Isaiah were thriving with new challenges, stretched with their college-like classes, contributing to their British football teams, and interacting with peers from very diverse backgrounds. And besides, I really liked being able to interact in English! To me, returning to Asia seemed like going backwards. But we believed it was God calling us, so we followed God's guidance.

In the summer of 2009 we said our good-byes to new friends in England, sold and gave away what we owned and moved to Thailand for the third time, this time in an extended leadership role. It was during this two-year assignment that as I read through the Bible, the word "bless" popped out more and more as I reflected on God's ongoing blessings in history. I also began to see the many ways He blessed us in our obedience to follow Him, even when it did not initially make sense to move from London.

I sensed He was prompting me to write a book, to proclaim His many blessings throughout His Story. My desire is that through God this blessing book will be accomplished. I pray that He will be honored with it, and we would live on in His blessings, being blessed and blessing others. My hope is that belief in the Lord will grow which would lead to thankfulness in the lives of His children. Lord, this book of blessings is a bit ambitious; please keep giving me Your wisdom as we build it page by page. You are so good to continue to bless me as I write; please bless all of us as we read. Amen.

Blessed to Magnify the Lord

Luke 1:46b-50 ESV

AUGUST 26

The joy inside Mary could not be kept there. In a song called the Magnificat, Mary poured out her great happiness to God her Savior: *"My soul magnifies the Lord, and my spirit rejoices in God my Savior, for he has looked on the humble estate of his servant. For behold, from now on all generations will call me blessed; for he who is mighty has done great things for me, and holy is his name. And his mercy is for those who fear him from generation to generation."* What a glorious reminder that we are blessed because of what God has done for us. Holy is His name! His name is worthy of our songs and praise.

The little Baby in Mary's womb would one day be her Savior. And He would be the Savior for all who would call out to Him for mercy. There is mercy for those who fear the Lord, mercy instead of what we deserve. August 26th is my birthday and as I grow older each year I'm more aware of God's many gifts in my life: the present of His Presence, the gift of mercy, and peace, and joy. God has done great things for me by giving me the loving family I was born into. He blessed me with Russell and then blessed us with a family of our own that continues to grow. I am so happy to have meaningful friendships with people all over the world and I see these relationships as a gift from God. Mary was blessed, and so is each one of us. May we magnify the Lord and take great joy in God our Savior!

Blessed with Voice to Bless the Lord

Luke 1:64 ESV

AUGUST 27

Several months had passed and at the end of the first chapter of Luke's first book, we read about the birth of the baby that leaped in Elizabeth's womb back when Mary visited. Now it is Elizabeth's husband Zechariah's turn to speak out a blessing. For the past nine months, Zechariah had been unable to talk because he doubted the angel who said that he would have a son. So when he was asked about naming his son, he wrote on a tablet, "His name is John." *And immediately his mouth was opened and his tongue loosed, and he spoke, blessing God.* How happy he must have been to get his voice back! I pray we would never lose our voice when we have the opportunity to sing forth the praises of God who is so very worthy.

My mind goes back to the many different times in my life when I have strived to learn a new language. Some people appear to be blessed and new languages seem to flow effortlessly; not so with me. Intentional language study can build up vocabulary and confidence. Intentional Bible study can increase wisdom and love for God. But in both cases the need to take the study and put it into loving action is essential to really live out the purpose of the study. Life changes when we give appropriate love to those God places in our path, those who need to know and see and hear and feel just how real and good God is. How happy I am when words do come together and my tongue is loosed and the things I say intersect with a kind deed and the outcome blesses God. After nearly a year of silence, Zechariah blessed God with his voice.

An added side-note: In August of 2014 our family gathered for what we thought was a surprise birthday party for Hannah, but we were all surprised when Hannah and Andrew announced that they were expecting a baby! In order for them to personally tell others, she asked me not to share the happy news for a few days. I felt like Zechariah during that time, but then the world heard, "I'm going to be a Grammie!"

We Have Deliverance and Redemption; Blessed to Bless

Luke 1:68 AMP

Are you as curious as I am to hear what it was that Zechariah first said now that he could speak? He began with: *"Blessed (praised and extolled and thanked) be the Lord, the God of Israel, because He has come and brought deliverance and redemption to His people!"* Zechariah ends his praise and prophecy by saying that his son John would prepare the way for the Lord, the Lord who will give light to those in darkness and guidance to the path of peace. We can be so thankful that the Lord Jesus still guides His children from darkness to peace. Praise God for how He rescues and redeems and redirects. Later John would indeed call out as one in the desert. Known as John the Baptizer, he prepared the way for the Lord and he urged people to repent for the Kingdom of Heaven is near. This was an exciting time and John raised a bit of a stir among the religious leaders of that day. But, I'm getting a little ahead of myself in God's Story.

Blessed to See Jesus Our Salvation

Luke 2:28-30 ESV

Jesus was born, peace and salvation and justice and power and compassion all wrapped up and lying in a manger. When it was time for the Baby's dedication, Mary and Joseph took Jesus to the Temple in Jerusalem. There in Jerusalem was a man named Simeon, devout and righteous, and he had waited his whole life for the coming Messiah. That day was just an ordinary day and then something extraordinary happened. Simeon's joy burst forth when he saw Jesus and *he took him up in his arms and blessed God and said, "Lord, now you are letting your servant depart in peace, according to your word for my eyes have seen your salvation..."*

What are we expectantly waiting our whole lifetime to experience? What joy are we longing for? Just picture taking God in your very arms and blessing Him. That is what Simeon was allowed to do. What a day that must have been. Jesus, You are an incredible blessing to behold.

Russell and I were living in Dallas and one Saturday joined others for Shabbat at Baruch Hashem Messianic Synagogue. It was my first time to worship Yahweh in a Jewish context and I loved the festive music and dancing. It was after a reverent reading and teaching of Torah that the unexpected happened. An eighty-something-year-old Jew from New York held his hands to his face and exclaimed, again and again, as happy tears freely flowed, "Yeshua! I have found Messiah!" My eyes too filled with tears of joy as this man saw with his own eyes that Jesus is Lord! He is our salvation.

A Mixed Blessing: Joy and Opposition

Luke 2:34 NLT

AUGUST 30

Jesus' first day in the Temple began with joyful praise and thanksgiving to God as Simeon proclaimed that his own eyes had seen salvation. Holding the eight-day-old Baby, he was looking at the Light of the world. He turned to address Jesus' stunned parents. *Then Simeon blessed them, and he said to Mary, the baby's mother, "This child is destined to cause many in Israel to fall, but he will be a joy to many others. He has been sent as a sign from God, but many will oppose him."* This "mixed blessing" must have been a challenge for the young mother to take in. Mary pondered all these things and more. Jesus was the Son of God yet He was an infant in her arms. She would live to see Him adored and opposed. Diverse responses to Jesus continue today. O come let us adore Him!

My own son, Isaiah, had just turned one year old when the five of us celebrated our first Christmas in North Carolina. Following my mom's Christmas tradition, I made rock candy and then we left the warm kitchen for an outdoor adventure. The kiddos were all bundled up as we approached the live nativity scene in our rural town. Laying decorated bags of the candy at the cradle in the makeshift stall, they were in awe of "Baby Jesus". I thought of Mary and all that her heart must have experienced in the thirty-three years that her Son lived on earth. The good times, the sad times, the times that may have seemed too hard to endure. God creates us with a wide range of emotion. Jesus is with us in all times and He remains a joy to many, just like Simeon said in his blessing.

Jesus; Blessed by God and People

Luke 2:51-52 MSG

AUGUST 31

Fast-forward twelve years. Jesus and his whole family made the annual excursion to Jerusalem to celebrate the Passover. When their group began the journey home, Jesus stayed behind without his parents knowing it, and spent His time with the teachers at the Temple. After three days of frantically searching for Jesus, Mary and Joseph found Him. If you have ever experienced the panic attack that comes when a child in your care is lost, you have more than likely felt the emotional rollercoaster of terrifying fear then relief and great joy when the child is found. We can almost hear that extreme emotion in Mary's voice when she and Joseph find Jesus.

Meanwhile, all who had heard Jesus at the Temple were amazed with Him. When his parents arrived *he went back to Nazareth with them, and lived obediently with them. His mother held these things dearly, deep within herself. And Jesus matured, growing up in both body and spirit, blessed by both God and people.* Jesus lived a blessed life; blessed does not always equate to easy. Often, blessings flow freely when we practice obedience but choosing obedience can be hard for us. Think of Jesus in His life, tempted beyond what we will ever face, yet He chose to obey. Even up to death on a cross.

Lord Jesus, You lived the life of love and obedience that we should live, but we don't. You died the death that we should have died because of our sins. Your goodness in exchange for mankind's badness is news too good to be true. Yet You are true, blessed by Your Father to bless the world with perfect love. Thank You! Thank You! Thank You! Amen. It is good though to remember that at this point in God's Story, Jesus is still a boy. Although we do not have a picture of Jesus climbing a tree, building His first birdhouse, or winning a soccer game, Jesus grew. He went through all the ages and stages, from infancy to manhood as He matured. Jesus, keep growing us, I pray.

Reflections

God's people, still in Babylonian captivity, needed hope so the first week of August we read of Job's story of extreme faithfulness in intense suffering. God's prophets provided assurance as the Israelites, now called the Jews, traveled back to their war-torn land. Haggai, Zechariah, Malachi, Ezra, and Nehemiah helped to restore the hearts of God's people and rebuild Jerusalem's walls. We then meet the main character in God's Story. Jesus, God's greatest blessing, comes to earth! Luke tells of the birth and early childhood of Jesus.

September

Blessings on the Poor in Spirit

Matthew 5:3 HCSB

SEPTEMBER 1

The cousins John and Jesus are now men; John fulfilled the prophecy to prepare the way for the Lord and Jesus began His ministry by preaching repentance for the Kingdom of Heaven is at hand. Jesus was baptized, was tempted after a forty-day desert fast, chose his twelve apprentices and taught about living life in a way that has meaning. In each of the Gospel accounts Jesus always does what is right. He is brave, smart, compassionate and powerful. He traveled extensively, meeting the needs of people. He healed all kinds of ailments, delivered others from demons, and returned sight and hearing to people who lacked these senses. He fed the masses and modeled the way to connect with His Father.

Now the time had come for Jesus' first formal and maybe most famous of all His teachings. With a crowd gathered around Him, He went up on a mountain, sat down and taught. And Matthew, one of Jesus' followers, recorded the sermon so all who later would read it would have the opportunity to be blessed. *"The poor in spirit are blessed, for the kingdom of heaven is theirs."* Whole books can be written about the meaning of this first "blessed" alone. Jesus could have stopped right here with this first teaching point and given a lifetime to ponder it, could we really know the implications of being poor in spirit and how that is a blessing, not to mention what it means to have the Kingdom of Heaven?

We are blessed when we realize we do not yet have all we can have when it comes to living in God's Spirit, and so we eagerly press into God. We will see the phrase, "for theirs is the Kingdom of Heaven" again. The first and also the final of those mountain top blessings bookend all the blessings in between. If you want to go a little deeper in your study of Jesus' teachings of how to live the blessed life, look up the daily verse in a different translation and read Matthew 5 in its entirety each day. Time spent with Jesus is blessed time indeed.

Blessed to Be Comforted after Mourning

Matthew 5:4 NKJV

Some have renamed this particular teaching of Jesus, the "Be Happy Attitudes", and a few modern translations use the word "happy" for "blessed". Mourners, the meek, those who really want righteousness, the merciful ones, the pure, those who are peacemakers - all of these are blessed, are happy. Even though outwardly it may not look or feel like it, when our hearts connect to the heart of God over these things, there can be a settled assurance, a rightness, a "happy" no matter the circumstance. Don't miss out on opportunities to be blessed.

> *"Blessed are those who mourn,*
>
> *For they shall be comforted."*

It may take weeping through the night but healing joy can come in the mourning. Yes, the mourning. It could be said that the comfort, relief, and freedom from grief comes through healthy mourning. We mourn because things are not the way they are supposed to be. There is often a process of grieving we experience before we feel comfort.

To really experience the blessedness that Jesus teaches about we should also mourn our sins. Not just brush them aside, but truly mourn how we choose our selfishness over God's goodness. When we take our sick feeling, the grieving we have because of sinful choices, to Jesus for forgiveness He changes our mourning to comfort. When His comforting comes, there is peace where once there was grief, and we know it as a blessing. Jesus is offering to His followers a new way of living life. A way that is blessed, a way that He alone can provide.

The Humble Are Blessed

Matthew 5:5 NLT

Those who are mild, patient, long-suffering, content, and meek are the kinds of people who are blessed to become the heirs of the earth. We are to be meek toward God and I wonder what the world would be like if each country in it were ruled by the humble? What would it be like if pride, arrogance and greediness no longer dictated the plan for the day? Picture people driving their cars with patience, workers content with their pay, co-workers, neighbors and family members actually esteeming others more highly than themselves. It makes me think of the Lord's Prayer: "Thy Kingdom come, Thy will be done, on earth as it is in Heaven."

God, give us that kind of goodness that is in Heaven while we are here on this upside-down earth. *"God blesses those who are humble, for they will inherit the whole earth."* I have heard it said that humility is shy; shine light on humility and she will look for a shadow. Then I saw it happen. On Tuesdays at noon a group of godly ladies, most closer to eighty years old than forty, meet faithfully to pray for missionaries around the world. I have learned so much from these ladies since joining them in the autumn of 2011. We studied a book together which taught us that we are to put on godly character like clothing, and the next lesson we would discuss focused on humility. Not one hand shot up quickly; not one voice boldly said, "Sure, I'm great at being humble, I will tell you all about it." These humble ladies have grown in their Christ-like maturity by spending time with Jesus. Jesus displayed patience, long-suffering, and contentment as a humble servant. Does a watching world see us wearing humility? I have a feeling it would look good on us.

Pursuing Righteousness is a Blessing

Matthew 5:6 AMP

SEPTEMBER 4

And then there are the hungry ones. They are not hungry for Tex-Mex or a good Thai meal or even for bread and water. They are hungry and thirsty for things to be right. They want life to be honest, decent and virtuous. *"Blessed and fortunate and happy and spiritually prosperous (in that state in which the born-again child of God enjoys His favor and salvation) are those who hunger and thirst for righteousness (uprightness and right standing with God), for they shall be completely satisfied!"*

What will it take to make us feel complete? Not lonely, not grabby, but fully satisfied and filled? By pursuing a right relationship with both God and people, we will be blessed. Here is a little caution to add: we will experience opposition on this quest to be fully satisfied with God's character of righteousness. Our choice to abstain from things that no longer bring about real satisfaction may cause others to feel defensive. But the rewards? Ahhhhhh. Blessed.

Mercy: Blessed to Receive, Blessed to Give

Matthew 5:7 MSG

SEPTEMBER 5

Mercy. What are some good mercy words? How about: compassion, kindness, forgiveness, sympathy, and empathy. We all want mercy, but do we really want to give it when others are in need of it? In God's economy, we are blessed to receive mercy when we are filled with mercy to the point it is flowing from us to others. Interesting! *"You're blessed when you care. At the moment of being 'care-full,' you find yourselves cared for."*

God's Story tells us we are more blessed to give than to receive, and here the blessing seems to work both ways. When we give mercy it opens us up so we can receive even more! God is the best at giving mercy -

undeserved goodness. When we think about all He has given, all that He has forgiven, and we allow gratitude, instead of guilt, to well up within us, we are at a good starting point for being able to give mercy.

Treating others the way we would like to be treated really can work for the good of everyone, especially where mercy is concerned. We need to take compassion and put it to action! Sending a heart-felt sympathy card makes sense, but what about extending kindness in traffic, offering forgiveness instead of letting a grudge grow, and listening from the other person's point of view? We are blessed when we care.

Blessed to See God

Matthew 5:8 NIV

SEPTEMBER 6

"Blessed are the pure in heart, for they will see God." To be pure means to be holy, set apart, clean, not mixed. Think of 100% pure orange juice; it does not have anything else added. God says, "Be holy" because He is holy and He is whole. He is not mixed when it comes to His motives. He says from the beginning we are not to add to Him. So do not worship Him and also worship idols of any kind. When our motives and lives are pure we will see God.

The year 2002 was the second time we lived in a village in China and as part of home schooling the kiddos we studied the Beatitudes. What helped us learn all eight of these principles Jesus taught was our attempt to draw them. The sixth of these blessings, "Blessed are the pure in heart, for they will see God," was illustrated by a pair of glasses with bright yellow and gold colors coming from them. We need to do what it takes to make the teachings of Jesus a part of our life.

Practicing purity does not stop when marriage starts nor does purity only refer to marital fidelity. Keeping a pure heart affects all of our thinking. Pollution of a variety of kinds can have significant damaging effects. But choosing to live pure, non-mixed lives is a choice that will bless us our whole life long. And what about the benefit? The pure in heart will see God.

Blessed to Be a Peacemaker

Matthew 5:9 ESV

I wonder if a cool breeze was peacefully blowing through the grass as Jesus continued to teach the gathered ones while they listened, taking it all in. Jesus is the Prince of Peace so it only makes sense that the children of God would long to be peacemakers too, like our Brother, like our Father. *"Blessed are the peacemakers, for they shall be called sons of God."* James, the half-brother of Jesus also understood and taught on this subject of peacemaking. He says that peacemakers will plant seeds of peace and reap a harvest of righteousness.

Do we love to be involved in a good conflict? Does it excite us to put another log on the flame in an argument? If our goal is not resolution, restoration and peace then it might be best to check our motives. Jesus says that the peacemakers will be the blessed ones. It is not too late, or too early, to get good at being a peacemaker. It will help if certain things like anger and contempt are thought of as working against the goal of being a peacemaker. Some of the best peacemakers have peace with God, and out of that settled assurance they can offer peace to others.

Being a peacemaker is a worthy prize to pursue. The treasure is eternal as well as immediate. Lord, I pray that You would make us instruments of Your peace. May we be so thankful to You for the mercy that You have shown us that we would be quick to overlook an offense when it comes to our feelings being hurt, or our pride being bruised. As much as it is up to us, help us to live at peace with those around us. Amen.

The Persecuted Ones Are Blessed

Matthew 5:10 KJV

The last of the beatitudes taught by Jesus that day on the mountain is very similar to His first one. The "blessed person" receives the Kingdom of Heaven. I love how Jesus does not sway from what He knows is needed. And what we need is awareness of, and entrance into the Kingdom of Heaven. Although it includes the place where the redeemed go when life on earth is over, there is more to it. The Kingdom of Heaven is wherever God, the King, is in charge and reigns.

If we are persecuted, wronged, offended, ill treated, or oppressed because we are on the side of rightness, Jesus tells us not to be all depressed about it, but to be happy. We are living in the place where God is in control. Stay on His side and at His side. He loves you and is giving to you His Kingdom. *"Blessed are they which are persecuted for righteousness' sake: for theirs is the kingdom of heaven."* As God reigns here and now, we have access to Him and His Kingdom, even though right now we do not see Him fully. There is the present blessing of knowing this and there is a blessing coming that is so worth holding on to. Hold on to hope in times of persecution. God is still King.

Blessed When We Live out Jesus' Teachings

Matthew 5:11-12a NIV

"Blessed are you when people insult you, persecute you and falsely say all kinds of evil against you because of me. Rejoice and be glad, because great is your reward in heaven..." This verse begins the more lengthy explanation Jesus gives to each of the teaching points He had just shared in Matthew 5:3-10. He started with the ending and then over the next few chapters Jesus filled out more of what it all means to be blessed.

Being blessed comes down to living life right, not just in actions like the law put forth in the Old Testament, but also in our innermost being where our thoughts are. Jesus is holistic; He desires all of me; all of you. Our wisdom grows as we take in and live out what Jesus teaches and He is good to spell out the plan in detail. I encourage you to take the time to read through Matthew 5-7 in one sitting and if you can, go outside with your Bible and pretend you are on a mountainside. See if you do not respond with amazement and astonishment like the crowds did when they first heard this good news message. Live blessed!

When you get to the pivotal verse of Jesus' message (the last verse of chapter 5), you will read in most Bibles the word "perfect" to describe both God and how we are to be. Here are my two favorite translations for that verse, for they help to better communicate what Jesus taught. "In a word, what I'm saying is, Grow up. You're kingdom subjects. Now live like it. Live out your God-created identity. Live generously and graciously toward others, the way God lives toward you." That one is from The Message, and the next one from the Amplified Bible also gives good clarification: "You, therefore, must be perfect [growing into complete maturity of godliness in mind and character, having reached the proper height of virtue and integrity], as your heavenly Father is perfect." For those who choose to live by Jesus' teachings there is great reward coming.

Blessed to Live the Way of Jesus

Luke 6:21-22 MSG

SEPTEMBER 10

Jesus holds a seminar similar to the Sermon on the Mount but this time the venue is along a plain. Luke is the one who recorded this teaching with all of its important insights. The down-to-earth way in which The Message translation puts it makes it easy to see why so many people eagerly followed Jesus and wanted to hear His teaching. Today we still have needs and Jesus still meets the needs of those who trust in Him.

"You're blessed when you've lost it all. God's kingdom is there for the finding. You're blessed when you're ravenously hungry. Then you're ready for the Messianic meal. You're blessed when the tears flow freely. Joy comes with the morning." Not exactly the first things that may come to mind when we think of living the blessed life, but then again, Jesus teaches to the heart of the situation. He goes deep where our needs really are and when we live His way, we are blessed.

Blessings Awaiting the Faithful Ones

Luke 6:22-23 NLT

SEPTEMBER 11

"What blessings await you when people hate you and exclude you and mock you and curse you as evil because you follow the Son of Man. When that happens, be happy! Yes, leap for joy! For a great reward awaits you in heaven. And remember, their ancestors treated the ancient prophets that same way." Adjusting our understanding of what can bring happiness is an important action to take.

Jesus' idea of blessings may surprise us, but it is good to remember that He was very aware of what was still to come in His own life. With the cross yet before Him, His joy was set beyond the pain of this world. He knew that taking on mankind's shame was going to be brutal. Dying stripped and stretched upon a Roman cross with thugs seemingly in charge is not the death anyone would desire. His hope was beyond those hours when the Father turned His face from Him.

Jesus knew His reward and knew the reason for His death. He lived and died on earth while He was obedient and Heaven-focused. When we are so much like Jesus that people who do not love Him take out their frustration and hatred on us, have hope. Aligning our way of seeing life in light of His truth can fill us with joy. God wants us to live blessed now, keeping in mind the reward that is yet to come.

Blessed to Forgive, Praying for Those That Hurt

Luke 6:27-28 NLT

If you have lived long enough, you have probably experienced the truth that hurt people hurt people. That painfully destructive cycle has unfortunately spun through the ages. How different life can be if we choose to follow Jesus' advice on this topic: *"But to you who are willing to listen, I say, love your enemies! Do good to those who hate you. Bless those who curse you. Pray for those who hurt you."*

Sabina was old when I met her, but age did not define her, joy did. Her family had been killed in Romanian Nazi concentration camps during World War II. Her husband, Richard Wurmbrand, had been tortured for Christ for over a dozen years while in several Romanian prisons. Richard spoke passionately at Russell's Bible school sharing how one night he met the brutal soldier who had killed his wife's family and lead him to repentance and trust in the Lord. Returning to his home and gently awakening his wife, Richard introduced this man to Sabina. She reached out with hands of peace to embrace her new brother in Christ. Sabina lived loving her enemies, praying for them to know God's forgiveness and blessing those who had caused her great pain.

Lord, I pray that the cycle of hurt can end with us. Please use us as instruments of healing to bless people even when our natural instincts are far from it. We need to remember how You forgave us and then call us to forgive others in order to live the way of blessing. This is hard. Please help us. We read about saints throughout history who have learned to trust You for justice and forgiveness. For some practical application right now, I pray for .... who has hurt me. God, help me to give the situation to You. Help me to do good and love appropriately with Jesus as my Helper. Amen.

Blessed to Follow the Golden Rule

Luke 6:37-38 MSG

SEPTEMBER 13

Treat others the way you would like to be treated. Matthew records "the golden rule" in the seventh chapter of the Gospel written by him and then Luke unpacked it some. Luke wrote: Jesus says, *"Don't pick on people, jump on their failures, criticize their faults— unless, of course, you want the same treatment. Don't condemn those who are down; that hardness can boomerang. Be easy on people; you'll find life a lot easier. Give away your life; you'll find life given back, but not merely given back—given back with bonus and blessing. Giving, not getting, is the way. Generosity begets generosity."* Good advice worth living by. Jesus is the best teacher ever! May the blessings boomerang back as we seek to bless God and bless people.

Not All Blessings Materialize on Earth

Luke 7:22-23 NLT (also in Matthew 11:4-6)

SEPTEMBER 14

Jesus gave his cousin John the affirmation he needed. We are at the point in God's Story when John the Baptizer is now in prison. Things did not go well for John when he rightly condemned Herod for marrying his own brother Philip's wife. So from a prison cell, John basically wanted to know, "Jesus, are you the Messiah or is someone else coming?" John desired reassurance that he had lived his life with meaning and purpose as he pointed people to Jesus.

Jesus gave this confirmation: *"Go back to John and tell him what you have seen and heard—the blind see, the lame walk, the lepers are cured, the deaf hear, the dead are raised to life, and the Good News is being preached to the poor. And tell him, 'God blesses those who do not turn away because of me.'"* Yes, John, your life has been worth it! Don't give up now. All of us, from time to time, need this kind of encouragement. Press on; know that God does care when we stand up for the sake of righteousness. He will bless us. Do not give up. Don't turn away. Not all blessings materialize on earth.

Blessed Rest for Those Who Yoke up with Jesus
Matthew 11:29 AMP

SEPTEMBER 15

What are we to do when our troubles are too heavy for us to lift, when we are too weary to go on? We are not to give up, or to text our complaint to those in our address book, but instead we are blessed when we go to Jesus. *"Take My yoke upon you and learn of Me, for I am gentle (meek) and humble (lowly) in heart, and you will find rest (relief and ease and refreshment and recreation and blessed quiet) for your souls."*

I love the definition here of rest: relief, ease, refreshment, recreation and blessed quiet. For me, there are few places that better paint a picture of this kind of rest than time spent in nature. So with the warm sunlight shining through the trees on a late spring 2012 afternoon in North Carolina, and a calm lake a stone's throw away, I felt at ease knowing that my Creator is in control. I relished the blessed quietness of the setting and peace seemed to wrap around me like a soft blanket.

Jesus' invitation recorded by Matthew suggests that this kind of soul rest is available when anyone with a heavy burden brings it to Jesus and the blessed quiet will come whether we are by a lakeside or not. Although the surroundings were serene, several of my friends - ladies I had not seen for years - came to me that weekend with hearts heavy and hurting. I remain thankful for arms for hugging and for wisdom that does not come from me, but from God's Word. Thank You Jesus; for in the midst of it all, we can come to You, learn from You, know Your love that will never leave us and in doing so, experience relief. Amen.

Blessed to Do God's Will

Luke 11:27-28 HCSB

SEPTEMBER 16

Blessed and more blessed. Jesus was in the middle of rebuking the religious leaders of the day. They had a crazy idea and accused Him of getting His power to remove demons from Satan. In the mix of this, a woman's voice cried out from the crowd, *"The womb that bore You and the one who nursed You are blessed!"* Jesus accepted what this woman said and he replied for all to hear, *"Even more, those who hear the word of God and keep it are blessed!"* It is interesting that Jesus does not at all deny that His mother is blessed, but He takes it one step further by saying that those who obey God's Word are even more blessed. Let's choose to live in blessed obedience, for that is true blessedness.

Blessed Eyes, Blessed Ears

Matthew 13:16 HCSB

SEPTEMBER 17

Jesus described the Kingdom of Heaven and taught many lessons by telling stories and parables, and after He shared the parable of the sower with a large group, the disciples asked Jesus why He spoke to the crowds in parables. Jesus replied that Isaiah's prophecy, which would have been familiar to those listening, is fulfilled about a people who will listen but not understand and look and yet not perceive. And then He says something so encouraging: *"But your eyes are blessed because they do see, and your ears because they do hear! For I assure you: Many prophets and righteous people longed to see the things you see yet didn't see them; to hear the things you hear yet didn't hear them."*

All of Israel's history was leading up to Jesus. Up until Jesus, the Israelites had leaders, some good, some not so good, but all were incomplete. God's fullness dwelt fully in Jesus. Were his followers ready to embrace this? Dear Lord, in these days I pray that we would have blessed eyes and blessed ears to understand Your teaching, line up our lives with it, and live with wisdom and joy. Amen.

Live Well, Live Blessed!

Mark 5:34 MSG (also in Luke 8:48 and Matthew 9:22)

SEPTEMBER 18

This story might sound familiar. Many years ago there was a woman who became very poor as she sought doctor after doctor for a dozen years, and longed for a cure from her constant bleeding only to find her health getting worse. She had heard enough about Jesus to want to be near Him so she joined the crowd following Him. Her faith moved her to action and she reached down and touched the hem of His robe, thinking, "If I can just touch His robe I will be healed." And she was! Now Jesus confronted the crowd, "Who touched Me?" She was terrified to single herself out. She also knew that she was healed. Would she flee in panic? No, instead she fell on her knees in front of Jesus. *Jesus said to her, "Daughter, you took a risk of faith, and now you're healed and whole. Live well, live blessed! Be healed of your plague."*

She had suffered long and reaching out to Jesus in faith healed her. Her joy was made complete by His words, "live blessed". What areas of our lives do we need to leave at the hem of Jesus' robe? Our healing may or may not be immediate, but the peace we have knowing we are not alone in our suffering gives us the strength to bravely go forward.

Isaiah passed his driver's test the summer of 2012, so he and I made a 1,000-mile trip from Texas to Michigan and enjoyed visiting old friends along the way. When we arrived, we had a family reunion and celebrated my oldest nephew's birthday. The following Sunday I sat between my mom and my stepdad as their priest wonderfully taught about Jesus as He encountered this specific woman of faith who had reached out for the hem of His robe. Although my issue was not bleeding, I related to the situation because migraine headaches affected my life for longer than a dozen years. As I pondered all of this, I was becoming more and more ill and I nearly passed out in church. And that was the beginning of yet another three-day migraine cycle. Three days and nights in bed, even with a head that is throbbing, allows a lot of time to think and pray. Jesus can heal; there is no doubt in my mind about that. I will not give up faith and I will praise Him with great joy when that time comes!

Blessed to Be Fed

Matthew 14:19 NLT (also in Mark 6:41; Luke 9:16; John 6:11)

SEPTEMBER 19

All four of the Gospel writers record this amazing event of how Jesus met the physical needs of the masses who followed Him. Matthew wrote that the evening picnic was on the heels of Jesus hearing that His cousin John had been beheaded, and Jesus was going off for some time by Himself. But as it often happened, crowds of needy people went where Jesus went, and Jesus, being who He is, had compassion. He healed and He taught and it was now past dinnertime at the remote place where they had all gathered.

Five loaves of bread, two fish and one prayer to God in Heaven was all it took for over 5000 men, not including all the women and children, to eat until they were satisfied. That was a meal no one would forget! *He told the people to sit down on the grass. Jesus took the five loaves and two fish, looked up toward heaven, and blessed them. Then, breaking the loaves into pieces, he gave the bread to the disciples, who distributed it to the people.*

Sunday Soup is kind of like our family's equivalent to fish and loaves. In our second home in China we had a freezer just big enough to hold a container for our weekly leftovers and it was in that home that we began our tradition of Sunday Soup. While baking bread before our house church met, I would simmer up the soup and by adding water and at times extra vegetables, we could feed however many joined to worship with us that day. May we follow Jesus' example and bless our food (meaning to offer thanks to God for what He provides) and be quick to share what we have so that others may also be satisfied. Jesus fed those who followed Him with what He taught and by meeting physical needs as well.

Seek the Giver Not Just the Blessing

John 6:23-24 MSG

SEPTEMBER 20

The crowd that was miraculously fed by Jesus the day before was getting hungry again. *By now boats from Tiberias had pulled up near where they had eaten the bread blessed by the Master. So when the crowd realized he was gone and wasn't coming back, they piled into the Tiberias boats and headed for Capernaum, looking for Jesus.* Unfortunately, some of these people were only trying to find Jesus because they wanted another free lunch. Jesus knew this and He told them not to live that way but instead to spend energy seeking the eternal life that can only be found in Him. What does God want for us to do? He wants us to believe in the One He has sent. Do not be a "bread-Christian" but instead follow after the One who is the Bread of Life! It is a good idea to seek the Giver of the blessing and not just the blessing. Living on the foundation of gratitude blesses us to be a blessing.

Jesus Multiplies Blessings

Mark 8:7 NLT (also in Matthew 15:36)

SEPTEMBER 21

As God's Story went forward, the teaching ministry of Jesus continued. Many followed after Him to hear His messages on how to live the blessed life. On this particular occasion after a three-day teaching conference in a remote place, the crowds had run out of food, again. Instead of sending them home hungry, Jesus took seven loaves of bread and after He had thanked God for it, passed the bread out to about 4,000 people. *A few small fish were found, too, so Jesus also blessed these and told the disciples to distribute them.* Jesus is good to meet the needs of those who follow Him because He is tenderhearted and His blessings multiply. We are not Jesus, but do we interact with others using our lives so that blessings are multiplied? Jesus tells us to do good deeds so that our Father in Heaven is made known. Blessing people also blesses God. Let's bless on!

Share the Blessing

Luke 10:6 NLT

SEPTEMBER 22

Now Jesus' students were about to experience some practical application of all that they had learned and all that Jesus had modeled. Jesus prepared them to take His teaching into neighboring towns so that others could learn what they had been taught. Seventy-two interns were divided in groups of two, and Jesus gave instructions and advised them to pray, to eat what was set before them, to heal the sick, and to let everyone know the good news that the Kingdom of God is near. His advice then is still applicable for us today as we seek to share God's goodness with those around us. Jesus told His students when they entered a new town, *"If those who live there are peaceful, the blessing will stand; if they are not, the blessing will return to you."*

What an incredible privilege it must have been to spread the message of Jesus in that day and time. What a privilege it still is for those who pray and go and give. If God has blessed you with good news to share, have fun as you share the blessing. My first mission trip was to a very rural area of Mexico in December 1989. Russell and I had been married about six months when we drove across the Texas border and we kept driving until the roads became dirt trails. I couldn't speak Spanish fluently but I learned the words "un regalo" and said them over and over as I passed out messages of good news. I believe God blessed me just as He blessed those who received the gift. Thankfulness grows when we remember that we do not just pass a gift on, but that we really are recipients of God's good gift of salvation. Jesus is the best *regalo* ever! My heart needs to be reminded often of this gift. I have a feeling I'm not alone with that need.

Blessed to See from God's Perspective

Luke 10:23 NIV

SEPTEMBER 23

When the seventy-two disciples Jesus sent out returned to joyfully tell Him all that had happened on their mission trip, Jesus was also filled with joy. Jesus prayed to His Father thanking Him for revealing important things to those who had child-like faith. *Then he turned to his disciples and said privately, "Blessed are the eyes that see what you see."* Do we see things from God's perspective? When we know Jesus, we cannot help but introduce others to Him too and doing this as part of a team reminds me of how it was done back in Jesus' days.

One of the things that brought me joy during our year of living in London was serving in a café that was housed in a renovated part of an ancient church. I loved walking through two lush green parks on my way to work, taking in God's beauty in creation and praising Him because it prepared me for whatever might come in the café. And I loved being a part of a team of people from several countries who also wanted to serve. Some days I served up the food and it was fun learning about British dishes. On other days I cleared tables or I would sit with the lonely or the drug-users or the elderly and talk with them. Because I had tasted and I knew that the Lord was good, it was easy to turn the conversation to Him.

But one dialogue became a bit heated when a fellow volunteer voiced his dislike for Christian do-gooders. When he asked what I thought, I asked him what he thought about the advances in medicine. I told him that if I had the cure for cancer I certainly would not keep it to myself but I would share it. How much more would I want to share the good news that Jesus came to rescue us from death to life! Jesus is not aspirin; He is the giver of life! Lord, please keep our eyes and ears open to

You. Choose us to be a part of the joyful team that You use to change the world, one person at a time.   Amen.

Blessed to Love My Neighbor

Luke 10:28 AMP

SEPTEMBER 24

And Jesus said to him, You have answered correctly; do this, and you will live [enjoy active, blessed, endless life in the kingdom of God]. Who was Jesus talking with and what were the questions and answers? It was on one occasion that an expert in the law asked Jesus, "What can I do to get everlasting life?" Jesus answered his question with a question, "What does the law of Moses say?" The lawyer replied, "Love the Lord your God with everything you've got—heart, soul, strength and mind—and love your neighbor as yourself." "Good answer!", Jesus replied. But then the man asked one more question. "Um, just who is my neighbor?"

The parable of the Good Samaritan followed. Blessed life can be boiled down to "love God, love people." When I wrote this in bold black letters on the front of the desk I used while homeschooling our kiddos in China back in 2002, it gave me the clarity to focus on the important things. There was a lot of time for questions and answers and my desire was to instill in my students the joy of learning. Not only were they each other's only classmates, there were no other foreign children in our town, so they also learned how to play and interact with those different from them. On some days, "loving our neighbors" came during "school-time" and they learned life lessons outside of the room that was filled with bookshelves, a time-line and maps drawn onto the concrete painted walls. Our children are grown now and living in a very diverse world. Neighbors move in and out. They may not look, believe or act like we do and yet Jesus still calls us to love our neighbor as ourselves. God, help us to daily refocus our attention on You and live to love those around us in ways for their good and Your honor. Amen.

Blessed to Live Ready!

Luke 12:35-38 HCSB

Jesus is coming back! It is important news and we do not want to miss out on the reward and blessing that awaits those prepared for Him. Jesus also says what will happen if we are not ready, and just to let you know, it is the very opposite of a blessing. If I knew you were coming through town I would be sure to have chili in the crock-pot or cookies baked up, ready for your visit. How much more excited I get thinking of the visit of our Lord Jesus!

This is how Jesus puts it: *"Be ready for service and have your lamps lit. You must be like people waiting for their master to return from the wedding banquet so that when he comes and knocks, they can open the door for him at once. Those slaves the master will find alert when he comes will be blessed. I assure you: He will get ready, have them recline at the table, then come and serve them. If he comes in the middle of the night, or even near dawn, and finds them alert, those slaves are blessed."*

Did you catch it? I missed it the first few time I read this through, but Jesus says He will serve the ones that are ready for the Master's return. But not everyone will be prepared, and no one knows when the time will be, but each day it gets closer. Expect the unexpected and until then may we humbly serve our servant King by serving one another. Live ready!

A Blessed Party is Coming

Luke 14:13-15 NIV

Tonight while I'm working on edits for this part of God's Story of blessings it is Super Bowl XLVII. Those Roman numerals equal 2013, and I'm only halfway embarrassed not to know which two teams are playing. Each year, during this season, there are all kinds of parties taking place as football games are watched and cheered. My supper bowl holds tomato soup and after a pleasant time of roller-skating on the bike trail, I'm enjoying the quiet evening alone. But, if I were to throw a celebration, I would want it to be a good one; a fun time for all who would come.

Jesus gives great advice for how to host a blessed gathering. He says, *"But when you give a banquet, invite the poor, the crippled, the lame, the blind, and you will be blessed. Although they cannot repay you, you will be repaid at the resurrection of the righteous."* Not all reward comes immediately, but blessing others, in this case, those who can't pay you back, brings a greater kind of blessing to the one who blesses initially. *When one of those at the table with him heard this, he said to Jesus, "Blessed is the man who will eat at the feast in the kingdom of God."* Now that's one party I sure do not want to miss! I may not know football, but I know God and I'm so happy to be on His team! I look forward to seeing you at the party!

Knowing Jesus Blesses Us

Matthew 16:17 AMP

SEPTEMBER 27

One day Jesus asked His disciples, "Who do you say I am?" Simon Peter answered, "You are the Messiah, the Son of the living God." *Then Jesus answered him, Blessed (happy, fortunate, and to be envied) are you, Simon Bar-Jonah. For flesh and blood [men] have not revealed this to you, but My Father Who is in heaven.* How blessed we are when we see Jesus for who He really is. Jesus, You are God's Anointed One. Savior of the world. Prince of Peace. Lord and Teacher. Jesus is the Son of the living God. And Jesus wants us to know Him. Do you?

1997 was our first Christmas in a village setting in China and it gave us many opportunities to ask that question to new friends and fellow students at the college where we were language students. In ways, the "commercial Christmas" was invading even this remote no-traffic-light area near the border with Burma, but few knew the name of the Man whose birth was being celebrated. How blessed our family was to unwrap the gift of the Christmas Story by sharing truth and offering hope that could last for all eternity.

Blessed to Run to Jesus

Mark 10:13-16 NLT (also in Matthew 19:13-15; Luke 18:15-17)

During our years of living in Thailand seeking to expand God's Kingdom through love and awareness of Him, Russell traveled a lot. A minority group in China was our major focus and after years of interaction Bible translation was just beginning among them. To help bring greater awareness to our praying partners, I wrote a prayer journal that focused on each of the sixty-six books of the Bible combined with the customs and needs relating to this particular group. The prayer journal became a book, *His First Bible*, and it was printed towards the end of 2006. Here is an excerpt from it highlighting how Jesus blesses:

In his biography of Jesus, Mark describes the ultimate Servant. Event after event we see Christ's character as he interacts with people. Tucked between Jesus answering the Pharisees' testing about divorce and His encounter with the ambitious young ruler, Jesus engaged not the powerful or the rich but the meek. His disciples were brushing these little people aside, thinking the Teacher was too busy to be bothered. But Jesus values children. Can you envision His arms open wide, while children run to Him drawn in by His love? "Let the children come to me. Don't stop them! For the Kingdom of God belongs to such as these. I assure you, anyone who doesn't have their kind of faith will never get into the Kingdom of God."

God's Kingdom belongs to those who long for His love and closeness. What a contrast between the religious know-it-alls and the children who are pure in heart. Jesus tells us our faith should be like that of children running into His arms. Lord, we thank You for still calling children of all ages and all nations into Your love. May we run to You, holding nothing back. We pray for the SD children to know You at a young age.

Jesus, teach us to learn from You never to be too busy to reach out to the little ones in our lives. What joy we would experience if we would follow Your example: *"Then he took the children into his arms and placed his hands on their heads and blessed them."*

Blessed Is the City
Who Welcomes Her Lord

Luke 13:35 NLT (also in Matthew 23:38-39)

SEPTEMBER 29

Some religious leaders told Jesus that He should flee Jerusalem if He wanted to stay alive. Hundreds of years earlier, the enemies of God's people had taken captives from Jerusalem and now was the time for One captive to set all mankind free. Jesus did not run away; instead He embraced what was before Him. He knew God's Story. He knows that God's Story includes making a mighty nation out of one person and blessing the world, over and over. Instead of fleeing, Jesus grieved over Jerusalem and said how He wanted to protect her like a mother hen would protect her chicks.

Then Jesus told the Pharisees, *"And now, look, your house is abandoned. And you will never see me again until you say, 'Blessings on the one who comes in the name of the LORD!'"* Here Jesus quoted from Psalm 118:26, a song He will sing with eleven of His twelve disciples right after the Last Supper. The time was growing close for Jesus' life purpose to be fulfilled. He did not take the easy way out, but He pressed on with the work yet before Him all the way to the cross. He indeed will come again. All blessings on King Jesus! May we bless in His name. May we bless Him for His steadfast commitment to all that is right.

Jesus Is the Blessed One

John 12:12-13 HCSB

Jesus' triumphal entry to Jerusalem was a very big event. Matthew, Mark, Luke and John each wrote about this day that we now celebrate as Palm Sunday. The scene had been set and the Holy Week began with Jesus the King of Everything riding into the religious center of the time on the back of a young donkey. *The next day, when the large crowd that had come to the festival heard that Jesus was coming to Jerusalem, they took palm branches and went out to meet Him. They kept shouting: "Hosanna! He who comes in the name of the Lord is the blessed One—the King of Israel!"* Hosanna is an expression of adoration, praise and joy. The crowds could not be happier; they were celebrating and they were there to participate in it all. Lord Jesus, You continue to be praise-worthy. May we live faithful to You in the time of celebration and in the time of trial that will surely come for those that truly follow You. Amen.

Reflections

In September we were so blessed to read from Jesus Himself how to live the blessed life. Jesus faithfully modeled those teachings as He healed, fed, and comforted people in various locations during His ministry on earth. He is strong and He is smart and He leads in ways so that His followers can also lead out with truth and love. His cousin John and His twelve disciples may have known Him best, but each of the gospel writers (Matthew, Luke, Mark and John) recorded the life of Jesus so that we too can know and be blessed by Him.

October

Blessed Is the King

Luke 19:37-38 ESV

Jesus obediently entered Jerusalem just the way the prophets foretold: on the back of a donkey. This week was going to change His life and it would change the lives of everyone who would believe in Him throughout time. What was on Jesus' mind as the donkey eased its way along the road that would lead to suffering? What would we have been thinking had we been one of those who walked beside Him?

The Catholic Church originated the Stations of the Cross, which poignantly depict the final hours of Jesus' life. The first outdoor encounter of the Stations of the Cross that I can remember was in a forest in northern Michigan. Heavy pine scent took the place of words as I walked from one station to the next. I was a young girl and I tried to imagine how painful it must have been for Jesus to die. As the sun streamed through the large trees, my family came upon a clearing, and there before us was the world's largest crucifix. The thirty-one foot high bronze Jesus on an even larger wooden cross had an impact upon me. Luke's Gospel account will record Jesus on the cross, but for now let's read the prelude of what would be world changing history.

As he was drawing near—already on the way down the Mount of Olives— the whole multitude of his disciples began to rejoice and praise God with a loud voice for all the mighty works that they had seen, saying, "Blessed is the King who comes in the name of the Lord! Peace in heaven and glory in the highest!" Does that sound familiar? When Jesus was born, an angelic choir sang out, "Glory to God in the highest, and on earth peace, good will toward men!" From His birth to His death and beyond, Jesus is announced with blessings and with an incredible amount of rejoicing. He knew His purpose and did not waver from it. The fourteenth, and generally the final Station of the Cross, portrays Jesus in the tomb. But He did not stay there! There is peace in Heaven and glory in the highest because death cannot hold our King.

Blessed Is He
Who Comes in the Name of the Lord

Matthew 21:9 AMP; Mark 11:9-10 NLT

OCTOBER 2

Matthew joined the other gospel writers and recorded the excitement that was felt by many as Jesus arrived in Jerusalem. Can you hear the multitudes cheering Him on? Those who loved Jesus and acknowledged Him as their King surrounded him. *And the crowds that went ahead of Him and those that followed Him kept shouting, Hosanna (O be propitious, graciously inclined) to the Son of David, [the Messiah]! Blessed (praised, glorified) is He Who comes in the name of the Lord! Hosanna (O be favorably disposed) in the highest [heaven]!* Everyone was enthusiastically getting caught up in the movement. Our King is coming! Our King is coming!

Mark also penned what happened that day: *Jesus was in the center of the procession, and the people all around him were shouting, "Praise God! Blessings on the one who comes in the name of the LORD! Blessings on the coming Kingdom of our ancestor David! Praise God in highest heaven!"* Was anyone besides Jesus prepared for the change of direction that each would soon encounter? Within the week emotions would swing wildly from joyfully celebrating His jubilant arrival, to fear, anger, betrayal, deep sadness, confusion, and pain. But for now, in God's Story, it was a joyful time for many people. If we had been there to witness it all, what would we have said in the crowds?

Blessed Is the Servant
Who Is Found Serving

Matthew 24:45-47 ESV

OCTOBER 3

A lot took place in that brief period between the road to Jerusalem and the road to Emmaus. Time was short and Jesus knew how to spend it

253

wisely. After a day in the Temple, Jesus used His time to tell His disciples about the end times. He warned them not to be fooled by false prophets because no one other than God the Father will know exactly when the last day or hour would be. Jesus said that those who are serving faithfully and are sensible until the end would receive a reward, a blessing. *"Who then is the faithful and wise servant, whom his master has set over his household, to give them their food at the proper time? Blessed is that servant whom his master will find so doing when he comes. Truly, I say to you, he will set him over all his possessions."*

Do you remember when Jesus mentioned this "be prepared concept" in an earlier parable? Now He is even more emphatic as He teaches those who love Him to be ready to serve faithfully right up until the end. Jesus not only told His students, but He would show them just what He meant. He is our living example. Thank You Lord Jesus for Your faithful life. You are not selfish or self-centered but humble, strong, and obedient. No one took Your life from You but You laid it down, sacrificed it voluntarily so that we may have life in You. Help us Jesus to ponder how You lived, cared, taught, and loved so that we can make the most of our days, serving bravely with compassion. Amen.

A Blessed Kingdom As Inheritance
Matthew 25:31-34 HCSB

OCTOBER 4

Jesus took the time for more teaching. There will be a final judgment and He gives us a peek at what that will look like. Could it be that He shared this so that when we have a choice to make, we would choose wisely? *"When the Son of Man comes in His glory, and all the angels with Him, then He will sit on the throne of His glory. All the nations will be gathered before Him, and He will separate them one from another, just as a shepherd separates the sheep from the goats. He will put the sheep on His right and the goats on the left. Then the King will say to those on His right, 'Come, you who are blessed by My Father, inherit the kingdom prepared for you from the foundation of the world.'...*

The stakes are high and the blessings are greater than we could ever imagine. Inheritance in a Kingdom prepared by God is going to be even better than any Disney princess movie ever made. But what will happen to those on His left? They will experience an unending and unimaginable separation from all that is life. Jesus goes on to tell how the actions lived out of love for "the least of these my brothers and sisters" made all the difference. Out of love are we caring for the hungry, the thirsty, the stranger, the one in need of clothing, the sick and the prisoner? If there is still a today, then there is still time. Let's open our eyes and our hearts, get involved and serve. The blessings will be now and forever more.

Blessed to Serve like Jesus

John 13:16-17 NLT

OCTOBER 5

First we need to know what we are supposed to do, and then we need to do what we are supposed to do. The outcome will be blessing. *"I tell you the truth, slaves are not greater than their master. Nor is the messenger more important than the one who sends the message. Now that you know these things, God will bless you for doing them."* Jesus taught this lesson to his disciples by giving them an example. During what would become known as the Last Supper, He knelt before each one and washed their feet. Jesus taught how to serve by serving. He taught love by loving. When He forgave, he demonstrated forgiveness, and He asks us to forgive others too. People will know we are His disciples if we love and serve one another. Knowing this truth is one thing; doing it is a whole other thing. But the blessing does not come in the knowing, or even in memorizing the chapter and verse, but in the doing, the serving.

Jesus is our Master and the message He gives us is His plan for abundant life: appropriately love God and people; repeat. Our guidebook, God's Word, will keep us on the right path and when we do get off track,

Jesus says to confess it and get back to a healthy relationship with Him and with people. Russell and I were at a marriage retreat just after we celebrated our fifteenth year of marriage. We gathered with other couples, some we knew, others we did not, and a ministry team from Chic-Fil-A, the Win Shape Foundation, met us at the resort setting in a Chinese city. In married life, sometimes we are gloriously on track and other times miserably off course. The humbling act of receiving a foot washing by Russell as part of the retreat was a very healthy re-set. May we not only remember the ways which Jesus taught, but carry the actions of His message. That is how a student honors his teacher. And Jesus is the best teacher I know.

Blessed and Broken for Us

Luke 22:18-19 MSG (also in Matthew 26:26-27; Mark 14:22)

OCTOBER 6

The Passover meal had been prepared in the Upper Room. Jesus had humbly washed the feet of His followers that were around the table and then He spoke the words that we often hear when we celebrate the Lord's Supper. *Taking the cup, he blessed it, then said, "Take this and pass it among you. As for me, I'll not drink wine again until the kingdom of God arrives." Taking bread, he blessed it, broke it, and gave it to them, saying, "This is my body, given for you. Eat it in my memory."* As often as we do this, may we always remember Jesus - broken for us, to have wholeness through Him.

The small youth group at a rural church in North Carolina grew in number and in maturity during the time Russell was the associate pastor and oversaw the youth ministry. I had the privilege of teaching this same group of teenagers on Sunday mornings, and we met in an attic room of the church which we dubbed the Upper Room. Week by week we read the Gospel of John as if we were acting out a play so each of us could better understand the interactions Jesus had with people. When we came to the part where Jesus was having His final meal with His friends, our Upper Room group sensed the seriousness of what was taking place. Jesus offered a new agreement. This new covenant was, and still is today, what He offers to those who trust Him: His lifeblood poured out for our death-sins to be forgiven. Jesus, thank You.

Jesus Is the Son of the Blessed One

Mark 14:61b-62 NIV

Jesus went from His last meal with His disciples to a garden where He prayed. It was in this garden where He was then betrayed and arrested. His friends fled in fear. Peter denied Him, and Jesus was brought before the Jewish Supreme Court to be questioned. *Again the high priest asked him, "Are you the Messiah, the Son of the Blessed One?" "I am," said Jesus. "And you will see the Son of Man sitting at the right hand of the Mighty One and coming on the clouds of heaven."* Jesus replied truthfully but the Jewish leaders called it blasphemy and insisted that He was worthy of death. But because the religious leaders did not hold power in the Roman world, the next step was to get the Roman government to authorize the death sentence for Jesus.

Again the high priest asked him, "Are you the Messiah, the Son of the Blessed One?" "I am," said Jesus. Two small words: "I am." Jesus really is who He says He is. Death did not hold the Author of life and He will come again because He is trustworthy. Will He come today? Oh, for the day when Jesus returns and all is made right! Until then, we trust Jesus who sits at the Mighty One's right-hand-side as the Messiah, the Savior of the world, and the Savior of our hearts. He is the Son of the Blessed One.

Blessed to Have Peace in Times of Pain

Luke 23:28-30 ESV

OCTOBER 8

Pilate, the Roman governor, did not find any reason to put Jesus to death, but because the Jews demanded crucifixion he complied. Jesus was mistreated in many excruciating ways on the road to His death. Exhausted beyond what most humans will ever experience, He began that journey carrying His own death weapon, the cross. Many people wept for Jesus; their love, confusion and anguish poured out in tears. *But turning to them Jesus said, "Daughters of Jerusalem, do not weep for me, but weep for yourselves and for your children. For behold, the days are coming when they will say, 'Blessed are the barren and the wombs that never bore and the breasts that never nursed!'"* Hard times would come and Jesus knew it. He also knew He would overcome. Through Him, we can too.

One of my favorite promises of Jesus was spoken by Him near the end of His life. I can picture Him with His disciples as they left the Upper Room and walked together to the garden. On the way, Jesus shared with them so much that it must have been hard to take it all in. Just before Jesus turned His eyes toward Heaven to pray, He told His friends, "in Me you may have peace. In this world you will have trouble. But take heart! I have overcome the world." As their world came tumbling down, did His follows remember His words? Do we experience peace when we know that Jesus overcame the world? Jesus was not taken by surprise, but when we are, let's remember His words of peace and follow His example of prayer.

In the spring of 2014, I experienced (in a way I had not yet encountered, even by watching Mel Gibson's *The Passion of the Christ*) just a little bit of the reality that was Jesus' as He died in agony. Lying in the emergency room with several bones of my ankle crushed, I thought of Jesus with not one, but both of his feet nailed to the cross, supporting the weight of His body and the weight of mankind's sin. In pain, I prayed to Him. His reply brought peace in the midst of suffering. "You are experiencing the pain of the world but remember that I overcame this world

258

of hurt, sin and even death. You are not going to have this pain forever. Trust Me. Take heart. In Me you may have peace."

Open Our Eyes to the Blessed One

Luke 24:29b-31 HCSB

OCTOBER 9

Jesus died on the cross that He had carried. His death paid for all the sins of all mankind. For my sins, your sins and beyond, He died. He died, but He did not stay dead. He is alive! And this news seems too good to be true. After God raised Jesus from the grave, Jesus met with several of His close friends who were all astonished to see Him. Then Jesus walked down a road with two of His own followers and talked about everything that had just taken place and explained so many things to them about Israel's history; God's Story. But on this seven-mile journey toward Emmaus, they did not know that it was Jesus with them. When they reached their destination they invited their travel companion in by saying, *"Stay with us, because it's almost evening, and now the day is almost over."* So He went in to stay with them. It was as He reclined at the table with them that He took the bread, blessed and broke it, and gave it to them. Then their eyes were opened, and they recognized Him, but He disappeared from their sight.

Sometimes I wonder, "What will it really take for us to see Jesus?" Lord, open our eyes to You. Lord, let us see that You are the blessing. Amen.

Blessed Are Those
Who Have Not Seen yet Believe

John 20:28b-29 ESV

OCTOBER 10

Thomas was with Jesus and the other disciples when they celebrated the last Passover together, but he wasn't with the disciples when Jesus initially met up with the group after His resurrection. Thomas found it hard to really believe that Jesus was alive again. Would we be quick to believe the stories our friends told us if we had not seen for ourselves? Thomas, like all of the disciples, had been through a lot. He needed proof. And Jesus provided just what Thomas needed. "Peace be with you", started off the conversation and then Jesus offered His hands and His side to Thomas so he would no longer doubt, but believe. Astounded, Thomas replied, *"My Lord and my God!" Jesus said to him, "Have you believed because you have seen me? Blessed are those who have not seen and yet have believed."*

We who believe in Jesus today are the "blessed ones" Jesus is talking about. We believe by faith and not by sight and in doing so, we are blessed by Jesus. I hope we can let that goodness soak in a bit. And then out of gratitude, live in His glorious Presence as we go through our days. It is natural to reach out to others when our hearts are continually filled with thankfulness for all that Jesus has done for us. There are still many people who have not yet seen. In what ways will they see Jesus in us? Will they too believe and be blessed?

Blessed to Live a Life of Great Joy

Luke 24:50-53 ESV

OCTOBER 11

Oh how those days must have sped by! Jesus was back and alive, answering questions and the disciples' trust grew. But the time had come in God's Story for Jesus to return to His Father and before He left, He gave the promise of the Holy Spirit. He also left His friends with instructions to share the good news: Jesus lived to love us, died to redeem us and rose again to conquer sin and death forever. His job on earth was complete and it was time to get back to Heaven, His home. Jesus was with His friends when He ascended. *He led them out as far as Bethany, and lifting up his hands he blessed them. While he blessed them, he parted from them and was carried up into heaven. And they worshiped him and returned to Jerusalem with great joy, and were continually in the temple blessing God.* I cannot even imagine how wonderful it must have been to receive that final personal blessing from Jesus. It led them to worship Him and true worship leads to obedience and we can read about the adventure of obedience in the Book of Acts. Let us live a life to bless God, and let's live it with great joy!

Shower of Blessings

Acts 3:19 MSG

OCTOBER 12

The Story does not end here! Soon after Jesus returned to His Father, His apprentices began the good work of spreading the good news about Him. Luke wrote the Acts of the Apostles as a historical record of how the Holy Spirit worked within the new and growing church. Peter preached on the day of Pentecost in Jerusalem and many people called on the name of the Lord to save them. Believers were baptized and the community was filled with great joy and deep caring. A crowd formed when Peter healed a crippled beggar and then Peter explained that this miraculous power came from God alone. He took the opportunity to tell the gathering Jews about Jesus and their need for Him. *"Now it's time to change your ways! Turn to face God so he can wipe away your sins, pour out showers of blessing to refresh you, and send you the Messiah he prepared for you, namely, Jesus."*

Oh, that we too would fully trust Jesus, and in doing so receive a fresh shower of blessings in our lives. Thai New Year festivities take place in mid-April each year and last about a week. The highlight for most people is a mobile, full-scale, water soaking party. Our first water splashing celebration was a lot of fun with our new Thai neighbors. It was a hot day, so riding around Chiang Mai's ancient moat in the back of a pick-up truck, splashing water and being splashed, felt good. Then it started to rain. Smiling, I told my neighbor Khun Ploi that God was water splashing with us too. Then with my limited Thai, I continued to build on what I had been sharing with her about Jesus being the way to God. I'm so thankful for God who cares for us and He indeed provides blessings that shower down in a multitude of ways. May the Thai people embrace Jesus and experience the refreshment that comes from all sin being wiped away.

Blessed to Turn from Sinful Ways

Acts 3:25-26 NLT

OCTOBER 13

Peter continued to talk to the crowd and he reminded the Jewish community of the story of Moses and the prophets and how they, the Jews, were connected to the past and how they would be blessed if they would turn from the wicked way they were living. *"You are the children of those prophets, and you are included in the covenant God promised to your ancestors. For God said to Abraham, 'Through your descendants all the families on earth will be blessed.' When God raised up his servant, Jesus, he sent him first to you people of Israel, to bless you by turning each of you back from your sinful ways."* This message that was offered up in hope earned Peter and his friend John a night in prison because the religious leaders did not want people to hear more about Jesus and His resurrection.

Who would not want to hear the good news of such a good blessing? Who would not want to be shown the way to life, especially if they were walking close to the edge of death's cliff? God, I'm so thankful that You place people in my life to tell me and show me how to turn from my sinful ways. May this good news continue to change lives, generation after generation. At one point, Peter denied even knowing Jesus. But Jesus provided a way for reconciliation, and with a clear identity, Peter courageously invited others into the covenant that You offered way back in the lifetime of Abraham. God, may we live bravely for You. Amen.

Great Blessings upon All

Acts 4:33-35 NLT

OCTOBER 14

For believers it was an exciting time to live! The Christian community was unified, and people shared the things they owned and made the good news known to others. Real needs were really being met. *The apostles testified powerfully to the resurrection of the Lord Jesus, and God's great blessing was upon them all. There were no needy people among them, because those who owned land or houses would sell them and bring the money to the apostles to give to those in need.* Our God is great in power and generous with grace and He gives us hope and a way to authentically live life with His hope.

I love looking back to Deuteronomy 15 when God's people were first entering the land He promised to them. We read how God so consistently desires that the poor be cared for. God's great blessings often flow when people are living in awareness, really searching out the great God of that blessing. Today, how can we connect to God, know His blessing, and bless others who are in need of blessing? A thankful heart is a great place to start. It is best for us not to hoard God's blessings but to allow them to flow through us. This takes practice. May we fold our hands in gratitude and open them up for godly giving and service.

Evidence of God's Blessing Fills Us with Joy

Acts 11:22-23 NLT

OCTOBER 15

Remain true to the Lord. This was part of the encouragement, advice, and news that Barnabas brought from Jerusalem to the church that gathered at Antioch. The early disciples were living very full lives, sharing with others the way to have full life in Jesus. They preached and taught; they healed those in need, and miracles gave credibility to their words. As the disciples followed the teachings of Jesus, more people began to follow Jesus' disciples. Unfortunately, this all made for some jealous religious leaders. A couple of the disciples were even imprisoned but were miraculously released by an angel. Stephen became the first Christian martyr and as persecution continued, the church scattered and yet continued to grow.

Saul was amazingly converted to Paul and joined Jesus' team to spread the good news that there was purpose to life. Up to this point in God's Story, the message was mainly told to the Jews. God's plan was for all nations to be blessed, and how surprised the church in Jerusalem was to hear that Greeks too were being brought into God's Kingdom. *When the church at Jerusalem heard what had happened, they sent Barnabas to Antioch. When he arrived and saw this evidence of God's blessing, he was filled with joy, and he encouraged the believers to stay true to the Lord.* When we think about those who have faithfully shared the love of God with us, I hope it fills us with joy. It is great news to know that God's love is for everyone; there are no exceptions. No one is too good and no one is too bad. Who will experience more of God's love through us today? May we be encouragers like Barnabas was back in the days of the early church.

David's Blessings Passed Down

Acts 13:34 HCSB

Paul, with Barnabas as his companion, set sail on the first of several missionary journeys. After sailing on from Crete, they were at a synagogue in Pisidia when Paul was asked to give a word of encouragement and he stood up to preach his first recorded sermon. I love how God's Story includes lots of "firsts." Paul began with the deliverance of their forefathers from Egypt, and continued through the history of the Jewish nation, right up to David, and then from David to Jesus, his descendant. I picture Paul pausing at this point and turning to the area where the God-fearing Greeks where gathered. In a loud voice for all to hear, Paul went on to say that God's promise to Abraham was to bless all nations, and that this promise is fulfilled through Jesus. *Since He raised Him from the dead, never to return to decay, He has spoken in this way, I will grant you the faithful covenant blessings made to David.*

Paul concluded his message of hope: it is through Jesus that the forgiveness of sins is proclaimed. God's Holy One will not see decay. People knew of King David. His life story was passed down from generation to generation and his psalms of praise to God were still being sung from the synagogue's hymnals. Yet David died and his body did decay. It was Jesus whom God raised from the dead, never to experience decay. Jesus is our sure blessing. When our future seems uncertain, hold on to the facts, and it is a fact that God raised Jesus from the dead. That changes everything!

The Blessing of Peace

Acts 15:33 NIV

For many new Christians (most of whom at this time had Jewish backgrounds), it was no small thing to see non-Jewish people being brought into God's Kingdom through faith in Jesus. Gentiles were thought of as "other", and some Jewish Christians from Jerusalem wanted the new Gentile converts to be circumcised and follow the law of Moses. They considered those steps necessary to be brought into the family of God. This caused quite a stir. After a meeting and a discussion, the resolution included the truth that people are saved by the grace of Jesus regardless of heritage or culture. Two prophets, Judas and Silas, hand-carried a letter with this news to the Gentiles in Antioch and they encouraged and strengthened the recently converted believers. *After spending some time there, they were sent off by the believers with the blessing of peace to return to those who had sent them.* When life is muddled at best or hostile at worst, there are few things more meaningful than the blessing of peace. May we seek to choose peace based on truth and in doing so be a blessing to others even when at first the issues may seem irreconcilable.

I'm thankful that biblical teaching was not only taught at the church we loved in Timberlake, North Carolina but something that was also practiced. Sweeping issues under the rug at home or at church is not a healthy way to go forward if our desire is real Christian maturity. But this growth is seldom without pain. Is it worth it to live having peace with God and peace with others? Peace allows the dirt under the rug to be cared for and the door to hope to open. Something that Russell and I enjoy doing, even up to this day, is returning to our own Antioch - the church family that faithfully sent us out with blessings in 1996, and supported our family as we served God in Asia. Returning is always a double blessing; we get to hear what God is doing in and through the church and also get to update our brothers and sisters with the things that God is doing in our part of His world. Each homecoming is full of joy because we treasure the same God who wants His children to live out the blessing of peace.

Those Who Have Faith Are Blessed

Galatians 3:8-9 HCSB

Paul traveled to many areas to share the good news, and as he taught and preached he lived life in community. He could not be everywhere at once, so he wrote letters of encouragement and correction to various churches he had started or in other ways had had an impact. Now each of us can learn from these letters written many generations ago. The people living in Galatia needed a reminder that it is by God's grace that anyone can be rescued. Everyone is made right by believing, placing faith in Jesus who is the One who does the rescuing. Paul reminded them: *"Now the Scripture saw in advance that God would justify the Gentiles by faith and told the good news ahead of time to Abraham, saying, All the nations will be blessed through you. So those who have faith are blessed with Abraham, who had faith."*

Praise be to God who has made a way for us! This is good news and it is so exciting to think that the blessings back in the days of Abraham are passed on to all who have faith, in Paul's day and in ours, and for the generations yet to come. All nations will be blessed. That is a big promise. But that is okay, our God is big. As we live out the blessings in the community we find ourselves in, may we live faithfully and expectantly with a desire to both learn and teach. God, help us in our days to not let the light go dim or the truth lose its saltiness. Amen.

Blessed through Faith

Galatians 3:10-14 NLT

Paul continued his letter reiterating that Christians are not given new life by obeying the law of Moses, but by living according to the way of Jesus. Whether we are new Christians or have been in God's family for a long time, it is great to think about the truth that Paul explains. *"But*

Christ has rescued us from the curse pronounced by the law. When he was hung on the cross, he took upon himself the curse for our wrongdoing. For it is written in the Scriptures, "Cursed is everyone who is hung on a tree." Through Christ Jesus, God has blessed the Gentiles with the same blessing he promised to Abraham, so that we who are believers might receive the promised Holy Spirit through faith." One day our faith will become sight. But now we live by faith with God's Holy Spirit living within us.

Our family has moved quite a bit. Yet wherever we go, God's Holy Spirit goes with us, within us. One day I was going through boxes that were stored in Russell's sister's home during the time we lived away from the US. What a blessing it was to find an old Bible from my own new Christian days and to read notes like this one- "Faith is: F-forsaking A-all I T-trust H-him." That is just what Paul sought to teach! Jesus came to reverse the curse and offer life to walking dead people. It is time to give up the prideful ways of thinking, that goodness in itself is adequate outside of God. Humankind needs redeeming, not just touch-up work. Can I trust that He is all I need and can I really believe that He died to rescue me? Jesus gave us new life with His Spirit to fill us where there once was sin and void. He removes our hollow meaninglessness.

Direct Blessing of God

Galatians 3:18-20 MSG

OCTOBER 20

Further explanation given in the letter Paul wrote to the church in Galatia shows us a couple of things. We can read just how strongly this community was driven to live by legalism and then read just how important it was for them, and for us today, to reflect and live gratefully based on what God has provided for us through His Son Jesus. *"What is the point, then, of the law, the attached addendum? It was a thoughtful addition to the original covenant promises made to Abraham. The purpose of the law was to keep a sinful people in the way of salvation until Christ (the descendant) came, inheriting the promises and distributing them to us. Obviously*

268

this law was not a firsthand encounter with God. It was arranged by an-
gelic messengers through a middleman, Moses. But if there is a middleman
as there was at Sinai, then the people are not dealing directly with God,
are they? But the original promise is the direct blessing of God, received by
faith." Let us live as grateful free people, free to love God and love others
in ways that please Him who has so richly blessed us.

Don't Lose Your Sense of Being Blessed

Galatians 4:13-15a HCBS

Paul mentioned a personal situation and asked those he taught in Galatia
to recall the love that they had for him and for one another. *"...you know*
that previously I preached the gospel to you because of a physical illness. You
did not despise or reject me though my physical condition was a trial for you.
On the contrary, you received me as an angel of God, as Christ Jesus Him-
self. What happened to this sense of being blessed you had?" Even though
the times were challenging, the church once had deep satisfaction and a
grateful spirit when Paul was serving among them. Hardships and trials
can bring about real bonding. Paul wrote a reminder of this because he
didn't want those he cared about to forget the joy that they once had together. He wanted them to go forward in peaceful blessedness.

Blessing and being blessed is God's plan for our life story, but at
times we forget, and other times our enemy would like to rob us of our
sense of being blessed. Thinking about God's love for us can help us assess the situation and calibrate our reactions appropriately. Then we can
choose to bless.

Back in the days before cell phones, the over-night bus from Kunming to Lijiang normally took fourteen hours to wind its way through
China's developing countryside. Our young family of five and a fellow
language student boarded with Oreo cookies - a rare treasure - to bless
our friends that we were going to visit. Some time around midnight the
bus stopped in the middle of nowhere. Thirty-something hours later,

after dynamite had cleared a dangerous mountain road landslide, we hugged our anxiously waiting friends. We were greatly relieved that our bus did not go over a cliff, like some do, and we all laughed about the gifts of cookies becoming our survival food. To this day when I enjoy Oreos I remember that trip, my gratitude to God for our safe travel, and for the bonding created because of the "trial". Remembering God can be the sweetest part of our days.

Wait for the Blessing

Galatians 5:5 AMP

OCTOBER 22

Do not give up hope! Paul did not write to his friends to condemn them but rather to encourage them to live life with joy and great hope. This expanded sentence shows that pressing on in God is so worth it. *For we, [not relying on the Law but] through the [Holy] Spirit's [help], by faith anticipate and wait for the blessing and good for which our righteousness and right standing with God [our conformity to His will in purpose, thought, and action, causes us] to hope.* Let's be thankful for the blessings we have received, and with hope wait for the blessings yet to come. And come they will to those who seek to live rightly with God. Anticipate His blessings like a child anticipates a birthday gift. God's blessings are presents that help shape us to be more like Jesus. Being like Him is very, very good for us.

I'm no longer a kid, but I still love birthdays. Back in 2001 I founded ABC (August Birthday Club) with two friends, and through the years it has been fun to include other women who have August birthdays too. I had a feeling that turning forty might be a challenging year for me so I bought journals that year for my birthday friends and I began to focus on a year of joy. As passages about joy filled my journal, my life reflected that joy with expanding hope. My fortieth year was a great growth year. I was intent on seeking out joy, wherever it could be found, in both the obvious places and in challenging situations too, and in doing so my faith

270

and trust increased. I'm excited about the blessings God still has for me, no matter what my age. Each completed year is evidence of His love in my life as His Presence is the most cherished gift.

Reap a Harvest of Blessing

Galatians 6:9 NLT

OCTOBER 23

Life gets hard. We are living in a world that is upside-down, where sickness, evil, confusion and death are very present to those who follow Jesus, and to those who do not. So, at times it might feel natural to want to give up on hope. Would it not be easier to live for self, rather than to press on growing character which seeks to be conformed to the image of Jesus? Paul knew this very human temptation and he rallied his readers with this battle cry: *"So let's not get tired of doing what is good. At just the right time we will reap a harvest of blessing if we don't give up."* We may not always have control over the situation at hand, but we always have a choice of responses. Choosing to do good will bring about benefits even if at present we do not see them.

Paul lived out what he had written as he set sail on his second missionary adventure shortly after writing this letter to the Galatians. I can imagine that traveling back in the New Testament days could be very draining, yet Paul pressed on. He knew his purpose, he had good to share, and his harvest of blessings was bountiful. Father, thank You for the example we get to read about in the life of Your servant Paul. You have not only used him to share Your good news first-hand in many unique situations, but You also allowed him time, sometimes while in prison, to write letters that continue to inspire and encourage us today. May we press on in the strength that You provide in the fields that You have prepared for us. May our harvests be joyfully abundant. Amen.

Glorious Blessedness yet to Come

1 Thessalonians 2:12 AMP

OCTOBER 24

Paul's goal was to establish new churches and train people to grow up in the character of Christ. He was on the go, traveling here and there, increasing the awareness of Jesus to all who would hear. But as busy as his days got, he still took the time to further counsel and encourage those at the newly established churches through his letters. Paul was thankful for the faith of the Thessalonians and he recognized that faith, hope and love were a part of their lives. Paul then continued to build up the believers at Thessalonica: *"...live lives worthy of God, Who calls you into His own kingdom and the glorious blessedness [into which true believers will enter after Christ's return]."* Paul does not want them, or us, to forget the eternal perspective even when suffering and hard times come.

Ruth, a believer among a people group that is beginning to hearing the gospel, is a wonderful example to me of someone who chooses to live worthy in spite of real hardships. Her persecution as a follower of Jesus Christ has been from the government, from village neighbors and even from her own family. Ruth is an integral part of a team that works diligently to translate the Bible into her language. In her joyful expression of living for God, she has turned many truths of God's Story into songs. As she faithfully teaches and sings from village to village, God's Kingdom is made bigger. We were blessed to hear her sing Paul's Thessalonian letters as she strummed her guitar in her humble home during Christmas of 2007. This sister understands what Paul wrote concerning the return of Jesus. Right now she experiences joy mixed with pain, but she knows there is a blessedness that is yet to come that will be glorious.

Unmerited Favor and Blessing

1 Thessalonians 5:28 AMP

Here are a few bumper sticker exhortations from Paul: Live in peace. Warn the idle. Encourage the timid. Help the weak. Be patient. Be kind. Be joyful. Be prayerful. Be thankful. Test everything. Hold on to the good. Avoid evil. Actually those would take a pretty big bumper and it might be a bit overwhelming to try to apply all of them at once. Paul knew this and he reminded his readers that God Himself is faithful and it is God who will bring about all of these needed life changes, and then some. Deliberately living for our Heavenly Father will reshape us as we become more aware of the difference between a selfish self and a holy God. God is trustworthy to lead us as we pursue Him.

It is easy to skim over Paul's conclusion to his letter and miss the weight of it. *"The grace (the unmerited favor and blessings) of our Lord Jesus Christ (the Messiah) be with you all. Amen, (so be it)."* God, through Jesus and with the written word of Paul's letter, is offering grace, undeserved mercy, to us. Years ago I learned a helpful acronym and hopefully it helps you to also make clear this concept of grace. GRACE can be described as God's Riches At Christ's Expense. This extended grace is not free, it cost Jesus His life. Jesus chose to obediently lay down His life so we could live. May we be attentive to God's Presence, His favor and blessing in our lives today as we seek to live like Him and for Him. Our Father, as we become increasingly aware of Your goodness and Your greatness, please help us to break (put to death) our old habits that do not lead to peace, kindness, joy. I pray we would avoid evil every chance we get, and thankfully and prayerfully turn to You who have so richly blessed us with new life through Your Son Jesus. Thank You for grace. Amen.

Shine Forth the Blessings of God

2 Thessalonians 1:12 AMP

OCTOBER 26

In his second letter to the Thessalonians, Paul prays that God may find them worthy and for God to fulfill every good purpose that comes about by faith. He prays this for a reason: *"...may the name of our Lord Jesus Christ be glorified and become more glorious through and in you, and may you [also be glorified] in Him according to the grace (favor and blessing) of our God and the Lord Jesus Christ (the Messiah, the Anointed One)."* Try to imagine the name of Jesus becoming even more glorious in and through us. Now try to envision us as His children becoming glorified in Him. "Glorious" is a word that is a little hard for me to picture. It helps me when I think of it this way: May we value Jesus more highly than anything else. Let's see Him as He is: heroic, brilliant, beautiful and triumphant and then make choices in our life that lead to elevating and celebrating Him. May His renown go forward in dazzling, noble and honoring ways. As we live to enjoy Him, may all these attributes and more shine forth in us as we reflect just how glorious He is! May God find us worthy instruments, useful for His good purposes. This is no small blessing that God desires for His children.

Blessed Letter of Recommendation

Acts 18:27b-28 MSG

OCTOBER 27

Evangelistic tour number three is about to begin for Paul, but he is not the only one going forth to share the good news. In Ephesus, after getting some training from Paul's colleagues, Priscilla and Aquila, a Jew named Apollos chose to take the message of hope to the Achaia province. Before he left, *his Ephesian friends gave their blessing and wrote a letter of recommendation for him, urging the disciples there to welcome him with open arms. The welcome paid off: Apollos turned out to be a great help to those who had become believers through God's immense generosity. He was particularly effective in public debate with the Jews as he brought out proof after convincing proof from the Scriptures that Jesus was in fact God's Messiah.*

A letter of recommendation may help open the door, but it takes faithful work to keep us employed! Just where is it in your life that God wants you to work for Him? No one can do everything, but every one of us can do something. May the many examples throughout the Book of Acts inspire us to get involved and do what we can to enlarge the Kingdom of God. Sometimes this takes some training - actually, it almost always takes some kind of new training. So embrace the opportunities that come your way to grow and to give of yourself. Has God been generous to you? Apollos turned out to be a great help. We each can be a great help too.

Bless Those Who Curse

1 Corinthians 4:12 NLT

OCTOBER 28

From Ephesus, where he stayed about three years, Paul wrote lengthy letters to the struggling church in Corinth. These correspondences sought to answer questions and gave training in godliness, even if it was from a distance. Paul did not want his followers to be deceived, but to build on the foundation that is found in Jesus alone. He brought to his readers' minds how he and his team lived among them and he warned them about pride that can so easily rob God and distort reality. Paul wrote, *"We work wearily with our own hands to earn our living. We bless those who curse us. We are patient with those who abuse us."*

Making rice taffy is hard work, yet that was one of the ways Hank made a living. He was a new believer and his family lived in a minority village in China. One day Hank was in the market hawking his wares offering samples to those doing their shopping. A man took the taffy, then arrogantly spit it out all over that day's inventory. Hank had a choice to make. The old Hank would have beaten the rude man, but the new Hank did not. Later, Hank shared this experience with a group of young men who also needed to learn that blessing and patience could be lived out. Returning evil for evil didn't have to be the way. When our foundation is firmly placed on God, we have the strength and the state of mind to offer a blessing instead of cursing, to patiently put up with insults. This shows a maturity from a life trained in God. He will judge all. Frequently recalling that our identity is as a child of the King will help give us a proper perspective as we actively live in a world that desperately needs to know Him.

The Blessing of the Master

1 Corinthians 7:39 MSG

OCTOBER 29

Paul addressed some very real concerns regarding marriage and singleness, and he passed on this advice to the church in Corinth because they had written to him about these situations. After talking about marriage, singleness, separation, and about helping spouses who are not yet believers, he addressed the issue of remarrying. *"A wife must stay with her husband as long as he lives. If he dies, she is free to marry anyone she chooses. She will, of course, want to marry a believer and have the blessing of the Master."* Marriage and other deep interpersonal relationships are the challenging ways we learn and live out the story of love and commitment. May our relationships honor God. I pray we would seek the blessing of the Master upon us as we live, loving in good and appropriate ways. Amen.

Share in the Gospel's Blessings

1 Corinthians 9:23 NIV

Paul writes about what he does, how he does it and for what reasons. In each of his interactions, whether it concerns food, freedom, income, self-discipline, temptation or loyalty, he says, *"I do all this for the sake of the gospel, that I may share in its blessings."* He has counted the cost, and has found that the blessings that come from following Christ far outweigh other things that might vie for his attention and affection. Paul is all about doing everything for the praise of God. May we live life with clear purposes and ultimate goals, because in the end, what really matters most? This radically God-focused lifestyle does not come about on a whim but requires careful thought. What have we been saved from? What have we been saved for? What does "for the sake of the gospel" mean? Is the cost worth it? What do we give up and what do we take up?

With serious compassion Jesus answered some of those questions by saying, "If any of you wants to be my follower, you must turn from your selfish ways, take up your cross, and follow me." He told this to His disciples as He sent them out with power to be change-agents for good. He shared the price of this discipleship to the crowds that gathered around Him. When a man seeking Jesus' approval who thought that he had met the requirements by the law heard directly from Jesus that he needed to put Him above his own riches and take up the cross to follow Him, he calculated that the cost was too high. Even though Jesus loved this rich, young ruler, He honored the man's choice and the man walked away sad. God, today You give to us the choice to follow You or not. I pray that we would grow in our confidence through Your Word and through Your Spirit, that You are worth the cost. I pray we would embrace afresh the good news that You love us and that no matter what, You are worth following. Amen.

Cup of Blessing

1 Corinthians 10:16-17 HCSB

OCTOBER 31

There were divisions when Paul was writing to the Corinthians and the challenge of loyalty still has an effect on people today. *"The cup of blessing that we give thanks for, is it not a sharing in the blood of Christ? The bread that we break, is it not a sharing in the body of Christ? Because there is one bread, we who are many are one body, for all of us share that one bread."* Paul focused on the Lord's Supper when Jesus used the bread and wine at the meal to make reference to Himself and the new covenant that He was making. Jesus was offering unity with the Father through Him. Actions speak very loudly and show just where our allegiances are. May we be unified in Jesus and remember that His death bought for us life - new life, blessed life, a life that is connected to Him and the Father.

This was the kind of new life Russell was teaching about at Nueva Esperanza, our first church for Hispanics. He emphasized the importance of loyalty to Jesus and Ricky had a hard choice to make. He loved God yet he loved the girl he was living with too. Long story short, with proper use of church discipline and faithful teaching that the Lord's Supper was for those who were following Christ in obedience, Ricky and the whole young church were built up. Repentance led to restoration and great joy. We at New Hope saw how new hope in God changed lives. Restored hearts celebrated the cup of blessing with thankfulness as we joined to share the Lord's Supper and remember all that Jesus has done for us.

Reflections

"Blessed is the King who comes in the name of the Lord!" In October we experienced Jesus' life during Holy Week, His death for our sins, His amazing resurrection and the blessing He gave for His followers right before He returned to Heaven. Jesus changed the way life was lived. Hope and peace, due to faith in Him, could not be contained but was actively shared. Bold new leaders like Peter and Paul preached and the early church formed and grew. Paul wrote to the new churches in Galatia, Thessalonica and in Corinth.

November

Blessed to Eat What Is Served

1 Corinthians 10:29b-30 MSG

NOVEMBER 1

In Paul's straightforward way of speaking, he tells the Corinthians to worry a whole lot less about what others think and a whole lot more about what God says. *"...I'm not going to walk around on eggshells worrying about what small-minded people might say; I'm going to stride free and easy, knowing what our large-minded Master has already said. If I eat what is served to me, grateful to God for what is on the table, how can I worry about what someone will say? I thanked God for it and he blessed it!"* Paul's teaching here has to do with food that has been sacrificed to idols. I don't think we have eaten idol food, but we sure have had our share of interesting meals. Often I'm asked to describe some of the weirdest food I've eaten while serving in Asia. One dinner comes to mind. While at the village home of good friends an intriguing trio was placed on the short, round wooded table: snakes and snails and mountain cat tails. We thanked God for the meal and He blessed our time of sharing His love as we shared special food. Paul gives us all good perspective about gratefully eating what is served to us. It can be a little mind stretching and take us out of our comfort zones to eat unfamiliar food, but seeking to connect to people of different cultures may open up doors for sharing with them Jesus, the Bread of Life.

Clear Communication Is a Blessing

1 Corinthians 14:16 KJV

NOVEMBER 2

Should unfamiliar language be used to communicate public prayer in church? Paul seeks to address the issue in a letter he wrote to those seeking to worship God in Corinth. This less modern version of 1 Corinthians 14:16-17 can help us to see a little more clearly the dilemma. *"Else when thou shalt bless with the spirit, how shall he that occupieth the room of the unlearned say Amen at thy giving of thanks, seeing he understandeth not what thou sayest? For thou verily givest thanks well, but the other is not edified."*

This seems to suggest that even if what is said is good, it is hard to agree or be helped by words that are not understood. Paul goes on to "sayest" that he is thankful that he speaks in tongues but when it comes to speaking in churches, he strongly encourages people to use a language that can instruct and be understood. We are to pursue love and by communicating in understandable ways, people can be strengthened, encouraged and comforted by God's truth. Father, may we bless You with both our spirit and with our mind, being sensitive to each situation. May we seek to live out of love so that the words that come from our tongue are so much more than a clanging cymbal. Thank You God, for listening to us when we pray to You. Please continue to guide us in truth and peace. Amen.

Send Folks off with a Blessing

1 Corinthians 16:10-11 NLT

NOVEMBER 3

The final greetings in this letter to the Corinthian church are tender and personal. Paul cares deeply about this gathering of people and wants them to be courageous in their faith and loving in their actions. He desires that people live with respect for each other, honoring others who are committed to the Kingdom's expansion. *"When Timothy comes, don't intimidate him. He is doing the Lord's work, just as I am. Don't let anyone treat him with contempt. Send him on his way with your blessing when he returns to me. I expect him to come with the other believers."* Even over an expansive distance, life is still best lived in the closeness of community. Love those around you and greet others as they travel through; be blessed and be a blessing.

Hospitality is not a southern thing; it's a biblical principle. I resolved in 2005 to live out the truths in a part of Paul's letter he wrote to those in Rome. "Practice hospitality" was one of those truths. Like other skills that we practice, we can grow to get better at them, even if it does not come natural at first. To help me be more concrete in this goal I began a Hospitality Notebook. How blessed I am to read through pages of visitors and to think back on the times we shared, some just over night and other stays more lengthy. I asked our guests to write down where they were coming from, where they were heading and something I could pray for them. Opening our home, no matter where it happens to be blesses our family because we learn more about people and the world from those traveling through it. And when the time comes to say good-bye, we aim to send the sojourners on their way with a blessing.

There will come a time when there will be no more traveling; all in the family of God will be safely home. Distance, time and language will no longer separate us. Nothing can separate those who are in God's family from the love of God that is in Christ Jesus our Lord, and one day all believers will be united again. What a wonderful family reunion that will be!

May the God of All Comfort Bless You

2 Corinthians 1:3-5 ESV

NOVEMBER 4

Paul writes a tribute to a wonderful God as he begins another correspondence to his friends living in Corinth. *"Blessed be the God and Father of our Lord Jesus Christ, the Father of mercies and God of all comfort, who comforts us in all our affliction, so that we may be able to comfort those who are in any affliction, with the comfort with which we ourselves are comforted by God."* Our God really is the God of all comfort and I am so very thankful that He is. Praise to Him who gives generously to us in our need, and fills us up so that we can give likewise. Paul then writes: "For as we share abundantly in Christ's sufferings, so through Christ we share abundantly in comfort too." Do not read this last bit too hastily. What does it mean to "share abundantly in Christ's sufferings"? I want the abundant comfort part, but do I have to go through the abundant suffering to get it? That is not an easy teaching.

It is so good to know that when we suffer we do not experience it alone. God is there with us and He knows how to provide comfort for our souls. At age forty-eight God saw fit for me to experience my first broken bones and after surgery, my first time to have stitches. Up until then, I thought I had compassion for people who suffered in these ways, but when I actually went through the pain, things changed. I changed. I see more depth in Scripture about pain and comfort and our need to draw near to God in times of suffering. My prayers for others who go through long painful healing now have more heart. And, through the experience, my awareness of what Jesus suffered for me has become more vivid. Suffering is just pain unless we use that time of suffering to draw ourselves near to God who is near us all the time. When we experience how God has comforted us through the suffering, we can offer meaningful comfort to others. This is yet another way of blessing.

Blessings Granted Due to Prayer

2 Corinthians 1:11 ESV

NOVEMBER 5

Living life connected to God is an individual decision and it involves the efforts and support of whole communities. If it takes a village to raise a kid, how much more does it take to raise and spread the concepts of living purposeful God-centered lives throughout the world? Paul, once again traveling, wrote his final letter to the Corinthians. He let them know how recent near-death experiences he and his team faced in Asia highlighted their need to rely on God and not on their own strength. He urged the Corinthian believers to be involved with his life and ministry by praying. *You also must help us by prayer, so that many will give thanks on our behalf for the blessing granted us through the prayers of many.* Prayer - connection to God, is essential and can be experienced corporately when the Body of

God lifts up the needs of the people of God. That way, everyone gets to celebrate God's blessings as He provides.

I'm so thankful to so many people who, with the desire to know Him and make Him known, have faithfully helped us by praying to God for various needs. As I write this, Russell is leading a mission trip to Brazil. As you read this please take the time to thank God for lives that are changed by people who are willing to go and share His goodness. We all personally know people we can pray for as they serve God in various roles, seeking to expand His Kingdom. May we praise God for everyone who will be around His throne - answers to our collective prayers. God blesses our partnership in prayer, in more ways than we could ever understand.

Double Blessings; Double Visits
2 Corinthians 1:13-16 NLT

NOVEMBER 6

Good visits can really be a blessing. We look forward to re-connecting with those we love, as God allows our paths to intersect, but sometimes the best laid plans still do not come about. Paul really wanted to go to Corinth so he could spend time with his friends there but seeing everyone face to face was impossible. His letters would have to do. *Our letters have been straightforward, and there is nothing written between the lines and nothing you can't understand. I hope someday you will fully understand us, even if you don't understand us now. Then on the day when the Lord Jesus returns, you will be proud of us in the same way we are proud of you. Since I was so sure of your understanding and trust, I wanted to give you a double blessing by visiting you twice—first on my way to Macedonia and again when I returned from Macedonia. Then you could send me on my way to Judea.*

Paul and his friends missed out on this double blessing of double visits and that makes me sad. But we can be thankful for Paul's many written correspondences. So much wisdom can be gained by reading and studying the letters he wrote to various churches, and let's encourage one another to apply the truth to our lives. God, help us not get distracted by specific issues meant for a certain time or place, but let us see Your timeless truths recorded for us in Paul's letters. Paul reminds us that our Lord Jesus is returning; let's live faithfully and expectantly for His return. Amen.

God's Abundant Blessings

2 Corinthians 9:8-11 NIV

NOVEMBER 7

And God is able to bless you abundantly... Paul could have stopped his sentence here and it would have been more than enough for us to know and believe that God is able, and that His blessings are abundant, and that He aims those abundant blessings our way. But Paul continues on *...so that in all things at all times, having all that you need, you will abound in every good work. As it is written: "They have freely scattered their gifts to the poor; their righteousness endures forever." Now he who supplies seed to the sower and bread for food will also supply and increase your store of seed and will enlarge the harvest of your righteousness. You will be enriched in every way so that you can be generous on every occasion, and through us your generosity will result in thanksgiving to God.*

May faith increase and lead us to obedient generosity. Generosity flows from our awareness and thankfulness to God who bountifully blesses us with all that we need. A close friend shared with us what he calls OHSP, which stands for open-handed stewardship policy. Allowing the blessings of God to flow through us and to others, pleases God. God, thank You for the many ways that You have enriched our lives. May we look for ways to be generous to people You place in our paths. Amen.

God Is Blessed Forever
and He Knows Our Hearts

2 Corinthians 11:30-31 ESV

NOVEMBER 8

"If I must boast, I will boast of the things that show my weakness. The God and Father of the Lord Jesus, he who is blessed forever, knows that I am not lying." Our Father God is undeniably eternally blessed. He knows our desires, our plans and our motives so there is no benefit in lying. I pray that boasting would come from our lips - the boasting that shows that Jesus is strong and able to provide just what is needed. We are dependent on Him. When we are weak, He is strong. Paul continued his letter and shared that God gave him a thorn in his flesh and he pleaded with the Lord to remove it. Paul wrote that Christ's power rests upon him when he is weak. As I have matured in my response to my migraines (or any other type of physical pain), I have even grown to be thankful for the disability. Don't get me wrong, I don't like pain, but similar to what Paul experienced, I have found that when I am weak, then I am strong. The strength doesn't come from me but from the Lord. All blessing, honor and praise and boasting to Him!

By-the-way, it was not long after Paul wrote this letter that he was able to pay the Corinthians a visit, just as he had hoped for earlier! It is such an encouragement to me to see how prayers are indeed answered. God's timing and our timing are not always in the same time zone and it was that way for Paul too.

Blessed to Choose Wisely

Romans 1:24-25 ESV

NOVEMBER 9

While Paul was visiting his friends in Corinth he wrote to the loved-by-God ones in Rome and introduced himself and explained more of the gospel. He had hopes to visit them in person so he wasted no time and declared that since the beginning of time, God has made His divine nature known so that there is no excuse for rejecting God. The godlessness and wickedness of mankind will be judged. *Therefore God gave them up in the lusts of their hearts to impurity, to the dishonoring of their bodies among themselves, because they exchanged the truth about God for a lie and worshiped and served the creature rather than the Creator, who is blessed forever! Amen.*

Erroneous thinking that exchanges the truth about God for a lie goes as far back as the Garden of Eden. From that lie, mankind has added many other lies that have become even more distorted, and in doing so have turned away from God to worship His creation. When we come to the point when we really believe that God will be blessed forever, our thinking and our actions change. God will remain. In this world we have choices to make. Choosing to live outside of God's truth has consequences both now and into eternity. It has always been that way. Heeding Paul's warning is a good choice. Please do not trade the truth for a lie.

Sins Are Covered; We Are Blessed!

Romans 4:6-7 HCSB

NOVEMBER 10

Paul wrote about the great joy and delight that awaits those who have been rescued - those who have received forgiveness of their sins, and he wanted to make it clear that the redemption that takes place is by faith and not by works. As he made his point to his readers in Rome, he brought up the fact that King David celebrated this same truth. *"Likewise, David also speaks of the blessing of the man God credits righteousness to apart from works: How joyful are those whose lawless acts are forgiven and whose sins are covered!"* All who have asked for forgiveness from God the Father through Jesus are blessed! We are then free to work, serve, and live in joy trusting that our sins are covered. Jesus covered all our sins with his blood - shed for mankind at Calvary, a real place outside of Jerusalem where His crucifixion occurred. Every blessing beyond what Jesus did for us on the cross is blessing upon blessing.

When the first SD believer understood the goodness of a loving, forgiving, holy God, he was amazed at God's generosity. But he could not fathom that redemption was a gift. Instead he wanted to do something to pay God back. He asked us, "What does God like? Does He want fruit? Rice? Meat?" Grace, apart from works, was explained with more clarity. God does not want or need food from us; He is the One who blesses His children with all that we need. Greater awe, joy and gratitude flowed from a forgiven heart that humbly accepted God's blessings. May we never lose our admiration of God who is worthy of all our praise. Are we joyful today because our lawless acts are forgiven? We who trust in Jesus have our sins covered! May joy and praise abound.

Blessed Happiness for the Forgiven
Romans 4:7-10 AMP

NOVEMBER 11

It is true that there is forgiveness of sins through Jesus, and Paul writes more about this in his letter aimed at both the Greeks and the Jews who made up the church in Rome. Paul explained that even those who do not share the same genealogical heritage as the Israelites were included in this great blessing that God offers to everyone. *Blessed and happy and to be envied are those whose iniquities are forgiven and whose sins are covered up and completely buried. Blessed and happy and to be envied is the person of whose sin the Lord will take no account nor reckon it against him. Is this blessing (happiness) then meant only for the circumcised, or also for the uncircumcised?* Good question, and the answer is found in the truth that this blessedness comes through faith alone. How do we achieve God's standards of righteousness? By faith. By faith like Abraham's. Righteousness is gained by faith.

Abraham was the father of the promise that God would bless all nations when those nations placed their faith, trust, belief in Him. Today, we are part of the "all nations". Do we trust Him today? Relationship is so much more than a one-time belief that took place at some point in the past. A relationship with God is a growing process where joy and blessing increase as we place our confidence in God in each new situation. Paul experienced the joy that his sins were forgiven. He knew God's Story when he quoted these passages from what David wrote in Psalm 32:1-2. He is excited and wants everyone to know this extremely good good news! There are a lot of pages to read between the Book of Psalms and Paul's letter to the Romans, and God's theme of blessing shows up over and over again. His invitation is extended to all generations and all nationalities. God's Story of blessings is the best!

God Is over All; Forever Blessed

Romans 9:5 ESV

NOVEMBER 12

Life is complicated. The Bible, God's Story from the beginning of life and His guidelines for how to live a blessed life, is complex but simple. Think about all the lives that have lived through the Old Testament up to the New Testament and every generation that has lived since. Mankind needs help. Right after he wrote a huge assurance that nothing at all can separate us from the love of God that is in Jesus, Paul shared something personal. Professional religious people, like Paul used to be, gave him great anguish. They didn't yet trust in Jesus as the Giver of the help they needed. Paul spoke to the people of Israel and said, *"To them belong the patriarchs, and from their race, according to the flesh, is the Christ, who is God over all, blessed forever. Amen."* Thanks be to God for His mercy that allows any of us to be adopted by Him. May the people of Israel not reject but wholeheartedly embrace God's provision through His Son Jesus. May all who have breath acknowledge that He will be blessed forever. In the complexity of life, how good it is to reflect on the simple, yet profound, truth that Jesus loves me, Jesus loves you.

God Blesses All Who Call on Him

Romans 10:12-13 NIV

NOVEMBER 13

One of my favorite T-shirts from Thailand says "same-same" on the front and "but different" on the back, a phrase that can often be heard by Thais as they describe something that is similar but not really the same. Paul could have used "different-different, but same" when he wanted to get his point across about people. There are differences between languages, cultures, customs, preferences, social status and physical appearance. But when it comes down to who we are as people created in the image of God, we are very much the same. *For there is no difference between Jew and Gentile—the same Lord is Lord of all and richly blesses all who call on him, for, "Everyone who calls on the name of the Lord will be saved."* Paul quoted what prophets of old had written.

Each one of us has the same need and that is to call out for Jesus to rescue us. This need was throughout history and this need is throughout our world today. It is beyond understanding to know the depths of just how richly He blesses everyone who relies on Him for redemption. Here's the deal: if you are saved you are blessed. A drowning man would take that deal, so how much more blessed is it to be rescued from the everlasting penalty of our sins? Jesus, You are our Rescuer, our Redeemer, and our Savior. We have a great need to be reconciled with God the Father and it is through You that we can have this peace that goes beyond all understanding. Nothing we have done is too bad for Your grace to cover, and nothing we will ever do is good enough to earn our way into a relationship with You. What must we do to be saved? Call on the One God has provided. Thank You Jesus for answering that call. Amen.

Don't Stumble over Blessings

Romans 11:9-10 NLT

A lawyerly tone is used by Paul in the middle of his letter to the people he hopes to meet in Rome. He doesn't argue for law or for deeds but for everyone to embrace God's grace. Passages from Deuteronomy, Isaiah and the Psalms give weight to his position. Paul built his case to show the history of the hard-heartedness of human beings and included a quote from King David: *"Let their bountiful table become a snare, a trap that makes them think all is well. Let their blessings cause them to stumble, and let them get what they deserve. Let their eyes go blind so they cannot see, and let their backs be bent forever."* Paul didn't bring this up to condemn the people who were still stuck in a trap regarding their thinking about the law and grace, but he wrote to offer hope and deliverance. May we never lose sight of the truth that every blessing is a gift from God. If we think our plenty comes from what we have earned, we too are like a snared animal. Instead, let's live in the freedom that comes freely to us from the One who paid a great price.

The Whole World Can Share God's Blessings

Romans 11:11-12 NLT

NOVEMBER 15

The "grace vs. law" debate continued and like all good lawyers, Paul did not ask a question that he didn't already have an answer to. Paul followed up his line of reasoning about the Israelites trusting in self rather than God, by asking, *"Did God's people stumble and fall beyond recovery? Of course not! They were disobedient, so God made salvation available to the Gentiles. But he wanted his own people to become jealous and claim it for themselves. Now if the Gentiles were enriched because the people of Israel turned down God's offer of salvation, think how much greater a blessing the world will share when they finally accept it."* The world is in for a great blessing when everyone accepts the goodness of God's offer of salvation. Just picture what it could be like if everyone loved God and loved people. If that is not our present reality, let's not give up hope! Instead, let's do our part by sharing and showing how we have been blessed and by repeatedly saying, "yes" to God's invitation to work with Him for the good of the world.

God Is the Root of All Blessings

Romans 11:17 NLT

NOVEMBER 16

Good communicators use relevant and relatable illustrations to better emphasize and clarify the concept they are trying to express. To get his next point across, Paul chose to paint the picture of tree grafting. The stem of one plant would be cut and then another cut stem would be bound to it so that the two sets may be joined to grow together from one root system. He wanted both Jews and Gentiles to know that every person could receive the blessings of God. *But some of these branches from Abraham's tree—some of the people of Israel—have been broken off. And you Gentiles, who were branches from a wild olive tree, have been grafted in. So now you also receive the blessing God has promised Abraham and his children, sharing in the rich nourishment from the root of God's special olive tree.*

Before moving back to the US, I went to the Sunday Walking Market in Chiang Mai for the last time. It was the summer of 2011. Scented candles, fresh roasting meat, the sound of ancient instruments and displays of creative art were some of the things I knew I would miss, so I walked slowly, taking it all in. I found the lady who had sold me colorful stone braided necklaces in the past, and I purchased six more. This blessed her. And it began my prayer to God to please give me new friends. I was about to move to a big city that I had never lived in before and our new nest would be empty, like in our first year of marriage. I was in a reflective mood and thought back to years earlier when our young family moved to a village on the edge of a Chinese town; we felt like outsiders. Over time though, relationships were formed and we began to be invited to festivals, marriages and funerals. We were grafted into their community, and eventually praise songs were written by villagers who became grafted into God's family through faith in Jesus. God had been faithful then to provide community (and He had done that for us with several moves) but would He provide for us in Houston too? Christmas came around for the second time after leaving our life in Asia, and I excitedly shared the story of God's goodness as I gave those necklaces to five women rejoicing with each how God had answered my prayers through them. The sixth necklace I wear as a reminder of God's blessings. May we never forget that God does not want there to be outsiders, but for everyone to be brought into His family, to be grafted in and share in the blessings of His rooted love!

Pray God's Blessings on Those Who Make Life Hard for You

Romans 12:14 NLT

NOVEMBER 17

Some concepts in God's Story are difficult to understand. Other concepts however are difficult to really do. I think that Romans 12:14 is not so much hard to comprehend, but very challenging to actually put into action. *Bless those who persecute you. Don't curse them; pray that God will bless them.* Not only are we to pour out happiness on those who harass us and treat us unjustly, but Paul tells us to talk to God about these people, asking Him to show them favor too. When we can do this, we get a better grasp on the forgiveness He has extended to us. So here are some ideas for practicing this good principle. When road rage strikes, try praying out loud in your car for the other driver instead of motioning a curse. If your boss or a co-worker or a teacher is demanding, take their names before God's throne as you walk into work or school, and especially before any specific meeting. Rudeness may be on the rise, but we as God's children do not need to swim in that same easy current. By staying close to God we can overcome and respond with sincere kindness.

When I was learning the Thai language, my first school closed down so I needed to switch schools. I found the new school's director very challenging to connect with and condescending toward my language goals and progress. I wanted to avoid him, so during my breaks, I walked laps around the block and would sometimes cry. While feeling sorry for myself in my less than supportive environment, God prompted me to pray for the school's administration and for its teachers. This simple act of obedience increased my closeness to God, and He helped me to see that there was more going on at the school that needed my prayer. Day-by-day, I began building deeper relationships with the Thai teachers, getting to better know them as individuals and I continued to pray for the director. Learning Thai was my main objective, but God did not want me to curse those who were making it extra difficult, but to bless them by praying and by caring. There are lots of ways we can put into practice Paul's admonishment to pray rather than to curse. People need changing and we are all people. God is the One who changes people best; let Him start with us and see how He opens up the opportunities for us to then compassionately love others, even those who persecute us.

A Clean Conscience Is a Wonderful Blessing

Romans 14:22 NLT

NOVEMBER 18

You may believe there's nothing wrong with what you are doing, but keep it between yourself and God. Blessed are those who don't feel guilty for doing something they have decided is right. This advice from Paul requires us to be mature as we relate to God and other believers. Paul is not giving a blank slate go-ahead to do whatever feels good, but instead he reminds us that God - not you or me, is the Judge of us and of others. It is best for us to take the time that is needed to know why we do (or don't do) what we do. Going forward with our thoughts and activities, being thankful to God for them, and not hurting others along the way, is a good indication that we have made a decent decision. A clean conscience is a wonderful blessing.

We Are Blessed Physically, Relationally and Spiritually

Romans 15:27-29 ESV

NOVEMBER 19

This is Paul's longest letter and maybe his most important one. In modern days, we type and can quickly edit what we've written. But try to picture Paul writing with pen and ink on an scroll using materials that would have been expensive and challenging to get from one person to another. It was quite a process and it is amazing how his words have been preserved for all these years. In his conclusion to his letter to the Romans, Paul lets them know that he wants to visit them when he takes a trip to Spain. But his immediate destination is Jerusalem because the Gentile believers in the Macedonian area have collected money to help the poor in Jerusalem and Paul would personally deliver it. Talking about the offering Paul adds, *"For they were pleased to do it, and indeed they owe it to them. For if the Gentiles have come to share in their spiritual blessings, they ought also to be of service to them in material blessings. When therefore I have completed this and have delivered to them what has been collected, I will leave for Spain by way of you. I know that when I come to you I will come in the fullness of the blessing of Christ."*

Mankind has spiritual needs, physical needs and relational needs. God is the One who designed us, and He is very aware of our needs. Jesus, during His Sermon on the Mount, taught His followers how to pray, and it is interesting that these three distinct areas come up in that model prayer. Our daily bread represents our physical needs. The need we have for two-way forgiveness reminds us that we depend on God for our relationship needs, to get along in healthy ways with people. Our spiritual needs are explained by the request for protection from temptation and the evil one. As we live and communicate with God in prayer, our ability to rely on His goodness grows. We become less egocentric and we can stop seeking to have our needs met in lesser ways. God filled Paul and used him to help provide what was lacking in the lives of many; may we be open and obedient to be filled and then used as well. Let's be thankful to God for our blessings and pray, as we pay it forward, so others too will know His goodness.

Blessed to Run with Joy

Acts 20:24 AMP

NOVEMBER 20

Back in 490 B.C., Greece came under serious attack by the Persian Empire and a great runner named Phidippides saved the day in the thriving influential city of Athens. Long story made short, the outcome also gave birth to the first marathon. About 550 years later, Paul was about to set sail from that part of the world, carrying a financial gift for the needy in Jerusalem. When he learned that the Jewish religious leaders in Syria were plotting to take his life he took the long way around. Instead of sailing the direct route he was able to reconnect with believers at various places along the coast of the Aegean Sea. As Paul trekked great distances, he strengthened and challenged new Christians with his teachings. Knowing the danger ahead of him, Paul shared with his Ephesian friends who met him along the way: *"But none of these things move me; neither do I esteem my life dear to myself, if only I may finish my course with joy and the ministry which I have obtained from [which was entrusted to me by] the Lord Jesus, faithfully to attest to the good news (Gospel) of God's grace (His unmerited favor, spiritual blessing, and mercy)."*

Phidippides ran his course and Athens was saved. I wonder if Paul thought about him as he pressed on with his course. Scottish athlete and devoted missionary to China Eric Liddell once said, "I believe God made me for a purpose, but He also made me fast! And when I run I feel His pleasure." God did not make me fast, but I sure do feel His pleasure when I run. I had been running for over twenty-five years when I ran my first and (to date) only marathon in northern Thailand. The center of Chiang Mai's ancient walled city was lit with lanterns and the minty smell of muscle cream filled the cool air. The stillness was broken by a sound like distant thunder: running shoes hitting the road. It was the start of my forty-two-kilometer course and excitement surged through all that was me. My feet went forward as the sun rose and God brought people to my mind to pray for as I ran. Family and friends cheered me on and I thought about how God's Word says we are to encourage one another to run the good race. I felt God's pleasure in a breeze and smiled, remembering Eric Liddell and how he faithfully lived his life. When the run became hard, Isaiah came alongside me, helping me keep pace. Sophie carried my iPod shuffle when that burden became too great for me to bear. Knowing the end was near, Russell joined us on the brick road calling out cadence to finish strong. Hannah's finish-line hug began the celebration; I had completed the race!

God, we all have different races to run and I pray that each of us would be strengthened by You to finish our course with joy. This takes intentional focus on You no matter what challenges lie ahead of us. May our story be faithful to Your Story as we live out the life You have blessed us with. Amen.

More Blessed to Give Than to Receive

Acts 20:35 ESV

NOVEMBER 21

The Ephesian believers wept as Paul departed because they knew they would not see him alive again. But Paul encouraged them and reminded them that it is all worth it when you live for what is right. Paul's words to them also give us inspiration: *"In all things I have shown you that by working hard in this way we must help the weak and remember the words of the Lord Jesus, how he himself said, 'It is more blessed to give than to receive.'"* It is so good to reflect on the life and words of Jesus; He gives proper perspective in the face of trials. I'm glad that Luke, who had been traveling with Paul and penned Acts, took the time to jot down this quote of Jesus. It gives us another thing to ponder about Jesus along with all that had already been written about Him by Luke and the other three Gospel writers. All the books in the world could not contain the full life of Jesus. Paul made other encouraging visits along the way, and then he pressed on to Jerusalem. Do we believe it is more blessed to give than to receive? Our actions will testify to our beliefs. When we bless those who cannot pay us back, we are choosing to live out the teachings of Jesus during our lifetime. There are so many ways to help the weak. How does Jesus want to use us today?

Blessing and Peace from God

Colossians 1:2 AMP

NOVEMBER 22

Well, Paul did make it to Rome, but not in the timeframe or along the route he had planned. While he was in Jerusalem the crowds tried to kill him and then Paul was arrested but was allowed to give his testimony about how Jesus changed his life. This led to a two-year imprisonment in Jerusalem. During his time in prison as he awaited trial, several prominent leaders heard the gospel from Paul. Paul appealed to Caesar and so he was sent to Rome and survived a shipwreck along the way. He lived under house arrest in Rome for another two years. These days, weeks and months were not wasted in self-pity, but lived with purpose. Paul empowered the believers in Rome and also served the Lord by writing letters.

Four of these wisdom-filled letters written during this time are included in the New Testament. Believers who lived in a heavily pagan-influenced area benefitted greatly when they received one of Paul's letters. *To the saints (the consecrated people of God) and believing and faithful brethren in Christ who are at Colossae: Grace (spiritual favor and blessing) to you and [heart] peace from God our Father.* The best way to share blessings and peace with others is to do so out of a heart that is filled with God's grace and peace. Paul was able to authentically offer grace and peace for he had contentment in less-than-best living conditions. His life is a good example for us. Let's not wait until the situation is just right to live the abundant life that Jesus offers.

It was also during his Roman imprisonment that Paul wrote to his friend Philemon and we get to read that letter a little later in God's Story. Tucked into the letter that Philemon received was a jewel of wise counsel. Paul said that as we share our faith, we will gain a full understanding of every good thing we have in Jesus. Let us share, and not stockpile, the good that we have, because when we do so, our understanding of this good makes more sense to us. May it lead us to be appreciative and to generously offer grace and peace to others.

Knit Together in Love and Blessing
Colossians 2:2 AMP

NOVEMBER 23

Be encouraged in faith, united in love and really unpack the treasures of wisdom that are hidden in Christ. That is what Paul desires for those who are growing in Christian maturity. The Amplified Bible expounds on this idea wonderfully: *[For my concern is] that their hearts may be braced (comforted, cheered, and encouraged) as they are knit together in love, that they may come to have all the abounding wealth and blessings of assured conviction of understanding, and that they may become progressively more intimately acquainted with and may know more definitely and accurately and thoroughly that mystic secret of God, [which is] Christ (the Anointed One).*

When we first moved to China, I saw knitters everywhere. Some were old ladies or young girls, some sat in small shops, others were squatting along the edge of the road, and some looked like they were sleeping but their hands were busy working a wide spectrum of yarn colors, knitting them into all sorts of practical items. Even though people have tried to teach me, I do not know how to knit. I am in awe of how a ball of yarn put onto two needles clinking next to each other produces a brilliantly creative and useful outcome. That is the picture of how we are to be as we develop in the process of loving God and loving people. Loving well, like knitting, requires training and skill, and it might come more naturally to some people than to others. But we all increase our ability to love (or knit) the more we practice. May this love of ours expand and never come unraveled.

Chained Blessings from Paul

Colossians 4:18 AMP

NOVEMBER 24

Many important points were made clear in Paul's short letter to the Colossians, including the truth that Jesus is supreme above all and that He should be the focus of our lives. An embrace of those facts will shape our relationship with Him and with people. Connecting with others in honest ways about both the good and the trying situations can be a great place to start to share God's faithfulness and care. Paul did this as he signed his letter: *I, Paul, [add this final] greeting, writing with my own hand. Remember I am still in prison and in chains. May grace (God's unmerited favor and blessing) be with you! Amen (so be it).* Paul did not gloss over the fact that he was in prison, and it was from that position that he wrote about God's grace. He was experiencing the goodness of grace and he wanted others to participate in God's blessing. When we correspond with people, may we ask for God's blessing and favor to be upon those who receive our letters. Blessings are a good thing to share! I love how Proverbs 25:25 communicates this idea in an easy-to-picture way. It says that good news from a distant land is like the blessing of cold water when you have a parched throat. Paul knew how to quench the thirst of others and he was good at offering Jesus who is Living Water for our souls, for our very lives.

God's Best; Christ's Blessings

Philemon 1:1-3 MSG

I, Paul, am a prisoner for the sake of Christ, here with my brother Timothy. I write this letter to you, Philemon, my good friend and companion in this work—also to our sister Apphia, to Archippus, a real trooper, and to the church that meets in your house. God's best to you! Christ's blessings on you! With a greeting like that, don't you want to dive right into the rest of the letter? That's what Paul hoped since the news he was sharing challenged his friend Philemon to make a choice. At stake was reconciliation and restoration with a person who had wronged Philemon in the past. So why is this letter addressed to so many people in addition to Philemon, and why do we get access to it now so many years after it was written?

I believe that we seldom make a big decision that does not significantly affect others in our community. Paul wanted God's Kingdom to expand in Philemon's life and also within everyone who met in his house church so that the whole community would be more like Jesus and be blessed. The strong argument that Paul makes is based on Christ's love and forgiveness. We as followers of Jesus should also seek to live out the godly principles of reconciliation and restoration. Regardless of the way the world would handle a situation or how our feelings might dictate, it is wise to consider what Jesus would want us to do. Philemon had been blessed not just to be blessed but also to be a blessing. Likewise our blessings should not end with us, they should extend to others.

Adopted and Blessed

Ephesians 1:3-6 ESV

The opening salutation of Paul's letter to his dear friends who lived in Ephesus is rich in blessings. He wanted them to be refreshed and to stop and think about some very good news. *Blessed be the God and Father of our Lord Jesus Christ, who has blessed us in Christ with every spiritual blessing in the heavenly places, even as he chose us in him before the foundation of the world, that we should be holy and blameless before him. In love he predestined us for adoption as sons through Jesus Christ, according to the purpose of his will, to the praise of his glorious grace, with which he has blessed us in the Beloved.* God is to be blessed for He has remarkably blessed us. And how has He blessed us? He has given us every spiritual blessing in the Heavenly realm. That is definitely a lot to take in. So Paul clarifies a bit by saying, "Be happy, be blessed." We are adopted by the Father of it all. This is all possible through Jesus who is treasured by God. We too are treasured; Praise God! We are adopted and loved and have the opportunity to grow up and be like our new Daddy.

Is being holy and blameless our goal? If our desire is to grow in maturity, it should be. If you need a little coaching, get it. Be enthusiastic in your pursuit for Christ-likeness, and do so knowing you are blessed! Years before Paul wrote this letter, Jesus taught His followers on a mountain what it meant to live a blessed life. In the middle of His sermon Jesus said we are to be perfect as our Heavenly Father is perfect. This "perfect" in the Greek language is teleios, which means mature or full-grown, having arrived at a set goal. We are blessed and equipped to be whole because this is God's plan for us. We can thwart that plan, however. The world offers a wide highway to travel on, but those who choose to go through the narrow gate, the way of proactively dying to selfishness in order to grow in godly maturity, are blessed beyond measure.

Promise of Blessings

Ephesians 3:6 NLT

NOVEMBER 27

Halfway through the letter to his Gentile friends in Ephesus, Paul emphasized that all people can become children of God. The word is spreading that both Israelites and non-Israelites could be connected to God, just as God said it would be when He gave the promise to Abraham. The gospel is for everyone! *And this is God's plan: Both Gentiles and Jews who believe the Good News share equally in the riches inherited by God's children. Both are part of the same body, and both enjoy the promise of blessings because they belong to Christ Jesus.*

No matter what our background is, we all can be adopted into the blended family of God! One is not born into God's family because they have parents or grandparents who go to church. We see in God's Story that the way into His family is through an individual belief in the good news that Jesus is the Way, the Truth, and the Life. No one comes to the Father except through belief in His Son who died on our behalf so that our sins can be forgiven. A great exchange takes place: Jesus removes our sins from us and we inherit His riches offered through the Father's grace. Our bad gone and His good given! Everyone can belong. There are no limits due to family history, location, status, or even poor personal choices. God extends His adoption plan to everyone and He often uses His children to share with others His plan. Belonging to Jesus is a blessing we can be happy about.

Bless with Your Mouth

Ephesians 4:29 AMP

NOVEMBER 28

Let no foul or polluting language, nor evil word nor unwholesome or worthless talk [ever] come out of your mouth, but only such [speech] as is good and beneficial to the spiritual progress of others, as is fitting to the need and the occasion, that it may be a blessing and give grace (God's favor) to those who hear it. What we say says a lot about us as individuals and the team that we support. God wants His team to use words that actually edify and bless those we are talking with. But this takes intentional speech therapy. Total immersion in the language and culture is the best way to learn a foreign language. If wholesome speech is not currently flowing from us, we can consider a detox from movies, books and social settings where foul language runs rampant. Instead, let's seek to put ourselves in environments where we can hear, read and practice speaking the language of Heaven.

Don't get discouraged if this new language doesn't come naturally overnight. It takes time to replace our polluted ways of thinking and talking with fresh and beneficial speech. But it is worth it. The Book of Proverbs gives lots of training tips, and so does Paul's letter to the Philippians. He advises us to think about things that are pure and noble and praiseworthy. When Peter, a good friend of Jesus, wrote about following in His steps, he said that no deceit was found in Jesus' mouth. If we want to love life and see good days we must keep our tongue from evil and our lips from unwholesome speech. James, another New Testament contributor, offered useful guidance on the subject of how to talk in ways that build up. We are blessed as we are used by God to relay wisdom in our speech during every occasion. God, help us to be a part of the blessing. May we be vocally thankful to be on Your team, to live as a member of Your family. Help us to speak the language of love. Amen.

Rejoice Again with Blessings

Philippians 1:2 AMP

NOVEMBER 29

The "rejoice again letter" was Paul's fourth prison correspondence. His joy was not that he would soon be released, but his rejoicing came through knowing, loving and serving the risen Lord. He began his letter with a blessing to the Christians in Philippi. *Grace (favor and blessing) to you and [heart] peace from God our Father and the Lord Jesus Christ (the Messiah).* From there he addressed selfless living, and being an active example of peace and forgiveness. How is peace and forgiveness lived out in the day-to-day of life? The year before Hannah graduated high school, Russell taught our house church practical advice from Paul's letter to the Philippians. He then wrote a booklet, *Joy Beyond Anxiety: The Philippians' Peace*, and a copy was given as a gift to each of Hannah's fellow graduates. On page forty he challenges us not to grab for control and start being anxious when we sense we need something, but instead: 1) Reflect with gratitude on the goodness of God. 2) Tell God what is going on (pray). 3) Ask for the help you feel you need.

May we learn that it is good to slow down and allow the assurance that God cares to fill us. He will provide all that we need to grow into the image of His Son. May this good news calm our racing minds. Then the peace of God will be with us: His favor, His heart-peace, His blessing.

Blessings Given Lead to Blessings Returned

Philippians 4:15-17 MSG

NOVEMBER 30

Paul has a good relationship with the church in Philippi. They were excited about giving generously and increasing God's Kingdom, and Paul did not want those brothers and sisters to lose that joy. *"You Philippians well know, and you can be sure I'll never forget it, that when I first left Macedonia province, venturing out with the Message, not one church helped out in the give-and-take of this work except you. You were the only one. Even while I was in Thessalonica, you helped out—and not only once, but twice. Not that I'm looking for handouts, but I do want you to experience the blessing that issues from generosity."* Blessings given are often blessings returned. I hope we don't get tired of the idea that we are blessed to be a blessing. It continues to be a major theme in God's Story. Let's not miss out on His goodness!

Reflections

Paul's Christian life was far from boring! In November we joined him as he continued on in his adventurous journeys of sharing God's good news message to all who would listen. When trouble comes his way and he is thwarted from travel he used the opportunity to connect meaningfully by writing letters. We now are privileged to read the blessings of God through Jesus that he originally penned to believers in Corinth, Rome, Colossae, to a friend named Philemon, and to gatherings of dear friends in Ephesus and Philippi.

December

Blessed to Live by God's Guidelines

1 Timothy 1:8-11 ESV

DECEMBER 1

Timothy was a young leader who Paul treated like a son. So Paul offered Timothy good training: *"Now we know that the law is good, if one uses it lawfully, understanding this, that the law is not laid down for the just but for the lawless and disobedient, for the ungodly and sinners, for the unholy and profane, for those who strike their fathers and mothers, for murderers, the sexually immoral, men who practice homosexuality, enslavers, liars, perjurers, and whatever else is contrary to sound doctrine, in accordance with the gospel of the glory of the blessed God with which I have been entrusted."* That is a lot to take in. But basically Paul is saying that there is a big difference between the lawless and their activities and a holy God. Living ethically is a blessing to those who practice integrity and to everyone else in society. God can change a chief of sinners into an ambassador for Jesus. The gospel transforms lives and God's Story provides guidelines for character growth. We serve a blessed God, and He wants us to live a blessed life as His children.

God is Our Blessed and Only Sovereign

1 Timothy 6:15b-16 HCSB

DECEMBER 2

At the close of a very constructive letter about Christ-like living, Paul continued to urge Timothy to pursue righteousness, godliness, faith, love, endurance and gentleness. He motivated him to fight the good fight of the faith, because God gives life. Gushing praise of God breaks forth from Paul, and he writes, *"He is the blessed and only Sovereign, the King of kings, and the Lord of lords, the only One who has immortality, dwelling in unapproachable light; no one has seen or can see Him, to Him be honor and eternal might. Amen."* God is truly worthy of praise and true praise is heard loud and clear in godly living. May we bless God with our lives day after day, choice after choice.

Paul says that both honor and eternal might belong to God who lives in unapproachable light. One day we will see Him. Until it is our turn to approach Him in all His glory, may we be found faithfully growing authentic God-like character. We can be dedicated like an athlete who values building strength and might. Paul tells Timothy that growth in godly character is good not only for this life but for the one yet to come. Picture the situations that God allows to come our way to be like a gym, and when we handle the circumstance wisely our faith muscles mature. Whether we like it or not we are in a fight against God's enemy. Being trained is critical. God, I pray that although we do not yet see You, we would keep our eyes, our focus, on You. You are our prize. Amen.

Blessed Hope; Jesus Returning

Titus 2:11-14 NIV

DECEMBER 3

Titus was living in Crete and could use some encouragement and a strategic planning seminar so Paul wrote a letter to him. Titus needed reminding (don't we all from time to time?) of what "blessed hope" is especially when he faced challenging tasks. *For the grace of God has appeared that offers salvation to all people. It teaches us to say "No" to ungodliness and worldly passions, and to live self-controlled, upright and godly lives in this present age, while we wait for the blessed hope—the glorious appearing of our great God and Savior, Jesus Christ, who gave himself for us to redeem us from all wickedness and to purify for himself a people that are his very own, eager to do what is good.* It takes discipline to say "no" to things that do not bring about lasting goodness, and say "yes" to Jesus who is our strength and our model for upright living. He is our Blessed Hope and He is returning!

As we anticipate Jesus' glorious appearing, we are encouraged to live redeemed lives with action and purpose, which grow both our joy and our freedom. Disappointment and frustration is a part of life, yet anger, bitterness or other unhealthy coping mechanisms are not a good way forward. Let's aim to use setbacks as an opportunity to go to God and depend more fully on Him for our needs. We are people who Jesus wants to purify. How eager are we to submit to this purification process?

Before beginning rewrites today I was praying, more like grumbling, to God about my immobility. It has been over fifty days (I'm trying to make the days count rather than just counting days) since the bicycle accident that has left me unable to walk and there's no projected walking date set. God knows that my desire is to depend fully on Him, and He also knows that a lot of my life has been lived in self-reliant ways. During my recovery He is showing me afresh His good, faithful, fulfilling love through His Presence, His Story and through a whole lot of people He has used to bless me. Will I accept His purifying lessons and fully trust Him? Waiting does not come naturally for me, and I do not think I'm the only one that struggles with this. God says we are to wait upon Him, He is the One who renews, restores, redeems and purifies. What is the next good step we can take today as we embrace our Blessed Hope? His grace is for us.

Send a Letter; Be a Blessing

Titus 3:15 AMP

DECEMBER 4

Who do we know who needs to be remembered by us today? Is there someone we could bless by sending a quick text message, a Facebook comment, an email, a card or even a handwritten letter? Encouraging one another is a way we impart godly love and blessings. *All who are with me wish to be remembered to you. Greet those who love us in the faith. Grace (God's favor and blessing) be with you all. Amen (so be it).* What a great way to end a good letter! Titus, a new pastor in Crete, was certainly blessed when he read Paul's pastoral advice and it gives us solid counsel today. Titus was glad that he was not forgotten as he served God in a faraway place.

In 1996, when our family first arrived in China, we communicated our prayer requests in handwritten letters mailed to those whom we loved. I would bike across the city to the post office where stamps were stuck on envelopes using a chopstick and brown goo. My letters were cryptic since we never knew if they would be opened and read before they left the communist country. Communication forms sure have changed since those days and how much more so since the time of Paul! With the help of technology, correspondence happens instantaneously to and from almost anywhere in the world. Prayer needs as well as praises for God's answers can be communicated without long delays. Then all who partner in sharing God's love and growing His Kingdom can together give the credit to Him, praising God for His grace. Let's continue to stir one another along with love and by good works, blessing as we go.

Kitchen Blessings

2 Timothy 2:20-21 MSG

DECEMBER 5

Like many sojourners, our family has moved a lot. For me, settledness in a new home comes when the kitchen has what it needs for me to make meals to serve my family and our guests. This can sometimes take a while; some of our kitchens literally had only the kitchen sink when we moved in. Eventually though, the room becomes useful and well-furnished and I feel settled. When it was time for Hannah to begin life on her own in college, I began to write *minickmenus*, a blog that has grown to include over 350 family recipes. Now that all of my kiddos have kitchens of their own, it is fun to hear how they access the blog to recreate meals we once shared around the same table. Try to picture what mealtime was like back in the days of the New Testament. I find it interesting that in Paul's second letter to Timothy he used a "kitchen" illustration. *In a well-furnished kitchen there are not only crystal goblets and silver platters, but waste cans and compost buckets—some containers used to serve fine meals, others to take out the garbage. Become the kind of container God can use to present any and every kind of gift to his guests for their blessing.* We can bless others with gifts from God when we become usable to God. What kind of container are we now? What are we training to become?

Blessed with the Crown of Life

James 1:12 ESV

DECEMBER 6

James, believed to be a half-brother of Jesus, is a to-the-point kind of man. As a leader in the early church, he addressed persecution and his words of wisdom hold true for all generations. *"Blessed is the man who remains steadfast under trial, for when he has stood the test he will receive the crown of life, which God has promised to those who love him."* His letter goes on to give advice for remaining steadfast. James teaches us to be unshakeable, wholehearted and firm in our convictions by gaining a realistic perspective of trials, temptation, and the need of putting faith into action. Each lesson builds on the other. But is it all worth it? Remaining resolute and loyal to God is a blessing in itself. If we need more motivation, let's ponder "the crown of life" that James says God promises to the ones who love Him. When the busy swirl of day-to-day obligations and pressures make it hard for us to contemplate the future that awaits us beyond this world's struggles, we are wise to pause and re-think priorities. Do our thoughts and behavior reveal a trusting, growing, dependent and joyful love of God? Nothing needs to separate us from that love. Embrace Him in the good and in the bad times because the testing will come. I like the expression "she passed" as a way of saying that someone has died. This world is our test; at the end of it I sure want to pass - pass with flying colors right into the Presence of God who knew me even before there was a me to know.

Blessed to Do Good Works

James 1:25 HCSB

Do we want to be blessed in what we do? James gives helpful direction. We cannot just listen to God's Word; we need to actually do what it says. That means taking it in, then working it out. This concept reminds me of a friend back in our Marine Corps days when Russell and I served in Spain. This young man would swallow several bodybuilding supplements with the desire to be buff but not take the time to lift weights in the gym. His body should have processed the supplements during sweaty workouts as his muscles were being built, but instead of bigger muscles, what his body produced was an unpleasant smell. We sure do not want to be stinky Christians by just taking in more information. We are blessed when we study God's Story and then live out what it says for us to do. *But the one who looks intently into the perfect law of freedom and perseveres in it, and is not a forgetful hearer but one who does good works—this person will be blessed in what he does.* We need to do more than just take in truth. Those who follow Jesus need to actively apply that truth, situation by situation. What good is the freedom Jesus provides if we do not live in it? Press on into blessedness. God, may our love for Your Word increase in us, not puff us up with knowledge but give us strength to live life effectively. I pray that our actions really would show what we believe and that loving You and loving people becomes our treasure. May our lives be a fragrant offering. Amen.

Do Blessings Flow from Us?

James 3:9-11 ESV

To make his message about training the tongue clear to his readers, James brings to life many visual aids. Animals can be trained, but can the tongue? *With it we bless our Lord and Father, and with it we curse people who are made in the likeness of God. From the same mouth come blessing and cursing. My brothers, these things ought not to be so. Does a spring pour forth from the same opening both fresh and salt water?* Do we want to be blessed? Don't curse. When we desire purity in our body and speech, we take action to rid ourselves of the hypocrisy that our enemy would like to trap us in. James desires us to thrive in the freedom that comes from living an unmixed life. Then we can in full confidence bless God and bless people.

Blessed to Persevere

James 5:10-11 NIV

DECEMBER 9

It is virtuous to be patient, but often we desire patience and yet want to bypass the very thing that grows our patience best: suffering. It was the same for those in the early church, so James helped them remember a man who was familiar with both patience and suffering. *Brothers and sisters, as an example of patience in the face of suffering, take the prophets who spoke in the name of the Lord. As you know, we count as blessed those who have persevered. You have heard of Job's perseverance and have seen what the Lord finally brought about. The Lord is full of compassion and mercy.* Job was blessed by persevering. The Lord is full of blessing, full of mercy, full of compassion. Hold tight to Him and to His promises. Nothing is wasted in our lives as we live out God's Story trusting fully in Him. Job was blessed. So were countless others who have persevered, suffered, grew in patience and in doing so knew the compassion and mercy of God. It is now our generation; our turn. How will we choose to respond to suffering?

Don't Pervert God's Blessings into Lawlessness

Jude 1:4 AMP

In his brief letter, Jude warns his readers not to become false teachers and not to be led astray by them. *For certain men have crept in stealthily [gaining entrance secretly by a side door]. Their doom was predicted long ago, ungodly (impious, profane) persons who pervert the grace (the spiritual blessing and favor) of our God into lawlessness and wantonness and immorality, and disown and deny our sole Master and Lord, Jesus Christ (the Messiah, the Anointed One).* Instead of listening or responding to those false teachers, we need to be built up in the faith, pray in the Spirit, and keep ourselves in God's love. We need to be wise and not let the wolf in sheep's clothing lead us away from the truth that is found in our Messiah and His teachings. How do we know if a leader is a wolf? Look at his offspring, or in other words, what kind of fruit is coming from his life? Jude was not the only one who warned of the seriousness of knowing who it is we choose to follow. Jesus made it clear that it will not end well for those who lead others astray.

Blessed to Be Born Again

1 Peter 1:3-4 ESV

God's Story is passed on through the perspective of Peter. He used to be a fisherman and then he had a change in careers. This was not a smooth transition for Peter, but an important one, and by the end of his life those who knew him learned about many blessings of God. Do you need a good reason to praise God today? Peter gives us several as he begins his first letter written to Gentile Christians who were living in a time of great hostility to the gospel. *"Blessed be the God and Father of our Lord Jesus*

Christ! According to his great mercy, he has caused us to be born again to a living hope through the resurrection of Jesus Christ from the dead, to an inheritance that is imperishable, undefiled, and unfading, kept in heaven for you..." Peter, the fisherman, also known as Simon and Cephas, wrote this. But Peter did not write this right away. First he needed to experience and then process those experiences.

Friendship with Jesus changes people. In John's Gospel we read that it was Peter's brother Andrew who introduced Peter to Jesus. Peter lived and learned what it meant to truly trust God by seeing Jesus in action. Jesus healed Peter's mother-in-law. Jesus led Peter up the mountain of transfiguration. Jesus told Peter where to fish and so many fish were caught it must have been talked about for years. Another time Jesus told Peter to catch a fish and that fish had a coin in its mouth which was used to pay taxes. Peter heard Jesus' sermons and was able to ask the smartest Man who ever lived question after question. And then, when the time came, Peter denied that he ever knew his Friend. But that is not where God's Story ended for Peter. It went on to see Peter's reconciliation with a resurrected Jesus. God's Holy Spirit filled Peter with boldness to preach and gave him a purpose worth living for. Praise be to God, who has so richly blessed His children, born into a hope that will not die, with an incredible inheritance guaranteed. God's mercy is great and the promise of what we have yet to receive is unimaginable by human minds. Thank You, Father God, for raising Jesus from the dead and through Him offering us abundant life and a living hope. Amen.

Payback Blessings

1 Peter 3:8-9 NLT

DECEMBER 12

Peter stressed the importance of unity within the community so that compassion and harmony could flow. Living this way will glorify God. Peter said at the close of his letter, *"Finally, all of you should be of one mind. Sympathize with each other. Love each other as brothers and sisters.*

Be tenderhearted, and keep a humble attitude. Don't repay evil for evil. Don't retaliate with insults when people insult you. Instead, pay them back with a blessing. That is what God has called you to do, and he will bless you for it." Like in other places in God's Story, we find that when we bless others (even when they don't "deserve it") God will bless us. Look for opportunities to bless, and all the more so, when blessing may seem far from what might come naturally.

Let God's supernatural love flow. From March of 2013 to March of 2014 I had a new job. While wearing a cute apron, I worked at a friendly self-serve frozen yogurt shop in our neighborhood. I loved riding my bike to work on quiet streets lined with large trees. Greeting guests and offering them samples of our yummy flavors was fun for me. Everyone is happy in a frozen yogurt shop, right? Well, early in my training, a guest impatiently fussed about a number of things and when she left the store, my team leader encouraged me not to let it get to me, as this lady was known for her grumpy, insulting attitude. My new mission was to show extra genuine kindness, blessing her until she could not help but to enjoy her fro-yo with a smile. When we have been blessed by God's love, how can we not desire to bless others, especially those who may not know Him yet? (By the way, the last time she came into the shop, she not only smiled and said kind words but she also left a generous tip!)

Blessed When Suffering for Righteousness

1 Peter 3:14a ESV

DECEMBER 13

Benjamin Franklin, in his *1757 Poor Richard's Almanac*, repeats a phrase that has become familiar: "God helps those who help themselves." Ben is not however, quoting the Bible. God helps those who are helpless. And when it comes to salvation, each one of us is in dire need of God's help. God does reward those who seek to do what is right. Sometimes it may feel like the unjust are receiving benefits while the godly are penalized. But always remember, God will have the final say, and His judgment is fair and true. *But even if you should suffer for righteousness' sake, you will be blessed.* Short and to the point, Peter's reminders go a long way to those who are being persecuted unjustly and this truth is good to keep in mind. Today is not the end. Keep calm and carry on in the ways that honor God. He sees and His Word says He will bless.

Blessed When Insulted Because of Jesus

1 Peter 4:12-14 NIV

DECEMBER 14

Dear friends, do not be surprised at the fiery ordeal that has come on you to test you, as though something strange were happening to you. But rejoice inasmuch as you participate in the sufferings of Christ, so that you may be overjoyed when his glory is revealed. If you are insulted because of the name of Christ, you are blessed, for the Spirit of glory and of God rests on you. Awareness and proper perspective can make all the difference in the way one lives through suffering. Peter, gentle with his words, lets his readers know that committing to a faithful Creator and continuing to do good is the direction to go for those who seek to follow Christ. One day the glory of Jesus will be made known to all.

When Russell teaches CrownHeartWorld, the whole biblical Story using three symbols in five columns, I love applying verses like this one from Peter. They fill in more details to our final hope. Column five show what is yet to come, when we will see God for who He is and all things will be restored. When we are complete, face-to-Face with our Creator and Redeemer, our hearts will never flip over into selfishness again. For now, though, those of us who have placed our faith in Jesus are still living in column four. In column four, we advance toward transformation and there is testing and suffering and the hurts of a world that is broken. But hold on to hope, there is over-rejoicing guaranteed in our future!

320

Blessings like Rain

Hebrews 6:7-8 NIV

It is unclear who wrote this letter to Christians with a Jewish background, but what does ring clear is the truth that Jesus Christ is superior to everyone and everything including all of the traditions within the Jewish heritage. *Land that drinks in the rain often falling on it and that produces a crop useful to those for whom it is farmed receives the blessing of God. But land that produces thorns and thistles is worthless and is in danger of being cursed. In the end it will be burned.* This illustration about the land is a warning to all of us against falling away from the goodness and redemption found in Christ alone. It is essential for us to check what it is that we are growing in our character and to live useful and not worthless lives. This letter written to the Hebrews is fascinating. It is filled with warnings and blessings and retells God's Story in a concise and powerful way. Give it a fresh read, circling the blessings for yourself, and be blessed!

God, I pray that we would not drift away from You but out of gratitude we would press on into purposeful and effective living. Let us not coast but produce a crop of goodness that blesses You and blesses those You place in our lives. Amen.

Remember God's Blessing to Abraham

Hebrews 6:13-15 ESV

God's promises are certain and true. We are firmly cautioned not to become lazy or seek to take matters into our own hands. Instead we are wise to imitate those who live faithfully and to trust the promises of God for ourselves. The writer of this letter hoped to refresh a specific promise made years ago for his readers, one that had impact on their lives, and still does on our lives today. *For when God made a promise to Abraham, since he had no one greater by whom to swear, he swore by himself, saying, "Surely*

I will bless you and multiply you." And thus Abraham, having patiently waited, obtained the promise.

Reminders about the past can give healthy encouragement to those in the present. "Team white van" made a long drive from Texas to Florida and allowed us to enjoy a great family Christmas gathering at Russell's dad's home. Along the way, we stopped in Pensacola where I met first Russ thirty years earlier. I loved reminiscing about our early days as a couple and telling our kiddos, each one now older than we were back when we first fell in love, about how I met their father. There were some turbulent times during the years leading up to sealing our love with a promise on our wedding day. By God's grace that promise stands. God models faithful promise keeping. He is just and will not forget our love toward Him and diligence toward loving others. Be strong until the end, for we can have confidence in Him. And as His Story faithfully tells, His promises include blessings!

Blessing Giver Is Greater Than Blessing Receiver

Hebrews 7:1, 6b-7 NLT

DECEMBER 17

To further clarify his point of the superiority of Jesus, the writer to the Hebrews retells the story of a Melchizedek, a priest, with a name that means king of justice and peace. *This Melchizedek was king of the city of Salem and also a priest of God Most High. When Abraham was returning home after winning a great battle against the kings, Melchizedek met him and blessed him... And Melchizedek placed a blessing upon Abraham, the one who had already received the promises of God. And without question, the person who has the power to give a blessing is greater than the one who is blessed.* The writer goes on to explain the priesthood of Jesus and how He is our permanent, powerful, and perfect priest. Others may bless us in our lifetime, like how Melchizedek blessed Abraham, but the blessing of Jesus extends into eternity. Father, how thankful we are that Your Story has an extensive history and it has room to include each of us. We who believe in You are blessed and no matter if we are returning home from winning a battle or are still in the midst of the fighting, You have overcome our sin and through Jesus it is paid for in full. Thank You for the blessing of being Your child. Amen.

Bless Those Who Come after Us

Hebrews 11:20-21 NIV

DECEMBER 18

The Great Hall of Faith chapter in God's Story begins with a definition of faith. Faith is being sure of what we hope for and certain of what we still do not clearly see. Faith and blessings are often interlinked. Abraham had lived by faith and passed blessings down to his son Isaac. *By faith Isaac blessed Jacob and Esau in regard to their future.* The next generation also experienced the faith/blessing combination. *By faith Jacob, when he was dying, blessed each of Joseph's sons, and worshiped as he leaned on the top of his staff.* When we live our lives by faith, being certain in God whom we do not see, we can bless those who come behind us. What a legacy to give: the example of a life lived faithfully. While on earth, we may never fully know just what kind of impact we've made. But there can be no impact for good or for God if we hide our light under a basket. Let's shine brightly for our Lord and King! Our children, our nieces and nephews, grandchildren, and neighbors need light in order to properly grow. Little seeds of faith require good soil, water and light. Let's allow the Gardener to use us in this process.

My mom was raised on a farm and she's still a wonderful gardener. Each season finds her doing what needs to be done to bring about beautiful blooms in her many flowerbeds. The first time Russell and I had a rental home with a little yard, I wanted to have flower gardens like my mom but found it very hard to while keeping up with three toddlers. Her wise words to me were to put flowered-printed dresses on the girls, bright colors on Isaiah, and spend my time playing outside with my young ones, for they were my flowers for this season. Through blended families, Mom is now the grandmother to fourteen grandchildren and one great-grand-son, and another great-grandchild on the way in April of 2015! She has watered those souls with prayers and shines her light on them as she spends time with each - in her gardens, in her kitchen, at their sporting events and on and on. I picture that when she leans against her hoe, like Jacob did on his staff, she is thankful to God knowing her "gardening" has made the world a more beautiful place.

Don't Exchange Eternal Blessing for Anything

Hebrews 12:16-17 HCSB

DECEMBER 19

It is imperative not to reject God's grace! We need to consider all that is at stake and no matter what, do not refuse the richness of forgiveness offered to us through the Son of the Most High God. The early Christians needed this warning just as we need it today. Along with that firm exhortation, the writer adds: pursue peace and holiness and pull out by the very roots any form of bitterness. *And make sure that there isn't any immoral or irreverent person like Esau, who sold his birthright in exchange for one meal. For you know that later, when he wanted to inherit the blessing, he was rejected because he didn't find any opportunity for repentance, though he sought it with tears.* Don't wait until it is too late; receive God's mercy today. His Story was written so we can not only learn from the errors of others but also see for ourselves the goodness of God's grace which calls us to repentance and trust. This then gives a life worth living. As we trust in the Lord at all times we will be drawn to Him rather than want to hide from Him.

Blessed to Have Eternal Life

1 John 5:13 AMP

When the apostle John was young, he walked beside Jesus and he penned his gospel account that is filled with distinctions between light and dark. As an old man John wrote letters to those who wanted to follow Jesus' teachings. There are so many things he could have shared as he pondered the past. He contemplated the present situation and addressed the need to love faithfully and to remain obedient to God's commands. John knew false teaching was a real enemy so he pleaded with his readers to practice discernment. Then John concluded one of his letters by giving needed assurance. *"I write this to you who believe in (adhere to, trust in, and rely on) the name of the Son of God [in the peculiar services and blessings conferred by Him on men], so that you may know [with settled and absolute knowledge] that you [already] have life, yes, eternal life."* What a blessing his words must have been then and how they remain a blessing to all who still yearn to follow Jesus today. We are blessed with eternal life. All praise to God! We do not need to wait until death ushers us into life; through God's Holy Spirit we can live with eternal life kind of hope even now. Jesus is the Key that opens the door.

God Gives Blessings, Mercy and Peace

2 John 1:3 AMP

Grace (spiritual blessing), mercy, and [soul] peace will be with us, from God the Father and from Jesus Christ (the Messiah), the Father's Son, in all sincerity (truth) and love. What do we really long for in our days? Is it not for our soul to be at peace with the God who created us for love? John's second letter is a mini version of his first one and his personal greeting for our goodness blesses all who read it. To live really comprehending that we have mercy instead of punishment from God is undoubtedly a blessing worth repeating. Forgiven sinners embraced by God Almighty. It is hard to fathom, but true. Do we have peace with God? He offers; will we accept?

Blessed When We Read Revelation

Revelation 1:3 HCSB

DECEMBER 22

When trying to decide if a book is a good one some readers will glance at the first chapter and if it captures their attention they continue turning pages. Others choose to read the last chapter and if it offers a satisfying conclusion, they will then invest in the rest of the book. With God's Book, the Bible, we can take either approach and discover His Story is one not only worth reading but worth living by. Genesis, the beginning of God's Story, records many blessings. The blessings do not stop there; they continue on generation after generation, situation after situation. Revelation, the conclusion of God's written Word to us, maintains this blessing theme.

John lived on a small island as an outcast for telling God's Story. In his nineties, he wrote down everything he saw, just as God told him to do. The final book in the Bible is challenging to fully comprehend but God rewards those who read and embrace its truth. *The one who reads this is blessed, and those who hear the words of this prophecy and keep what is written in it are blessed, because the time is near!* The time is more nearer today than it was yesterday. May we be encouraged to love God's blessings and journal them for ourselves and for the generations yet to come. We can take good comfort in knowing that the time is near. God is near. Live fully in the God of the blessings!

Blessed Be the Lamb Forever!

Revelation 5:12, 13b ESV

Suddenly, John is transported to Heaven. I wonder what that must have felt like! John had just recorded interesting and eye-opening messages to seven different churches, messages that critiqued each for what they had done well and for what they had failed to do. Today, churches can be more effective when leaders read this information and needed adjustments are implemented. While in Heaven, John was escorted by an angel. John sees amazing, hard-to-express things that human minds can only somewhat imagine. But what he hears is loud and clear: on-going praise to God the Father and Jesus. *"Worthy is the Lamb who was slain, to receive power and wealth and wisdom and might and honor and glory and blessing!"*

Then every living creature everywhere (in Heaven, on earth, under the earth and in the sea) all joined in with the praise chorus: *"To him who sits on the throne and to the Lamb be blessing and honor and glory and might forever and ever!"* What an incredible foretaste we are privy to as we read God's Story. If we allow our minds and hearts to take in all that John tried to describe, we too cannot help but to worship. Lord Jesus, You are worthy to be praised forever and ever. All blessing is Yours. All honor, glory and might belong to You. We will join the masses to praise You throughout all eternity. May our lips and lives praise You even now. Amen.

Blessing and so Much More Belong to God

Revelation 7:12 NLT

There is a promise for those in Heaven that brings such hope: God will wipe away all tears. All who love God will experience full and abiding comfort. One day, multitudes from every nation, tribe, people and language will worship Him. The angels will join in with the praises. *"Amen!*

Blessing and glory and wisdom and thanksgiving and honor and power and strength belong to our God forever and ever! Amen." And the praise goes on! When we notice people who are different from us, try to see them as God sees them. See them as people Jesus died for - those who, if they bow their knee to the King of kings, will join the multitudes to receive His peace. May we be active in extending God's hope, one person at a time. Honest transparency helps us as we seek to share God's Story with others. Even though I know the joy of what the future holds, some days on this earth I still slip into melancholy.

The dark, cold afternoons of London winter contributed to my sense of discouragement so I prayerfully considered my options and then I joined a gym. Each day before going I would ask God to give me a friend to share His goodness with and He faithfully provided many opportunities for meaningful conversations. After one workout, I met Fariba, a beautiful Iranian who was also new to the gym. Fariba and I had fun exploring London together, learning from each other and discovering what we each valued. About a month before Easter, Fariba asked me what I was giving up for Lent. I told her depression. My depression is not the kind that requires medical care. When I choose to focus on Jesus as my Hope, my dark mood lifts. In a gym we train our bodies; in God's Word we train our minds. When a pity party breaks out, stop, and invite in thankfulness. Hopefulness and gratitude are good workout partners for the mind and at times we need to do more repetitions of both. When it is our turn for Heaven, let's be in good shape to join the faithful around God's throne. May we be strong in lifting up His praise because all glory and wisdom, thanksgiving and honor belong to Him. He is the One who gives us strength and power to live now in hope and to actively share it.

Blessed Rest yet Before Us

Revelation 14:13 NIV

Trumpets, angels, plagues, battles, evil enemies and God's faithfulness; the next few chapters of God's Story, as recorded in the Revelation of Jesus Christ, stretches one's imagination to say the least. God's judgment and hostility toward the adversary's assaults cause havoc on the earth. But God remains in control. In spite of everything that is taking place at the coming of Jesus and with Satan's war against Christ's church, there is hope for the faithful and blessings as well. From Heaven John heard a voice say, *"Write this: Blessed are the dead who die in the Lord from now on." "Yes," says the Spirit, "they will rest from their labor, for their deeds will follow them."*

Mary, the mother of Jesus, had rest from her labor the night Jesus was born in a manger so long ago. Jesus encourages us to come to Him to find rest from our labor when we give our burdens to Him. All of us long for rest in spite of the variety of labor pains that we presently experience. And the kind of rest that comes to those who die in the Lord is a blessed rest indeed. But for now we have life, and the things that we have done and the ways we have blessed others will not be forgotten. Let us go forward in faithfulness to our Lord. Thank You, Lord Jesus, for we can come and adore You! You have taken fear out of death. There will come a day when we will rest in lasting peace. Your life, death and resurrection made it possible for those who trust in You to have reconciliation, peace, and joy. Joy to the world, the Lord of rest has come. Amen.

Blessed Are the Watchful Ones

Revelation 16:15 NLT

God's righteous punishment continues against everyone who obstinately remain in their wicked ways: those who will not repent of their rebellious actions and give glory to God. Seven angels will go forth on the earth to pour out seven bowls of God's wrath. The destruction will be final and there will come a thorough cleansing of the world from sin. Those who remain alert and watchful for God will be blessed. *"Look, I will come as unexpectedly as a thief! Blessed are all who are watching for me, who keep their clothing ready so they will not have to walk around naked and ashamed."*

This statement from Jesus reminds me of Adam and Eve at the beginning of God's Story. When they disobeyed God their eyes were opened to their nakedness and they no longer had joy and peace but were ashamed. God wants us to trust Him and obey Him; He has provided a way for us to give up our shame. Jesus died in our place, and the sin and shame of all of mankind was nailed to His cross. Because God's love is greater than our sin, God raised Jesus from the dead and we can be dead to sin and alive to walk and live in new life. This news is good! May we live in awareness of God, intentionally and bravely practicing perseverance in the trials we face every day. May we be ready, humbly relying on God, no matter what comes our way. For we know that Jesus is coming! Let's live expectantly!

Wedding Invitation Blessings

Revelation 19:9 NIV

DECEMBER 27

John's role as a scribe continues and he writes a great encouragement of what is yet to come. *Then the angel said to me, "Write this: Blessed are those who are invited to the wedding supper of the Lamb!" And he added, "These are the true words of God."* Remember the wedding in Cana that Jesus attended at the beginning of His earthly ministry? John was at that wedding. When Jesus performed His first miracle, turning water into wine at that marriage celebration, John was there. When the angel in Heaven told him about the wedding supper that will take place in the future, I wonder if he thought back to the Cana wedding. Just what did he picture?

Think back on the wonderful wedding celebrations you have been to throughout your lifetime. Recall the happiness of shared love as the groom and his beautiful bride are joined together in holy matrimony, beginning their lives as one. Then there are the weddings written about in novels and we read the story describing all the great and blissful details: the prince and princess overcoming insurmountable odds and they victoriously live happily ever after. We have watched moving weddings in movies when we cry happy tears, or maybe we've followed the pomp of royal weddings with all the grandeur of riches. Even a combination of the best of these events will be colorless in light of the marriage feast of the Lamb! The invited ones will be blessed beyond measure. Believe it! God's Story is not a fairytale.

Blessed Resurrection

Revelation 20:6 HCSB

DECEMBER 28

At last, Satan, the enemy of old, will be seized, bound and thrown into the abyss, locked away for 1,000 years. Now more fascinating things happen. The faithful-to-God ones (people who had been beheaded due to their testimony about Jesus, those who had not worshiped the beast or accepted his mark) will come back to life! *Blessed and holy is the one who shares in the first resurrection! The second death has no power over them, but they will be priests of God and of the Messiah, and they will reign with Him for 1,000 years.* Satan, for the last time, is set free to deceive and then is thrown into the lake of fire. God will then judge everyone, both the living and the dead.

God's Story is anything but boring. But as we read it, we need to keep in mind that we are a part of it; we will be judged by how we choose to live. God, I pray that we would choose wisely. You have provided so much for us in the way of knowledge and nearness, in provision and blessing. But You do not control us like puppets on a string. You allow us choice, even if that may mean choosing against You. God, have mercy upon us and those we love because Your judgment is coming. No one can stand against You in their own strength; we need the covering of Jesus. May we humbly bow before You. Amen.

Amazing Blessings to Inherit

Revelation 21:7 NLT

DECEMBER 29

God is preparing something incredible: a new Heaven. The descriptions tell us that it will sparkle and shine with precious stones and gold. There will no longer be barriers to love. The glory of the Lord will illuminate and life will be fully satisfying. The new Heaven is the guaranteed blessing for all who have their names written in the Lamb's Book of Life. Real joy will abound. No tears. No pain. No mourning. God promises: *"All who are victorious will inherit all these blessings, and I will be their God, and they will be my children."* There will be the absence of sorrow and the fullness of joy! We will see God face-to-Face in our new unbelievably stunning home. The curse of sin and the fear of death will be gone forever.

The death of Ben still makes my heart ache. Ben was about eleven, a little older than our Sophie, when we first met him. We rented the Thai house that his mother had built and our friendship with his family grew deep over the years. A compassionate son, friend to many, Ben's genuine smile bridged cultures. He had a way of making everyone feel at ease. It was fun cheering alongside his father as we watched Ben, in his number eight jersey, play soccer with skill, passion and integrity. Then came a Thursday morning when his life tragically ended in a motorcycle accident while he was on his way to school. Grief unimaginable. After several days of Buddhist rituals, the community gathered for his cremation. And when I thought I could cry no more, fresh tears formed as a friend of Ben's family, a famous saxophonist, played *Amazing Grace* in the stillness of that blue-skyed setting. God, do I know Your grace that is beyond amazing? Will I be with You surrounded by joy, alive in peace, as one who has inherited Your blessings?

The Obedient Are Blessed

Revelation 22:7 NLT

Although the conclusion of God's Story is about our bright future we are still living in a world that is upside-down and broken. John also lived in a broken world and everything that he saw and heard concerning the new Heaven seemed too good to be true. Finding the goodness hard to take in, John, in awe, bowed down to worship at the feet of the angel who had shown to him these marvelous things. The angel, however, was quick to tell John not to worship him but to worship God alone! God is the worthy One. Trustworthy, praiseworthy, bless His holy name forever! Are you like me curious about the time frame for when this all will take place? We may not be able to mark the date on our calendar, but we do know that the time is closer now than when John first wrote about it.

Jesus says, *"Look, I am coming soon! Blessed are those who obey the words of prophecy written in this book."* When Jesus says we are blessed for obedience I want to obey. Throughout God's Story we see how generous God is, over and over again lavishing His extravagant love upon those He created. And like all good fathers He desires for His children to grow up to maturity. Jesus is God in the flesh, come to the world to show us what it means to grow up: to be holy (set apart) and full of compassion, kindness, humility, and joy. Our strength to be this, and so much more, really does come from Him. God's training in righteousness leads to great freedom; we can be free to live a satisfying life that pleases Him. Our Father does not keep us guessing about what makes Him happy. We can detect God's love language throughout His Story, and right up through to the end we read that Jesus has the same love language: obedience. "If you love Me, obey My commandments."—Jesus.

Blessed to Receive the Tree of Life

Revelation 22:14 HCSB

DECEMBER 31

God's first blessings came to mankind in a beautifully fresh garden filled with good food to eat and unhindered love. As we experience His Story personally and throughout history, we see that God is good and He blesses us with way more than food. God's final recorded blessings will take place in a spectacular garden city. One of my favorite cities to run in is Singapore, an island city-state in South East Asia about eighty-five miles from the equator. Among the skyscrapers and busy sidewalks are spacious parks with ancient trees that provide cooling shade in a land of interesting diversity. As clean and green as Singapore is, it cannot compare to what is yet before us. In God's perfect timing everything will be made new. The future Holy City's foundations will be rare jewels that glimmer and I get so excited trying to picture what it will feel like to run on streets made of pure gold! Planted along the crystal clear river flowing with the water of life is the Tree of Life. This tree will yield both fruit and healing.

Those who belong to God will live forever in His protection, provision and love. In Jesus we are fully blessed. Because of Him we know true love and have hope even as we wait with eager expectation for everything that is still before us. Our future hope is real and God's Story concludes with His children being blessed. Jesus declares, *"Blessed are those who wash their robes, so that they may have the right to the tree of life and may enter the city by the gates."* Jesus says He is coming quickly. Come, Lord Jesus, come! May the grace, joy, peace and favored blessings, of the Lord Jesus be with God's people now and forever more! Live Blessed! Amen.

Reflections

December holds the exciting conclusion of God's Story of blessings. We get keen insights from those who wrote letters as the church continued to grow, both in number and in maturity. Paul, James, Jude, Peter, the writer to the Hebrews, and John all penned messages of hope, encouragement, and loving warnings to those they deeply cared about. The final blessings that await us in Heaven seem too good to be true. But they are. God is true and His blessings remain forever.

Blessing
By Hannah Minick

Blessings be
upon the One who taught my tongue
what blessings are,
the One who said "Taste, taste and see
see that I am good."
Submerging me in the explosive power
of his oceanic love
and the weight of grace did not destroy
but redeemed, purified
pulled me through flames
to emerge
gasping, laughing, loving
whole
for the first time.
Lord, you taught me to give
now teach me to take
take deep draughts of you
like air after choking
water after running.
My heart feels drained
each drop pushed loose
through conduits long dug to faraway ears
distant reaching hands
and it's your love that taught me,
your love that gives me words
but I've run myself dry
straight into the ground.
Dust to dust.
Ashes to ashes.
Lord, I have wept with the weeping.
Will you teach me to laugh again?
I am a gaping mouth.
The only thing left in me I spend
to call out blessing.
Blessings upon the LORD,
the One who blesses beyond belief.
Bless him my soul.
Bless me, my All.

In the light of your Presence, I bless your name.

Dear Reader,

We have come to the end of our journey through The Blessing Book. I pray that you have been blessed by reading of God's faithful love throughout His Story and that you are encouraged by His love and blessings for you.

One of the joys we have is the ability to interact with others in our world. I have provided contact information via **TheBlessingBook.com** if you would like to know more about a person or a ministry introduced to you in the book. Feel free to keep the spirit of blessing flowing as you connect with people both near and far.

Thank you for allowing me to guide our blessing tour. May we all continue on in our quest to be a blessing, knowing we are wonderfully blessed by God.

With love,
Karla